THE SOVIET UNION, EASTERN EUROPE AND THE THIRD WORLD

EDITED BY

ROGER E. KANET

University of Illinois at Urbana-Champaign

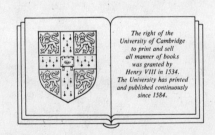

The right of the
University of Cambridge
to print and sell
all manner of books
was granted by
Henry VIII in 1534.
The University has printed
and published continuously
since 1584.

CAMBRIDGE UNIVERSITY PRESS

Cambridge

New York   New Rochelle   Melbourne   Sydney

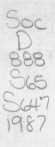

Published by the Press Syndicate of the University of Cambridge
The Pitt Building, Trumpington Street, Cambridge CB2 1 RP
32 East 57th Street, New York, NY 10022, USA
10 Stamford Road, Oakleigh, Melbourne 3166, Australia

First published 1987

Printed in Great Britain at the University Press, Cambridge

British Library cataloguing in publication data
The Soviet Union, Eastern Europe and the Third World. – (International Committee for
Soviet and East European Studies).
1. Developing countries – Foreign relations – Soviet Union   2. Soviet Union – Foreign
relations – Developing countries   3. Soviet Union – Foreign relations – 1975–
I. Kanet, Roger E.   II. Series
327.470172'4   D888.S65

Library of Congress cataloguing in publication data
The Soviet Union, Eastern Europe, and the Third World
Selected papers from the 3rd World Congress for Soviet and East European Studies, held in
Washington, DC, Oct. 30 – Nov. 4, 1985, sponsored by the International Committee for
Soviet and East European Studies and the American Association for the Advancement of
Slavic Studies.
Includes index.
1. Developing countries – Foreign relations – Soviet Union – Congresses.   2. Soviet Union –
Foreign relations – Developing countries – Congresses.   3. Developing countries – Foreign
relations – Europe, Eastern – Congresses.   4. Europe, Eastern – Foreign relations –
Developing countries – Congresses. I. Kanet, Roger E., 1936– . II. World Congress for Soviet
and East European Studies (3rd : 1985 : Washington, DC) III. International Committee for
Soviet and East European Studies. IV. American Association for the Advancement of Slavic
Studies.
D888.S65S647   1988   327.4701724   87-12497

ISBN 0 521 34459 X

Selected papers from the Third World Congress
for Soviet and East European Studies
Washington, DC
30 October–4 November 1985

Sponsored by the

INTERNATIONAL COMMITTEE

FOR SOVIET AND EAST EUROPEAN STUDIES

and the

AMERICAN ASSOCIATION

FOR THE ADVANCEMENT OF SLAVIC STUDIES

General Editor
R. C. Elwood
Carleton University

EDITORIAL COMMITTEE MEMBERS
Oskar Anweiler, Ruhr-Universität Bochum
Christopher Barnes, St Andrews University
Thomas J. Blakeley, Boston College
Deming Brown, University of Michigan
Marianna Tax Choldin, University of Illinois at Urbana-Champaign
J. Douglas Clayton, University of Ottawa
Z. F. Dreisziger, Royal Military College of Canada
Dennis J. Dunn, Southwest Texas State University
N. J. Dunstan, University of Birmingham
F. J. M. Feldbrugge, Rijksuniversiteit te Leiden
John P. Hardt, Library of Congress
Roger E. Kanet, University of Illinois at Urbana-Champaign
Mark N. Katz, Kennan Institute
Stanislav J. Kirschbaum, York University
David Lane, University of Birmingham
Carl H. McMillan, Carleton University
Arnold McMillan, University of London
Richard Peace, Bristol University
Peter J. Potichnyj, McMaster University
Tom M. S. Priestly, University of Alberta
Don Karl Rowney, Bowling Green State University
Fred Singleton, University of Bradford
Benjamin A. Stolz, University of Michigan
John W. Strong, Carleton University
Beatrice Beach Szekely, White Plains, NY
William Mills Todd III, Stanford University
John Westwood, University of Birmingham

THE SOVIET UNION, EASTERN EUROPE AND THE THIRD WORLD

Soviet policy towards the countries of Asia, Africa and Latin America has undergone substantial expansion and change during the three decades since Khrushchev first initiated efforts to break out of the international isolation in which the USSR still found itself in the immediate post-Stalin years. Over the course of the past thirty years the Soviet Union has expanded significantly both the geographical range of its involvement with developing countries, and the intensity of its political, military and economic activities. Moreover the USSR has increasingly acted in consort with "allies" such as Cuba and the countries of Eastern Europe. The studies in the present volume examine various aspects of recent Soviet and East European policy towards the Third World.

The five chapters in Part 1 deal with broad aspects of Soviet policy including major trends in political relations, Soviet reassessments of the nature and prospects for revolutionary change in the developing countries, Soviet support for clients confronted by internal insurgencies, and the Soviet use of information policy and propaganda in the Third World. Part 2 deals with various aspects of Soviet and East European economic involvement in the Third World, while Part 3 includes case studies of Soviet policy towards Syria and India.

Roger E. Kanet is Professor of Political Science, University of Illinois at Urbana-Champaign.

Contents

List of figures   *page* vii
List of tables   viii
List of contributors   ix
Foreword by R.C. Elwood   xiii
Preface by Roger E. Kanet   xv

PART I: THE THIRD WORLD IN SOVIET FOREIGN POLICY   I

1 The Soviet Union and the Third World from
   Khrushchev to Gorbachev: the place of the Third
   World in evolving Soviet global strategy
   Roger E. Kanet   3

2 Revolutionary change in the Third World: recent
   Soviet reassessments
   Elizabeth Kridl Valkenier   23

3 Anti-Soviet insurgencies: growing trend or
   passing phase?
   Mark N. Katz   42

4 The Soviet Union and the New World Information Order
   Paul Roth   70

5 Soviet propaganda and the process of national liberation
   Roger E. Kanet   84

v

PART 2: CMEA ECONOMIC INVOLVEMENT IN THE THIRD
     WORLD   115

6   Soviet economic policy in the Third World
    Heinrich Machowski and Siegfried Schultz   117

7   Eastern Europe and the Third World: Economic
    interactions and policies
    Laure Després   141

8   The non-European members of the CMEA: a model
    for developing countries?
    Giovanni Graziani   163

PART 3: THE SOVIET UNION IN THE MIDDLE EAST AND
SOUTH ASIA   181

9   Soviet policy toward Syria in the Andropov era
    Robert O. Freedman   183

10 Indo-Soviet security relations
    Jyotirmoy Banerjee   211

    Index   228
    *Publications from the Third World Congress for Soviet and
    East European Studies, Washington, 1985*   233

Figures

5.1   Channels of Soviet propaganda and active measures   *page* 87
5.2   Pro-Soviet International Front organizations   90
7.1   Trade of Bulgaria with the Third World   159
7.2   Trade of Czechoslovakia with the Third World   159
7.3   Trade of the GDR with the Third World   160
7.4   Trade of Hungary with the Third World   160
7.5   Trade of Poland with the Third World   161
7.6   Trade of Romania with the Third World   161
7.7   Trade of The Six with the Third World   161

Tables

6.1 Soviet foreign trade with the Third World, 1970–84   119

6.2 Share of the USSR in Third World trade by major commodity groups   121

7.1 Trade balances of the East European countries with the West and with the Third World   142

7.2 Ranking of the top ten partners of The Six in the South   144-6

7.3 Trade balances of the East European countries in trade with oil exporting countries and with Latin America   147

7.4 Arms sales of the East European countries to the Third World   150

7.5 Clearing agreements in force between the East European countries and the developing countries   152

7.6 Trade balances of the East European countries with the Third World in 1983 according to the types of settlements   153

8.1 Geographic distribution of foreign trade of Mongolia, Cuba and Vietnam   165

8.2 Share of individual European CMEA countries in non-European members' trade with CMEA, 1983   166

8.3 The top ten trade partners of Cuba and Vietnam, 1983   168

8.4 Commodity composition of Soviet trade with Cuba, Mongolia and Vietnam   170

8.5 Cuban exports of sugar   173

8.6 Share of CMEA LDCs in Soviet imports of selected commodities, 1984   175

Contributors

JYOTIRMOY BANERJEE is Reader in International Relations at Jadavpur University in Calcutta, India. He is the author of two books and numerous articles on Soviet and East European foreign policy, including *India in Soviet Global Strategy* (1977), *GDR and Detente: Divided Germany and East–West Relations* (1981), and "US–USSR and the New Arms Race," *IDSA Journal* (1982).

LAURE DEPRÉS is Maitre de Conférences in the Faculty of Economic Sciences of the University of Nantes, France. During the academic year 1986–87 she was an Olin Fellow at the Russian Research Center of Harvard University. She has published on various aspects of Soviet economics, including *Une théorie soviétique de l'hyperinflation: l'économie d'émission, 1918–1924* (1980), *Les ventes d'armes et la coopération militaire entre l'URSS, les pays socialistes européens et les pays en voie de développement non membres de CAEM* (1985), and "L'estimation des ventres d'armes de l'URSS par la méthode des résidus," *Revue d'Etudes Comparatives Est–Ouest* (1985).

ROBERT O. FREEDMAN is Professor of Political Science and Dean of the Peggy Meyerhoff Pearlstone School of Graduate Studies of Baltimore Hebrew College. He has written a number of books and numerous articles on the Middle East and Soviet policy in that region, among them *Soviet Policy Toward the Middle East Since 1970* (1982, 3rd edn), and is the editor of *The Middle East Since Camp David* (1984) and *The Middle East Since the Israeli Invasion of Lebanon* (1986).

GIOVANNI GRAZIANI is Associate Professor of Economics in the Institute of Management of the Faculty of Engineering, University of Padova, Italy. He has written extensively on the CMEA and on East European foreign trade, including *Comecon, domination et dépendences* (1982), "Des multinationales à l'Est?" in *Revue d'Economie Industrielle* (1984), and "Commercial Relations Between LDC's and the USSR," *Cambridge Journal of Economics* (forthcoming).

ROGER E. KANET is Professor of Political Science and a member of the Russian and East European Center at the University of Illinois at Urbana-Champaign. He has written widely on various aspects of Soviet and East European foreign policy. Among his edited books are *The Soviet Union and the Developing Nations* (1974), *Soviet Foreign Policy in the 1980s* (1982), and *Soviet Foreign Policy and East–West Relations* (1982).

MARK N. KATZ is a Research Associate at the Kennan Institute for Advanced Russian Studies, Woodrow Wilson International Center for Scholars in Washington. He has published extensively on Soviet policy in the Third World, including *The Third World in Soviet Military Thought* (1982) and *Russia and Arabia: Soviet Foreign Policy Toward the Arabian Peninsula* (1986).

HEINRICH MACHOWSKI is Senior Economist at the German Institute of Economic Research, Berlin. He is the author of numerous studies of Soviet and East European economic policy and foreign trade, including the following that have appeared in English: "International Economic Organization within COMECON: Status, Problems and Prospects," in *COMECON: Progress and Prospects*, NATO Colloquium (1977), "Soviet–West German Economic Relations: The Soviet Perspective," in *Economic Relations with the Soviet Union: American and West German Perspectives*, edited by Angela Stent (1985), and "The Soviet Union," in *Economic Warfare or Detente*, edited by Reinhard Rode and Hanns-D. Jacobsen (1985).

PAUL ROTH is Professor at the University of the Federal Armed Forces, Munich, Federal Republic of Germany. He is the author of a number of articles and books on the Soviet use of the mass media for propaganda purposes, including *Sow-Inform: Nachrichtenwesen und Informationspolitik der Sowjetunion* (1980), *Die kommandierte öffentliche Meinung: Sowjetische Medienpolitik* (1982), and *Cuius regio – ejus informatio: Moskaus Modell für die Weltinformationsordnung* (1984).

SIEGFRIED SCHULTZ is Senior Economist at the German Institute of Economic Research, Berlin. He is the author of numerous publications in German and English on development economics, international trade, protectionism and East–South relations. Publications in English include "CMEA Countries: Economic Relations with the Third World," *Intereconomics* (1986), "The Re-liberalization of World Trade: Some Ideas for Reducing Trade Barriers against Industrial Products from Developing Countries," *Journal of World Trade Law* (1984), and "Protectionism in International Trade in Services," *EADI-Bulletin* (1985).

ELIZABETH KRIDL VALKENIER is Resident Scholar at The W. Averell
Harriman Institute for Advanced Study of the Soviet Union and
Adjunct Professor in the Department of Political Science of Columbia
University in New York City. She has written extensively on Soviet
economic policy in the Third World, including *The Soviet Union and the
Third World: An Economic Bind* (1982), "East–West Economic Competition in the Third World" in *East–West Tensions in the Third World*,
edited by Marshall D. Shulman (1986), "The USSR, the Third World
and the Global Economy," *Problems of Communism* (1979).

Foreword

The articles selected for publication in this volume were chosen from among those presented at the Third World Congress for Soviet and East European Studies held in Washington, DC, from 30 October to 4 November 1985. The Congress, which was sponsored by the International Committee for Soviet and East European Studies and the American Association for the Advancement of Slavic Studies, attracted over 3,000 scholars from 41 countries. This figure represents a two-fold increase over the number of delegates who attended either the First Congress in Banff, Canada, in 1974 or the Second Congress in Garmisch-Partenkirchen in 1980 and reflects the revival of Slavic studies throughout the world.

More than 600 papers were formally presented or distributed at the Washington Congress. From among the substantial number submitted for possible publication in this series, the Editorial Committee has selected 160 to appear in 15 volumes. Five volumes are being published in the social sciences: three by Cambridge University Press and two by Lynne Rienner Publishers. Five volumes devoted to history and literature are being published by Slavica Publishers while the remaining five in education, law, library science, linguistics and Slovene studies are appearing as part of established series or as special issues of scholarly journals. The titles of all these publications will be found at the end of this volume.

As general editor for the Third Congress I should like to express my sincere appreciation to Donald W. Treadgold, the program chairman, and Dorothy Atkinson, executive director of the AAASS, who were responsible for the efficient organization of the Washington Congress; to Oskar Anweiler and Alexander Dallin, the past and current presidents of the International Committee, for encouraging the publication of these proceedings; and to Roger Kanet, the general editor for the first two congressses, whose advice has been invaluable to his successor.

Thanks also are owing to the Congress participants who submitted their papers for consideration, to the Editorial Committee that selected those to be published, and to the editors of the various volumes.

R. C. Elwood
General Editor

Preface

Soviet policy toward the countries of Asia, Africa and Latin America has undergone substantial expansion and change during the three decades since Khrushchev first initiated efforts to break out of the international isolation in which the USSR still found itself in the immediate post-Stalin years. Over the course of the past thirty years the Soviets have expanded significantly both the geographic range of their involvement with developing countries and the intensity of their political, military and economic activities. Moreover, they have increasingly acted in consort with "allies" such as Cuba and the countries of Eastern Europe. The studies included in the present volume examine various aspects of recent Soviet and East European policy toward the Third World.

The five chapters in Part 1 deal with broad aspects of Soviet policy. In the first chapter Roger Kanet examines the major trends in Soviet policy over the past thirty years. Elizabeth Kridl Valkenier is concerned especially with recent Soviet reassessments of both the nature of and prospects for revolutionary change in the developing countries, while Mark N. Katz discusses the problems faced by the Soviets in their support for "client" states currently confronted by internal insurgencies. In the two final chapters in Part 1 Paul Roth and Roger Kanet examine aspects of Soviet information and propaganda policy. While Roth notes the Soviet use of the concept of a New World Information Order to try to control Western news and information media, Kanet deals with the place of propaganda in Soviet policy in the Third World.

The three chapters that comprise Part 2 are concerned with various aspects of Soviet and East European economic involvement in the developing world. Heinrich Machowski and Siegfried Schultz provide an overview of Soviet economic policy toward developing countries, while Laure Després adds a treatment of the East European component of CMEA trade. Finally, Giovanni Graziani finds that the trade patterns of the non-European members of the CMEA are virtually identical to those of other developing countries with the industrialized West.

Part 3 includes two case studies of Soviet policy toward Syria during Andropov's year of leadership of the CPSU, by Robert O. Freedman, and of the military-security aspects of Soviet relations with India by Jyotirmoy Banerjee.

The editor wishes to express his appreication to all who have facilitated the preparation of this volume. These include, first of all, the authors of the individual chapters and those whose comments at the Washington Congress of the Committee for Soviet and East European Studies resulted in improvements in the original manuscripts prepared for presentation at the Congress. Thanks go, as well, to Professor R. C. Elwood, the General Editor of the volumes resulting from the Washington Congress, and to the members of the editorial committee who read and commented on these and other papers that were submitted for consideration for possible inclusion in this volume and in a possible second volume on Soviet foreign policy that did not materialize. Finally, I am especially endebted to Ms Mary Hack and Mr John Sullivan who assisted in editing the papers and to Ms Deborah Campbell who has maintained her sense of humor despite having to type and retype portions of the manuscript.

ROGER E. KANET
Urbana, Illinois

PART I

The Third World in Soviet foreign policy

I

The Soviet Union and the Third World from Khrushchev to Gorbachev: the place of the Third World in evolving Soviet global strategy

ROGER E. KANET

Since the end of the Second World War the conflict between the United States and the Soviet Union has been the single most important factor influencing the nature of the international political system. Within a relatively short period of time after the conclusion of hostilities in Europe and Asia the two countries were engaged in a struggle for influence that focused, initially at least, on Europe. Within only a few years the Soviets managed to create a zone of satellite states in Europe which they dominated; moreover, in Asia, communist parties allied to the Soviet Union came to power in China, North Korea and North Vietnam.

Despite the significant increase in Soviet influence in the regions bordering Soviet territory and the growth of Soviet military power during the decade after the Second World War, when Stalin died in 1953 the Soviets were still in a position of substantial inferiority in comparison with the United States. The USSR was still a regional power whose major international competitor, the United States, commanded far superior resources and dominated the international system politically, militarily, and economically. Postwar Soviet expansion had played a crucial role in stimulating the creation of an American-centered system of alliances in Europe and Asia, all of which were oriented toward preventing the further extension of Soviet power and influence. As a result of the creation of this alliance system US military forces were stationed around virtually the entire periphery of the communist world, from Germany in the west, through the Middle East, and as far east as Korea and Japan.

Not only had the United States expanded significantly its political, economic and military role in international affairs in the years since the

3

war, but its major allies, Great Britain and France, were still global powers with interests and capabilities scattered throughout most of Asia and Africa. With the exception of its political and economic contacts with other recently-established communist states, the Soviet Union remained isolated from the remainder of the international community. Relations with newly independent states in Asia were virtually nonexistent, in large part as a result of Stalin's refusal to view their leaders as more than mere "lackeys" of Western imperialism. Overall, therefore, in spite of the improvement in its relative military position in the postwar period, the USSR remained politically isolated and inferior militarily and economically. Instead of reducing the security concerns of the Soviet leadership, postwar developments had, in fact, fed the traditional Russian paranoia concerning security. The Soviet Union remained, in the eyes of its leaders, a beleaguered bastion of socialism surrounded by a hostile – and militarily superior – capitalist world. Stalin's primary approach to the problem of security had followed the long-standing Russian policy of expansion and consolidation of control over regions adjacent to Soviet territory. But limited capabilities, the eventual reaction of the West, and the internal demands of the Soviet system itself had prevented the Soviet Union from expanding its zone of control much beyond those territories occupied by the Red Army at the conclusion of the Second World War, with the partial exception of China. In the years immediately following the war Soviet efforts had focused mainly on consolidating their position in Eastern Europe, although even here they continued to face resistance as events in the years 1953–56 indicated.

From the perspective of the late 1980s, the position of the USSR in the world has changed dramatically since Stalin's death. Not only is the Soviet Union no longer isolated within its postwar empire, but it now also possesses state interests of a worldwide character and is capable of projecting military, political, and economic power in most regions of the world. During the past decade it has proved both its concern for developments in areas far from the boundaries of the postwar Soviet empire and its ability and willingness to use the means necessary to influence those developments – as evidenced by Soviet activities in Angola, Ethiopia, Southeast Asia, Central America and Afghanistan.[1] Soviet interests and involvement in events far from Soviet territory, however, extend beyond the purely military. Soviet commentators continually emphasize the crucial role of the USSR in the solution of virtually all the major problems that face the international community.[2] Other indications of the expanded position of the Soviet Union in the world include the major shift in the relative military balance between it and the United States and the substantial political reorientation of much of the so-called non-aligned movement during the past twenty years, or so.[3]

The purpose of the present discussion will be to provide an overview of the evolution of the Soviet Union during the past thirty years from the position of a strictly regional power – though one with significant military capabilities and substantial untapped potential to expand its role in the world – to a global actor in the international political and security systems. Moreover, we shall demonstrate the important place that competition with the United States has held in Soviet efforts to expand their activities and influence in the countries of the Third World – or, phrased differently, the crucial role that the Third World has come to play in Soviet competition with the United States. The most important factors that explain the ability of the Soviets to expand their role in world affairs so dramatically include a persistent commitment by the Soviet leadership since the mid-1950s to break out of the bonds of US and Western containment and to expand the active role of the Soviet Union in the world; the steady and continuing buildup of Soviet military capabilities; the collapse of the European colonial system and the ability of the Soviets to profit from conflicts between the West and the developing countries;* and the basic failure of the United States and its major allies to recognize and respond immediately to what the Soviets refer to as the changing international correlation of forces.[4]

INITIAL ATTEMPTS AT SOVIET GLOBALISM

Among the first changes introduced by the post-Stalin leadership were those concerning the overall policy of the Soviet state toward the outside world. In Europe the USSR reestablished relations with communist, but maverick, Yugoslavia and reduced the level of tension in East–West relations. "Peaceful coexistence" replaced the "two-camp" thesis as the foundation of Soviet relations with the members of the NATO alliance in part, at least, to reduce the isolation of the Soviet Union and as a prelude to an eventual Western recognition of the existing political realities in postwar Europe. In its policies towards the developing world the new leadership introduced comparable innovations. No longer were countries such as India and Egypt viewed as mere dependencies of Western imperialism, but rather as independent states whose interests

---

* The terms "Third World," "developing countries," and "less-developed countries (LDCs)" are used interchangeably in this volume and refer to the non-communist states of Asia, Africa and Latin America (with the exception of Japan, Israel and South Africa).

overlapped in many areas with those of the Soviet Union and the other members of the redefined "Socialist Community."

In the mid-1950s Khrushchev initiated the attempt to expand the Soviet role in international affairs. In the Middle East, for example, the beginnings of Soviet military and economic support in Afghanistan, Egypt, and later in other radical Arab states, effectively challenged Western dominance and reduced Soviet isolation in that region of strategic significance to Soviet security. The wave of decolonization that swept over Africa in the decade after Ghanaian independence in 1957 found the USSR willing to proffer assistance to a variety of new African states. The attempted deployment of missiles in Cuba in the fall of 1962 was probably the high point of Khrushchev's efforts to challenge US dominance in world affairs; however, it also indicated most clearly the continuing inferiority of the position from which the Soviet Union was operating. In the early 1960s the Soviet Union still lacked the economic, military, and political capabilities necessary to compete effectively in most regions of the world. The United States still commanded substantial strategic superiority, and this superiority forced the Soviets to move especially cautiously – and even to retreat – in situations of direct conflict such as the Cuban missile crisis. Moreover, the absence of an effective Soviet capability to project conventional military power outside its own area of control meant that Soviet leaders had great difficulty in supporting clients or allies outside the core region of Soviet power. In 1956, for example, it was primarily US opposition to the joint British–French–Israeli attack on Egypt – not Soviet threats to intervene – that brought the Suez War to a conclusion. In 1960 the closing of the airport in Leopoldville by UN officials in the Congo effectively cut off Soviet support for the forces of Patrice Lumumba. In the mid to late 1960s Soviet-oriented political leaders in several African countries were overthrown with virtual impunity. In sum, in this period the Soviet Union was unable to provide the type of effective support that would permit it to stabilize throughout the Third World regimes which it viewed as friendly and generally supportive of Soviet interests.

The Khrushchev era witnessed a major break from the past in terms of the expansion of Soviet interests and the attempt on the part of the USSR to play a greater role in the international system. However, the results of this change in policy were at best mixed. Even though the Soviets had begun to close the military gap between themselves and the Americans and had built the foundations for the development of relations with a number of Third World countries, these relations remained fragile and provided the USSR with few concrete returns on its investment of support. Moreover, the Soviet empire itself was beset with serious internal fissures.[5] The Albanians and Chinese had already withdrawn completely from the Soviet-oriented "Socialist Community"; the Romanians successfully resisted Soviet pressures to follow a joint line in foreign affairs; and other East European countries were experimenting with their domestic political and economic systems. The accession of Cuba to the Soviet network of states and the reduction of the Western monopoly of contacts with the developing states, though clearly beneficial to Soviet interests, did not balance these losses.

In late 1964, as Brezhnev came to power in the Soviet Union, the position of the USSR in the non-communist international system was stronger than it had been a decade earlier. Still, the USSR remained primarily a regional power. Its interests and, in some cases, its commitments had expanded beyond the confines of Stalin's empire, but inadequate capabilities severely limited its ability to affect significantly events in other areas of the world.

Even prior to Khrushchev's overthrow several developments occurred that would prove to have a major impact on the growth of the role of the Soviet Union in the international system. Most important was the initiation by the early 1960s – reinforced by the débâcle of the Cuban missile crisis – of a program of military buildup in both the nuclear and conventional arenas and the Soviet military expansion into areas that until that time were outside the range of Soviet military capabilities. Especially significant was the new commitment to the creation of a blue-water navy and long-range air transport and air reconnaissance capabilities, as well as the development of a network of overflight and "basing" rights that would eventually give the Soviet Union the ability to project power in areas far beyond Soviet territory.[6]

A second development important for the expansion of the Soviet role in international affairs related to the collapse of the European colonial empires and the "radicalization" of many of the newly independent states. Conflicts of interest between the industrial West and the less developed countries provided the Soviet leadership with possibilities of expanding their involvement in countries or regions that earlier were closed to them. Related to this was the reduction of Western power – and involvement – in much of the Third World, as evidenced by the British withdrawal from the regions "east of Suez."

THE FOUNDATIONS OF THE NEW SOVIET GLOBALISM

Among the most important and visible developments in Soviet–American relations that have influenced the expansion of the international role of the USSR have been the growth of Soviet military capabilities and the resulting shift in the overall balance of military capabilities between the two superpowers. Initially the Soviets emphasized the expansion of their nuclear strategic capabilities in order to offset the superiority of the United States at the beginning of the 1960s. Early in the decade efforts were made to assure the survivability of Soviet nuclear forces with the construction of reinforced missile silos, the placing of missiles at sea, and the development of a first-generation missile defense system. By the mid-1960s the Soviets had begun to expand their own strike capabilities, and by the end of the decade had reached something approximating strategic parity.[7] Since the beginning of the 1970s, therefore, the nuclear power of the United States has been largely neutralized by countervailing Soviet strategic capabilities. This "balance of terror" has, in effect, provided the Soviets with an international strategic environment in which they have been able to employ their expanded conventional military – as well as political and economic – capabilities in ways that they view as conducive to the protection and expansion of their own state interests. Rather than making conventional military capabilities obsolete, as some Western commentators had argued during the 1960s, the nuclear stalemate between the superpowers has in fact reestablished an environment in which conventional weapons can be employed – at least in certain circumstances.

In addition to the expansion of Soviet strategic capabilities begun in the Khrushchev era and continued until the present, the Soviets have also built up their conventional military capabilities – both in Europe and throughout Asia and Africa and even Latin America – to the point where they can now project power throughout a substantial portion of the world. As already noted, among the most important aspects of this development has been the construction of both an ocean-going navy and a worldwide merchant fleet that also engages in military-related reconnaissance. Although the development of the Soviet fleet became most visible only after Khrushchev's fall from power, the decision to develop a surface fleet was made prior to the Cuban missile crisis.[8] By the 1970s the Soviets had created a naval capability that permitted them to play an important military role in various international crisis situations, such as the 1971 Indo-Pakistani War, the Middle East War of 1973, and other conflicts.[9]

In addition, they had also signed agreements with a number of developing countries that gave them access to the naval facilities necessary for the maintenance of this new fleet. The production of long-range transport aircraft and the acquisition of overflight rights and the use of landing facilities provided an important complement to the expanded naval power.[10]

Another important aspect of the expansion of the Soviet Union as a global power has been the continuing commitment of the Soviet leadership to the extension of the Soviet role in world affairs. In the mid-1970s, for example, the Soviet Minister of Defense enunciated the broadened view of the role of the Soviet military when he stated that "the historic function of the Soviet armed forces is not restricted merely to their function in defending our Motherland and the other socialist countries." Aggression by the Western "imperialist" states should be resisted "in whatever distant region of our planet" it occurs.[11] The changed correlation of forces in international affairs, the Soviets have argued, permits the USSR to provide support to the just cause of national liberation and to progressive regimes threatened with intervention by the Western imperialists or their reactionary stooges in the developing world. No longer is the capitalist West able to act with impunity in undermining progressive regimes or in supporting revolutionary movements.

Finally, at least since the overthrow of the government of Salvador Allende in Chile in 1973, the Soviets have expanded their support for "national liberation movements" and various terrorist organizations. Even though their ideological orientation and immediate goals may not coincide with many of these organizations, the Soviets have apparently decided that support for terrorism undermines the long-term interests of pro-Western states in the Third World and of the West itself.[12]

SOVIET GLOBALISM IN PRACTICE

Since the beginning of the 1970s the Soviet leadership has continued to view Europe and East Asia as areas of crucial significance to its security and has, therefore, pursued its efforts to expand the USSR's military capabilities *vis-à-vis* both NATO and the People's Republic of China, especially by deploying a new generation of intermediate-range nuclear missiles. At the same time, however, Soviet policy toward the West has been oriented as well toward reducing the tensions that characterized relations during the 1950s and 1960s. The detente policy of the 1970s fits well with the USSR's overall drive to expand its worldwide role, since part of its purpose was to reduce the likelihood of Western – especially American – response to the extension of Soviet involvement throughout the Southern Hemisphere. The Soviets hoped to be able to convince the West that improvements in direct bilateral relations between East and

West were far more important for the latter than developments in other regions of the world. They expected that the leaders of the Western alliance system would be unwilling to risk the benefits of detente – in particular economic benefits for economies that were suffering from the effects of "stagflation" – by attempting to counter Soviet activities elsewhere in the world.

In many respects this Soviet objective benefited from events in the Third World over which the Soviets themselves exercised only minimal influence. First, the continuing drive toward independence in the developing world and the inability of moderate governments in many countries to deal effectively with the problems of economic backwardness and political instability combined to bring to power throughout portions of Asia, Africa, and the Western Hemisphere a group of governments more strongly anti-Western than their predecessors. This provided the Soviets and their Cuban and East European allies with opportunities to gain access to – if not always influence in – a substantial number of developing states. At the same time the position of the United States and its Western allies deteriorated significantly throughout the Third World.

Associated with the relative change of position of the Soviet Union and the West in developing countries during the 1970s was the unwillingness or inability of the West, including the United States, to pursue a coherent course of action in its policies. The US débâcle in Vietnam, the Watergate scandal, and the exposure of various CIA activities all played a role in the mid-1970s that made it virtually impossible for the US government to initiate an effective response to Soviet activities in the Third World. Moreover, given the political environment of detente and the apparent conviction of some US leaders that the period of superpower conflict characteristic of the Cold War had come to an end, the political atmosphere in the United States was not conducive to checking Soviet attempts to expand their international role by taking advantage of conflict situations throughout the Third World. In both Angola in 1975–76 and in Ethiopia two years later the Soviets assumed correctly that they would be able to intervene without the danger of American counteraction, since the United States did not have the will to challenge the expansion of Soviet involvement in regions then considered far from the centers of primary US interest.

In the Third World itself the Soviets indicated during the 1970s that the political and military foundations that they had laid during the prior decade provided them with the capabilities to project power in order to support outcomes that they deemed favorable to their own interests. In Angola, Ethiopia, and Southeast Asia, for example, Soviet (and Cuban) support was essential in either bringing to power or consolidating regimes friendly toward and dependent on the USSR. By the middle of the 1970s the Soviet Union had become a state with both global interests and global capabilities. In Angola and again in Ethiopia it demonstrated the ability to provide allies with significant military assistance and proved that this assistance could be adequate to change the local balance of power in favor of Soviet clients. In return, the Soviets have acquired access to naval and air facilities useful in potential future conflicts with the West. Since the early 1970s the Soviets have continued to provide substantial support to political movements or countries of potential importance to their strategic and global interests, despite what seems to be a preference for supporting "progressive" regimes and movements. Although an upsurge of Soviet involvement in Sub-Saharan Africa occurred in the mid-1970s, Soviet interest is still concentrated heavily in the arc of countries bordering the southern flank of the USSR. Here the Soviet goal has remained the reduction of Western influence and military capabilities and the concomitant expansion of the military and political capabilities of the Soviet state. This has meant that the USSR has continued to provide military and political support to such countries as Iraq, Syria and South Yemen. In several cases they have signed treaties of friendship and cooperation with important South Asian, Middle Eastern and African countries (for example Iraq and India). In fact, during the 1970s they even increased their efforts to improve relations with countries formally allied with the West, such as Turkey and Iran (prior to the overthrow of the Shah) by offering economic assistance and even military sales as a means of reducing these countries' dependence on their Western allies – in particular the United States. Another important element in Soviet policy has been the search for access to both naval and airport facilities that would enable them to expand the reach of their military capabilities.

Ever since the initial establishment of contacts with Third World states more than thirty years ago the Soviets have relied heavily on the provision of economic and military assistance as means of developing and consolidating relations.[13] In general the terms of Soviet assistance are favorable when compared with commercial loans available to emerging nations on the international market, though the Soviets offer virtually no nonrepayable grants and all aid is provided in the form of credits for the purchase of Soviet goods and equipment. Soviet trade with Asia and Africa has grown rapidly as well, though an important aspect of this trade has been the degree to which it has been related to the provision of economic assistance. With relatively few exceptions (e.g., the purchase of rubber from Malaysia and grain from Argentina) trade has resulted from agreements between the Soviet leaders and their Afro-Asian counterparts which include the commitment of Soviet economic and technical assistance. Examples of this type of agreement have been those with Egypt and India which called for the Soviet Union to provide capital equipment on the basis of long-term credits. These loans were to be repaid with the products of the recipient country over a period of twelve years at an interest rate of 2.0–2.5 per cent. Such agreements have been especially attractive to those countries which have had problems obtaining the convertible currency necessary to purchase on the world market machinery and equipment needed for economic projects.

By the end of the 1970s, the relative position of the two major power blocs in the Third World had changed markedly. The collapse of the Western colonial empires and the ensuing rise of numerous anti-Western political regimes in the developing world, unilateral Western military retrenchment, and various other developments resulted in the contraction of the Western military presence and of Western political influence throughout most of Asia and Africa. At the same time the Soviets were able to establish a network of economic, political and military relationships that permitted them for the first time in their history to play the role of a global power with worldwide interests and the capabilities to pursue many of those interests effectively. The change in the relative position of the Soviet Union in the international political system stems in part from the continued buildup of Soviet military power and the willingness and ability of the Soviet leadership to take advantage of the conflicts between the less developed states and the major Western powers.[14] Already in the 1970s the Soviets were able to employ their newly developed military power to support distant and dispersed political and strategic goals. Examples include the use of the Soviet fleet in the Bay of Bengal to demonstrate support for India in the 1971 war with Pakistan, the transport of large numbers of Cuban troops to Angola four years later to support the Popular Movement for the Liberation of Angola (MPLA) and a virtual repeat of this operation in Ethiopia in 1978, and the provision of substantial military supplies to revolutionary groups in Central America in the 1980s.

By the beginning of the 1980s the Soviet Union was truly a superpower with the ability to influence developments in areas far from Soviet territory. Although the primary means available to the Soviets in their attempts to accomplish their short and long-term objectives throughout the Third World has been the provision of various forms of military support, that support has been accompanied by a wide range of other Soviet activities – relations with revolutionary movements and political parties, modest amounts of economic assistance, political support in various international forums and a vast assortment of propaganda activities.

SOVIET POLICY IN THE THIRD WORLD SINCE BREZHNEV

When Brezhnev died in fall 1982 Soviet policy toward the Third World had already entered another period of reassessment. In a number of countries with which the Soviets maintained close ties insurgencies undermined internal stability and required the continued provision of Soviet (as well as Cuban and East European) security support.[15]

Moreover, the Reagan Administration had already initiated efforts to counter what many of its members viewed as the unchallenged expansion of Soviet involvement in, and domination over, areas of strategic importance for the long-term interests of the United States and its major allies. Finally, the Soviet invasion of Afghanistan in late 1979 had called forth widespread condemnation among Third World states and had tarnished the "anti-imperialist" image that the Soviets had so assiduously attempted to cultivate. By the 1980s Soviet analysts had already begun to question the optimism of the prior decade concerning likely developments in the Third World.[16] For example, writing in late 1984 concerning the problems facing national liberation movements in the Third World, a prominent Soviet analyst had stated:

The roads of freedom are difficult, agonizingly difficult. And in some measure, to some extent, these difficulties are inevitable. Because, as historical experience shows, the transition from the old to the new and the rise of society to higher levels of civilization have never been easy, smooth or free of collisions, losses and sometimes tragic zigzags.[17]

The importance of the reassessment is most visible in the Party Program of the CPSU approved at the 27th Party Congress in March 1986. While the earlier 1961 program had spoken with great optimism about prospects for liberation and the role of the USSR in supporting the liberation struggle, the new program discusses the revitalized role of neo-colonialism and imperialism in the Third World and notes only that the "CPSU supports the just struggle waged by the countries of Asia, Africa and Latin America against imperialism . . .", and that the "Soviet Union is on the side of the states and peoples repulsing the attacks of the aggressive forces of imperialism and upholding their freedom, independence and national dignity." Progressive states are informed that the tasks of building a new society are primarily their own responsibility, although the "Soviet Union has been doing and will continue to do all it can to render the peoples following that [socialist-oriented] road assistance in economic and cultural development, in training national personnel, in strengthening their defences and in other fields."[18] Another example of the more modest level of Soviet commitment to national liberation can be seen in General Secretary Gorbachev's mentioning merely Soviet "sympathies" for the aspirations of people who are attempting to overthrow the yoke of neo-colonialism in his first speech as new leader of the CPSU.[19]

What is clear from the recent discussions among Soviet analysts concerning the Third World and even more evident from the authoritative pronouncements from the very top of the Party is the fact that the Third World is no longer given the central position in overall Soviet foreign policy that it received under Brezhnev. The results of the expanded Soviet activism in the Third World in the late 1970s have been disappointing from a Soviet perspective. Moreover, the economic and political costs of that activism have now become evident. The Soviets have entered a period in which they are emphasizing the consolidation of the positions that they gained in the 1970s in countries such as Angola, Ethiopia, and Vietnam. They are apparently not prepared to take on significant and costly new initiatives in the foreseeable future; however, they have not indicated that they are likely to consider withdrawing direct or indirect support for clients such as the puppet regimes in Afghanistan and Cambodia.

Soviet activism in the Third World in the latter stages of the Brezhnev era resulted in large part from a coincidence of several factors already discussed above: the acquisition of strategic nuclear parity, the extension of Soviet power-projection capabilities, the opportunities presented to the USSR by the collapse of the Portuguese empire in Africa and the radicalization of a number of other developing countries, and the malaise that engulfed the United States in the wake of Vietnam and Watergate. The Soviets took advantage of these factors to extend significantly their involvement in various Third World conflict situations where their ability to provide military support was important in the successful acquisition or retention of power by their new-found clients. This was all part of the much heralded "changing international correlation of forces" in favor of socialism and the Soviet Union which was referred to in virtually all Soviet assessments of global developments in the late 1970s.[20]

As a result of their support for revolutionary movements and governments the Soviets obtained some important military advantages through access to military facilities in strategically significant regions of Southeast Asia, Africa and the Middle East. However, most of their new clients were small, weak, and dependent upon continued Soviet support for their very existence. While this weakness represented an asset for the Soviets' ability to exert influence and even control, it also meant that these countries soon became a substantial drain on Soviet resources. Even prior to the death of Brezhnev, Soviet commentators and analysts began to recognize that the benefits that the USSR had gained from their "successes" in the Third World were counterbalanced, in part at least, by a new series of problems.

The first of these problems derives from the growing cost of supporting clients. A group of American analysts, for example, has estimated that the costs of Soviet empire – including Eastern Europe and the growing subsidies to Cuba and Vietnam – had reached somewhere between $35 billion and $46 billion dollars annually by 1980.[21] In more recent estimates direct economic aid from the Soviet Union and Eastern Europe (with about 80 per cent coming from the former) for 1984 came to about $700 million for Cuba, $1.2 billion for Vietnam, and $600 million for Mongolia. In addition, price subsidies for Cuba were worth more than $4.2 billion in 1984.[22] Added to this are the costs of military and economic support provided to countries such as Ethiopia and Afghanistan, neither of which is able to cover the costs of Soviet supplies with their own exports. It is essential to recall that the growing costs of Soviet overseas commitments occurred precisely at the time that the Soviet economy was suffering from falling economic growth rates.

During his brief tenure as CPSU General Secretary, Iurii Andropov made a number of statements that appeared to question the benefits for the USSR of extensive involvement in the Third World. He made it most clear that the Soviet Union was not likely to expand its economic commitments to socialist-oriented developing states when he stated: "We contribute also, to the extent of our ability, to economic development. But on the whole their economic development, just as the entire social progress of those countries, can be, of course, only the result of the work of their peoples and of a correct policy of their leadership."[23]

Besides the growing concerns about the economic drain on the Soviet economy resulting from commitments to Third World clients, Soviet analysts have recognized the fact that the successes of national liberation movements in coming to power in the 1970s have not been matched by successful efforts to create viable political–economic systems. In most of these countries economic production has fallen off since the mid-1970s, and most of the governments are faced by continuing indigenous challenges to their authority (in part, as in Nicaragua, Afghanistan, and Angola, supported from the outside). As recent Western surveys of Soviet literature on the Third World have demonstrated, the Soviets have been quite frank in recognizing the difficulties facing the vanguard parties that have come to power with Soviet assistance.[24]

A third set of problems that faces the Soviets, in part as a result of their Third World "successes" of the 1970s, derives from the deterioration of their relations with the United States. The new party program, for example, notes with concern the interrelationship between the renewed "aggressiveness" of the West in the Third World and the contradictions between the socialist and capitalist states.

The message that emerges from recent Soviet discussions about the Third World is that the Soviets are concerned about the staggering costs of maintaining their "empire" and about the inability of their weaker clients to achieve political and economic stability. They have already initiated efforts to divert some of the economic burden to their East European allies – with only limited success, given the problems facing most of these countries.[25] Moreover, they have become increasingly selective in the amounts and types of support that they are willing to provide to existing clients, e.g., Mozambique and Angola. Despite Soviet concerns about the cost of their involvement in the Third World and about the weakness and instability of most of their major Third World clients, there is no evidence that Gorbachev and his associates are likely to initiate a policy of withdrawal from prior commitments. Although the Soviets have refused to provide the economic and security backing required by the embattled regime of the late President Machel of Mozambique, elsewhere they have continued to extend substantial new support to established Third World clients and allies. In Syria they have not only replenished the arsenal destroyed by the Israelis in the air war of 1982, but have also committed a substantial number of Soviet military technicians to man the new equipment.[26] In Afghanistan the Soviets have continued to pour in manpower and resources in an attempt to defeat or demoralize the mujahedin resistance and to stabilize the puppet communist government.[27] They have continued to support Vietnam in the latter's attempts to pacify Cambodia,[28] and have increased their overall assistance to Nicaragua since the beginning of the decade.[29] Finally, the have agreed to provide India with a wide range of new weapons (including the licenses to produce advanced Soviet military aircraft) on very favorable terms, in order to forestall India's turning to the West for such equipment.[30]

Overall the post-Brezhnev leadership of the USSR has continued the policies toward most Third World clients that were initiated under Brezhnev. If anything, the costs of supporting established clients (such as Cuba, Angola and Vietnam) and of maintaining ties with important allies (such as India) have risen. Although the desire to reduce costs has been voiced increasingly, the immediate demands of retaining and consolidating the Soviet positions in the Third World have overridden this desire. Although they have been unwilling to make major new commitments – in part, most likely, because of the lack of opportunities – they have fulfilled and even expanded commitments made earlier.

They have also increased their efforts to improve relations with large capitalist states in the Third World. Their continued cultivation of relations with India is an example of this aspect of their policy, as have been their attempts to expand relations with countries such as Brazil and Argentina, even when those countries were ruled by the military.[31] Yet the problem that the Soviets face as they attempt to court these countries results from the relative lack of resources with which to compete with the West. In the 1970s they were able to capitalize on their major strength – the ability to provide security support – as they established close ties with countries in Asia, Africa and the Middle East. As they attempt to expand relations with the large, basically stable Third World states, the overall weakness of their economy represents a major drawback. Not only do they lack the investment capital and the technology sought by these countries, but increasingly they are in competition with them for export markets in the West.[32] Thus, prospects for Soviet success in this area are not at all clear.

CONTINUING LIMITATIONS ON SOVIET POLICY

Despite the significant expansion of Soviet capabilities and the new role that the USSR has been able to play in international affairs, its power and influence are still limited. First of all, the new Soviet position in the Third World depends heavily on the coincidence of Soviet interests with those of "client" states. The expulsion of the Soviets from both Egypt and Somalia during the mid-1970s indicates the degree to which the Soviets depend on the good will of such client states. Second, even with large-scale Soviet support some Third World states have been unable to accomplish the primary goal of creating a stable political system. In Angola, for example, ten years of Soviet and Cuban support have not resulted in the elimination of major domestic opposition to the MPLA, and the government would collapse without the continued support of its communist allies. President Machel of Mozambique negotiated a security arrangement with the government of South Africa and turned to Western Europe for financial support because of the inability or unwillingness of the Soviets to expand their commitments.

Another illustration of the inability of the Soviets to accomplish their goals – at least more than partially – has been in Afghanistan. The failure of Taraki, and later Amin, to consolidate their rule in Afghanistan during 1978 and 1979 eventually resulted in the Soviet decision to intervene directly. Despite the introduction of massive military power the Soviets have not succeeded, after almost seven years, in eliminating widespread opposition to the puppet regime in Kabul. Moreover, the Soviet invasion and continued military presence in Afghanistan resulted in substantial condemnation, even from developing countries, which in the past generally supported the Soviet Union. Perhaps the most important long-term cost of the Soviet invasion of Afghanistan has been the evidence that it provided to leaders of developing states of the expansionist nature of the Soviet state.

Elsewhere in the Middle East the Soviets have been largely frozen out of the major developments in the Arab–Israeli conflict for more than a decade after the October War of 1973. Only by committing themselves to the support of the members of the Rejectionist Front in the late 1970s were they able to continue to play a role – albeit quite marginal – in developments in the region. However, that role was played largely on terms set by the Arabs. Dependence on the Soviets did not prevent Syria from intervening in the Lebanese Civil War of 1975–76, contrary to Soviet wishes at that time. Nor did Soviet displeasure prevent Iraq, which depended almost entirely on Soviet weapons until its efforts in the late 1970s to diversify its sources, from invading Iran in the fall of 1980. Events in Lebanon and in Syria since 1983 indicate that, although the Soviets provide virtually all the military hardware and substantial numbers of military "advisors" for Syria, the government of President Assad continues to makes its decisions largely independent of Soviet wishes. Finally, the recent bloody struggle between rival Marxist factions in South Yemen – the closest Soviet ally in the Middle East – demonstrates the problems faced by the Soviets in influencing "client" states.

When we turn to the position of the Soviet Union in the international communist movement we find the most serious challenges to its expanded role in the international system. Despite three changes in Soviet leadership since 1982 and a major shift in Chinese domestic and foreign policy, Soviet relations with China have not improved significantly over the past decade. The Chinese still represent a challenge to Soviet interests in Asia and have been among the most vocal critics of detente with the Soviet Union and of Soviet expansion throughout the Third World. Evidence of the likelihood of greater Chinese cooperation – even in the military realm – with the United States, Japan, and Western Europe is viewed with great alarm in Moscow.

In the global military realm, the deployment of intermediate-range nuclear missiles by NATO in the 1980s and the revitalization of US military capabilities by the Carter Administration and, even more vigorously, by the Reagan Administration have presented the Soviets with a whole new series of problems. Unless the new Soviet leadership is willing either to negotiate seriously on limitations and reductions in nuclear weapons or to expend an increasing percentage of its GNP on armaments, it will be faced with the prospects of falling behind the United States in a renewed arms race.

Besides the external factors that are likely to restrict the continued expansion of the Soviet role in world affairs, the weakness of the Soviet economy has limited the degree to which the USSR can compete effectively with the West in influencing international economic developments. To date the Soviets have been required to adapt themselves to the existing international economic system as a means of participating in world trade. Soviet economic relations with both the West and the developing countries are carried out within an international economic system dominated by the Western industrial countries. In fact, the growth of East–West economic relations during the 1970s created a certain degree of interdependence of the two groups of countries. The Soviets and their East European allies have discovered that they are no longer immune to developments in the international economy such as inflation or recession.

It is not likely that the Soviets will be able in the coming years to solve the basic structural problems of their economy. Moreover, the probability of increasing difficulty in meeting their (and their East European allies') growing energy needs bodes ill for high growth rates; finally, the precipitous drop in the world market price of oil has cut substantially into the Soviet ability to cover the cost of needed Western imports. With continued low levels of economic growth most likely, the Soviets will find it difficult to make additional commitments of the sort that they have already made to Cuba, Vietnam, Angola, Ethiopia, and Afghanistan.

Yet, having noted the problems that the Soviets continue to face in their attempts to extend their global influence and to affect events in regions both near to and far from their own borders, it must be noted that the power base from which the Gorbachev regime is able to operate in world affairs is substantially stronger than that which Khrushchev inherited from Stalin in 1953 or that which Brezhnev took over from Khrushchev eleven years later. Most important is the fact that the Soviets have devoted major efforts to building up both nuclear strategic and conventional military capabilities and have demonstrated over the course of the past fifteen years, or so, that they are willing to employ that enhanced military power in a variety of ways and in conjunction with other capabilities in the attempt to accomplish their objectives. Limitations still exist on the ability of the USSR to act globally – but the availability of extensive military capabilities has enabled the leaders in the Kremlin to challenge Western interests throughout the world in ways that would have been unthinkable only twenty years ago.

NOTES

1 Although Afghanistan borders on the core area of Soviet power, the Soviet invasion of that country in late December 1979 represented an extension of the Soviet willingness to use military power in order to serve Soviet state interests. Until the invasion, the direct use of Soviet military power had been limited to the areas under direct Soviet control since 1945, i.e., in Eastern Europe.

2 See, for example, the argument of B.S. Fomin of the Institute of Economics of the World Socialist System in Moscow that "no stable and viable world economic system is possible without the equal participation of the socialist states, and without a just consideration of their specific interests." B. S. Fomin, "The New International Economic Order as Viewed in the CMEA Countries," in *Eastern Europe and the New International Economic Order: Representative Samples of Socialist Perspectives*, Ervin Laszlo and Joel Kurtzman, eds. (New York: Pergamon Press, 1980), p. 7. Similar statements can be found in all Soviet commentaries on the development of a New International Economic Order.

3 See US Department of Defense, *Soviet Military Power* 1985 (Washington: US Government Printing Office, 1985). For an excellent discussion of changes in the political orientation of the non-aligned movement, see William M. LeoGrande, "Evolution of the Nonaligned Movement," *Problems of Communism*, vol. XXIX, no. 1 (1980), pp. 35–52.

4 For a discussion of the Soviet view of the nature and importance of the international correlation of forces, see Michael J. Deane, "The Correlation of World Forces," *Orbis*, vol. XX (1976), pp. 625–37; see also Sh. Sanakoyev, "The World Today: Problems of the Correlation of Forces," *International Affairs*, no. 11 (1974), pp. 40–50.

5 Ghita Ionescu, *The Break-Up of the Soviet Empire in Eastern Europe* (Baltimore: Penguin Books, 1965).

6 For a brief discussion of the development of Soviet power projection capabilities, see W. Scott Thompson, *Power Projection: A Net Assessment of US and Soviet Capabilities* (New York: National Strategy Information Center, Agenda Paper no. 7, 1978), pp. 10–19. See also Roger E. Kanet, "L'Union soviétique et les pays en voie de développement: le rôle de l'aide militaire et de transferts d'armes," in *L'Union Soviétique dans les Relations Internationales*, Francis Contes and Jean-Louis Martres, eds. (Paris: Economica, 1982), pp. 415–64. Rajan Menon cautions against exaggerating the ability of the Soviets to project military power in the face of US competition. See his "Military Power, Intervention, and Soviet Policy in the Third World," in *Soviet Foreign Policy in the 1980s*, Roger E. Kanet, ed. (New York: Praeger, 1982), pp. 263–84.

7 For a discussion of these points, see Carl G. Jacobsen, *Soviet Strategic Initiatives: Challenge and Response* (New York: Praeger, 1979), pp. 1–8.

8 See Norman Polmar, *Soviet Naval Power: Challenge for the 1970s*, rev. edn (New York: Crane, Russak, for National Strategy Information Center, 1974), pp. 40–45.

9 For a number of studies of the use of the Soviet fleet in international conflict situations, see Michael McGwire, Ken Booth, and John McDonnell, eds., *Soviet Naval Policy: Objectives and Constraints* (New York: Praeger, 1975); Michael McGuire and John McDonnell, eds., *Soviet Naval Influence: Domestic and Foreign Dimensions* (New York: Praeger, 1977); and Bradford Dismukes and James M. McConnell, eds., *Soviet Naval Diplomacy* (New York: Pergamon Press, 1979). For an excellent analysis of the political role of Soviet military power, see Stephen S. Kaplan *et al.*, *Diplomacy of Power: Soviet Armed Forces as a Political Instrument* (Washington: The Brookings Institution, 1981).

10 For discussions of the new Soviet capabilities, see Thompson, *Power Projection*, and Jacobsen, *Soviet Strategic Initiatives*, esp. pp. 51–72. For a reasoned argument that one must be careful not to exaggerate the facilities that have been made available to the Soviets, see Richard Remnek's appendix in *Soviet Naval Diplomacy*, Dismukes and McConnell, eds. See also, Kanet, "L'Union Soviétique."

11 Andrei Grechko, "The Leading Role of the CPSU in Building the Army of a Developed Socialist State," *Voprosy istorii KPSS* (May 1974), translated in *Strategic Review*, vol III, no. 1 (1975), pp. 88–93.

12 For a brief recent overview of the place of support for international terror in Soviet foreign policy, see Samuel T. Francis, *The Soviet Strategy of Terror* (Washington: The Heritage Foundation, 1985), rev. ed.

13 See Roger E. Kanet, "Soviet Military Assistance to the Third World," in *Communist Nations' Military Assistance*, John F. Copper and Daniel S. Papp, eds. (Boulder, CO: Westview Press, 1983), pp. 39–71.

14 Several recent books examine Soviet involvement in Third World conflicts in some detail. See, for example, Stephen T. Hosmer and Thomas W. Wolfe, *Soviet Policy and Practice Toward Third World Conflicts* (Lexington, MA: Lexington Books, D.C. Heath, 1983); Joachim Krause, *Sowjetische Militärhilfepolitik gegenüber Entwicklungsländer* (Baden-Baden: Nomos Verlagsgesellschaft, 1985); and Bruce D. Porter, *The USSR in Third World Conflicts: Soviet Arms and Diplomacy in Local Wars, 1945–1980* (Cambridge: Cambridge University Press, 1984).

15 For a discussion of guerilla insurgencies targeted against Soviet-supported states, see Mark N. Katz, "Anti-Soviet Insurgencies: Growing Trend or Passing Phase?", Chapter 3, below.

16 Among the most comprehensive recent treatments of changing Soviet interpretations of the Third World are Jerry F. Hough, *The Struggle for the Third World: Soviet Debates and American Options* (Washington: The Brookings Institution, 1986), Danial S. Papp, *Soviet Perceptions of the Developing World in the 1980s: The Ideological Basis* (Lexington, MA/Toronto: Lexington Books, 1985), and Thomas J. Zamostny, "Moscow and the Third World: Recent Trends in Soviet Thinking," *Soviet Studies*, vol. XXXVI (1984), pp. 223–35.

17 A. Bovin, "Difficult Roads of Freedom, *Izvestiia*, 12 November 1984, p. 5; translated in *The Current Digest of the Soviet Press*, vol. XXXVI, no. 48 (26 December 1984), p. 48.

18 "Programma Kommunisticheskoi Partii Sovetskogo Soiuza. Novaia Redaktsiia," *Pravda*, 7 March 1986, p. 7; translated in *New Times*, no. 12 (31 March 1986), p. 43. The previous party program, published in 1961, had spoken of a mighty wave of national liberation revolutions that were "sweeping away the colonial system and undermining the foundations of imperialism." *Pravda*, 2 November 1961.

19 *Pravda*, 11 March 1985.

20 See Michael J. Deane, "The Correlation of World Forces."
21 See Charles Wolf et al., The Costs of the Soviet Empire (Santa Monica, CA: The Rand Corporation, no. R-3073/1-NA, September 1983), p. 19.
22 Foreign and Commonwealth Office, London, "Aid to the Developing World," Background Brief (April 1986), p. 3.
23 "Speech of the General Secretary of the Central Committee of the CPSU Comrade Iu. V. Andropov," Kommunist, no. 9 (1983). See, also, Andropov's earlier article entitled, "Under the Banner of Lenin, Under the Party's Leadership," Izvestiia, 23 February 1979. The party program approved in 1986 used virtually the same wording as that of Andropov when it noted that "every people creates, mostly by its own efforts, the material and technical base necessary for the building of a new society, and seeks to improve the well-being and cultural standards of the masses." "Programma Kommunisticheskoi Partii," p. 7.
24 See note 16.
25 For a discussion of East European economic relations with the Third World, see Roger E. Kanet, "Patterns of Eastern European Economic Involvement in the Third World," in Eastern Europe and the Third World: East vs. South?, Michael Radu, ed. (New York: Praeger, 1981) pp.303-32; see, also, Roger E. Kanet, "East European Trade in the 1980s: Reorientation in International Economic Relations," in The Economies of Eastern Europe and Their Foreign Economic Relations, NATO Economics Directorate, ed. (Brussels: NATO Economics Directorate, 1987).
26 For a perceptive discussion of Soviet–Syrian relations, see Robert O. Freedman, "Moscow, Damascus and the Lebanese Crisis of 1982–1984," in Superpower Involvement in the Middle East: Dynamics of Foreign Policy, Paul Marantz and Blema S. Steinberg, eds. (Boulder, CO: Westview Press, 1985), pp. 87–132; see also Freedman's "Soviet Policy Toward Syria in the Andropov Era," Chapter 9, below.
27 One of the best studies of the Soviet role in Afghanistan is Henry S. Bradsher's Afghanistan and the Soviet Union, 2nd edn (Durham, NC: Duke University Press, 1986); see, also, Joseph G. Whelan and Michael J. Dixon, The Soviet Union in the Third World, 1980–85: An Imperial Burden or Political Asset? (Report prepared for the Committee on Foreign Affairs, US House of Representatives, by the Congressional Research Service, Library of Congress). (Washington: US Government Printing Office, 1985), pp. 69–86.
28 Whelan and Dixon, The Soviet Union, pp. 114–21.
29 For a good discussion of Soviet military support for Nicaragua and for revolutionary groups in Central America that places that support in the overall context of Soviet military aid policy, see Krause, Sowjetische Militärhilfepolitik, pp. 366–73; see, also, Mark Falcoff, "Marxist–Leninist Regimes in Central America and the Carribbean," in Uri Ra'anan et al., Third World Marxist–Leninist Regimes: Strengths, Vulnerabilities, and US Policy (New York: Pergamon-Brassey's International Defense Publishers, 1985), pp. 45–82; Daniel Abele, "The Soviet Commitment to the Sandinistas," Radio Liberty Research, RL 2698/86, 18 July 1986.
30 See Whelan and Dixon, The Soviet Union, pp. 130–33.
31 For a discussion of Soviet relations with Argentina, see ibid., pp. 356–64.
32 For an excellent examination of the issue of growing competition on the world market between newly-industrializing states and the members of the CMEA, see Kazimierz Poznanski, "Competition between Eastern Europe and Developing Countries in the Western Market for Manufactured Goods," in East European Economies: Slow Growth in the 1980s, vol. II: Foreign Trade and International Finance (Selected papers submitted to the Joint Economic Committee, Congress of the United States), John P. Hardt and Richard F. Kaufman (Washington: US Government Printing Office, 1986), pp. 62–90.

2

Revolutionary change in the Third World: recent Soviet reassessments*

ELIZABETH KRIDL VALKENIER

An increasingly sober and far-ranging review of the nature of Third World radicalism and its relationship to scientific socialism marks a significant change in Soviet perceptions about the USSR's ability to manipulate anti-imperialism to its advantage. Dating from about 1980, this re-examination is related to Moscow's difficulties in imposing a Marxist regime in Afghanistan, the unexpected turn of the Iranian revolution from an anti-American upheaval into Islamic fundamentalism, and the mounting concern for the performance of the Soviet economy.

Official statements give only partial and conflicting evidence of an altered outlook. In the past three years, for example, the May Day slogans, which reaffirm the regime's domestic and foreign policy objectives, have given up many ritualistic claims about revolutionary change in the Third World. They no longer single out the radical states that have chosen the path of socialist orientation; the adjective "invincible" has been dropped from the reference to the Soviet Union's alliance with the national liberation movements; and the "struggle against imperialism" is not mentioned as the goal of international solidarity. Yet, these claims have not disappeared altogether from other pronouncements.

To get a better sense of the on-going reassessment one must turn to the writings of Soviet experts on the Third World. Many of them are prominent in academic and Party institutions that help formulate foreign policy. Among these people the change of mood is unmistakable. It is a far cry from the high expectations for the prospects of socialism in the developing countries and the resulting shift in the "world balance of forces" in favor of the USSR that was first evident under Khrushchev and again in the mid-1970s after the collapse of the Portuguese empire.

* Reprinted with permission from *World Politics*, vol. XXXVIII, no. 3 (1986), pp. 415–34.

Aside from the fact that Soviet research institutions work for various government agencies, two factors make the skeptical re-evaluation relevant to the conduct of Soviet foreign policy.

1   Prominence and publicity are given to the questioning of the old assumptions and to the new, undogmatic interpretations: they are not buried in small-run academic publications but also appear in the pages of the Party daily and the theoretical press.

2   There is a certain congruence between the concerns and the arguments advanced by the skeptical experts and those of Gorbachev.

Both favor a pragmatic approach that underscores the primacy of economic imperatives over ideological desiderata. This chapter outlines the various components of the recent reassessment and briefly discusses its implications for Soviet policies toward the developing countries.

SOCIALIST ORIENTATION AND SOCIALISM

The evident loss of confidence in the prospects for 'socialist orientation" illustrates better than any other issue the nature and extent of Moscow's disenchantment with the course of revolutionary change.

"Socialist orientation" is more or less synonymous with the earlier term "non-capitalist path." It first became current in the late 1960s to show how the radical non-communist less developed countries (LDCs) were progressing toward socialism. At the start, the theory and practice of socialist orientation were analyzed almost exclusively in political categories. Appropriate political institutions – especially a disciplined revolutionary democratic or vanguard party – were deemed essential for devising, implementing and sustaining a program of progressive socio-economic change. The question of appropriate economic policies was either by-passed or ignored, as the proceedings of an academic conference held in 1970 show: "A characteristic feature of every type of non-capitalist development is that socialist transition starts with the superstructure . . . The political superstructure subsequently creates conditions for restructuring the socio-economic base."[1]

By the end of the 1970s that formulation had been reversed. It was now seen that the gap between political aspirations and socio-economic realities seriously impeded the construction of socialism in backward countries. The dilemma was well stated in a monograph published in 1978:

The political goals demand the speediest possible subordination of the economic basis to the revolutionary democratic superstructure through the all-around development of the state section, elimination of foreign and local enterprise from the national economy. But the economic circumstances dictate a different political line – attracting foreign and local capital for the development of the national economy.[2]

Recognition of this gap and of the ensuing difficulties spawned a myriad of conferences, studies and publications that sought to redefine the concept of socialist orientation in terms that were more convenient to the USSR. The check-list of genuine Marxist–Leninist features absent in the radical states grew longer at the same time as the proper relationship between them and the Soviet Union was specified.

A collective volume published in 1982 provides an authoritative guide to the results of the reassessment.[3] The galaxy of authors alone – K. Brutents and R. Ulianovskii (who served under B. Ponomarev in the Central Committee's International Department), Anatolii Gromyko and E. Primakov (who direct the African and the Oriental Institutes respectively), among others – assured its importance. Moreover, the book continues to be cited as furnishing a definitive interpretation of "socialist orientation" and its theses are seen as solidly applicable in 1986 no less than in 1982.[4]

The work is noteworthy for the care it takes to spell out how far states of socialist orientation fall short of genuine socialism, the difficulties they face along their progressive course, and the nature of their relations with the USSR. To begin with, it is stated unequivocally that although socialist orientation is a progressive form of statehood, it can in no way be equated with the actual establishment of socialism. At best, it designates policies oriented toward socialism; it is definitely a pre-paratory, pre-socialist stage.[5]

The enumeration of the obstacles that beset the non-capitalist path makes it clear why the Soviets now regard socialist orientation as only the first, tentative step in the direction of socialism. The book is explicit about the numerous interrelated problems posed by the economic, social and political underdevelopment of most of the radical states. (Significantly, rather than acknowledge the advances scored by countries like Algeria, it prefers to focus on far weaker states like Afghanistan or the Congo People's Republic.) Social conditions, such as widespread illiteracy and the lack of sharp class differentiation, make it difficult to attain high productivity or to introduce progressive economic reforms.[6] The enumeration of embedded obstacles substantiates another argument: namely, that the choice of socialist orientation is a process that is reversible.[7]

Concerning the relationship of the states of socialist orientation to the USSR and the socialist community, the book makes a very revealing assertion – one that had not been elaborated before. It draws a clear distinction between the early travelers on the non-capitalist path (Mongolia and the Soviet Asian republics) and the present-day radical states as to the support they can expect from the USSR:

The peculiarities of current-day non-capitalist development . . . consist . . . in the fact that the countries which proclaim socialist orientation are not closely tied, geographically, economically and politically, to the victorious socialist revolution . . . or to the world socialist system, as were the pioneers of the non-capitalist development.[8]

A comparison of Boris Ponomarev's guidelines for Third World radicals at a conference in 1980 (which Brutents, Gromyko and Primakov also attended) with the 1982 analysis shows the evolution in Soviet reconsiderations.[9] Though Ponomarev's speech indicated that the CPSU was worried about the prospects for socialist orientation, it still concentrated on detailing the steps that would help avoid mistakes and overcome difficulties. Two years later, the brunt of the argument fell on the obstacles. Similarly, even though Ponomarev discussed the economic preconditions that would help steady the leftist course, he nevertheless stressed the ways to strengthen the political apparatus. At that juncture, it was still believed that firm political control was the determining factor. The collective volume, by contrast, held that economic and social conditions in many radical LDCs made political control quite problematic. Finally, Ponomarev underscored the knitting of ties with the socialist countries as one of the seven preconditions for the successful preservation of "progressive positions." By 1982, the precondition of close ties was being radically redefined.

THE VANGUARD PARTIES AND SOCIETY

A general apprehension about the states of socialist orientation proceeding too precipitately in building socialism and about the malfunctioning of the state apparatus was evident by 1980.[10] Uneasiness about the radical parties' claim to be full-fledged socialist parties surfaced later and become quite pronounced under Andropov.

One article, written on the anniversary of the 2nd Congress of the Russian Social Democratic Labor Party, concluded:

It seems to us that it would be correct to consider the ruling parties of the socialist oriented states as parties of the working people in the sense that they (1) consist basically or exclusively of the representatives of the working masses; (2) reflect the interests of the urban and rural working people, and (3) arm themselves with the ideology of scientific socialism. At the same time, these are not yet fully formed proletarian parties – in their composition, structure, experience, political consciousness – but parties completing the transition from revolutionary democratic to Marxist–Leninist.[11]

It is symptomatic of the recent trends that Soviet specialists have started to examine systematically the shortcomings of the vanguard parties. For most authors the basic difficulty derives from the nature of society in these states; or to put it in Soviet terms, "the incomplete process of class formation."[12] Thus, at the July 1983 conference on the working class in the LDCs, only a minority argued the view that a "more or less" sizable modern working class had been formed in the countries of Asia and Africa. Most participants took issue not only with this contention but also with the claim that the proletariat in the Third World was becoming the vanguard of the all-national struggle. Instead, critics of the old dogmatic notions objected to the mechanistic application of Western models and pointed to the pitfalls in delineating the proletariat by purely economic or numerical indicators. They held that such an approach ignored cultural traditions and the "social psychology" of this stratum in the liberated countries.[13]

In the absence of the requisite class basis, the mere proclamation of adherence to Marxism–Leninism is not sufficient to turn a vanguard party into a genuine and correctly functioning socialist party.[14] Some authors lay stress on the long time it will take for socio-economic preconditions to ripen so as to assure an adequate level of organizational maturity. Significantly, they stress this factor more than the inclusion of communists in the party.[15] Others state the need for immediate preparatory steps. First, the party ranks must be broadened with members from the working class that is being formed and from the cooperative peasantry. Second, intensive educational and ideological work must be undertaken to eradicate the traditional (i.e., tribal or religious) outlook in the membership. Third, cadres must be trained who can correctly evaluate both the achievements and the mistakes of the revolutionary struggle.[16]

Freer discussion of the social realities in the radical states raises questions about the character of their leadership. Some writers stress how the social structure makes it difficult for leaders to communicate effectively with the population and to carry out ambitious reform programs.[17] Others discuss the distortions of power inherent in a situation where there is such a marked gulf between the masses and the ruling group. Regarding the latter situation, some specialists draw attention to the "predominant role of strong personalities."[18] But others examine the wider implications of elitism. Here Vladimir Li's recent book-length analysis is outstanding in investigating the processes that result from the misuse of power – how the political gap between the masses and the ruling elite is filled by the proliferating bureaucracy.[19]

Reassessment of the prospects for the vanguard parties is not limited to analyzing problems and excesses. A further topic, with practical policy implications, has surfaced in print. Moreover, it was raised by Rostislav Uli'anovskii, a conservative expert in charge of relations with Third World radicals in the Central Committee's International Department, who had previously not been critical of the revolutionary democrats. But, by 1984, he too showed exasperation with the "leftist" political excesses perpetrated by Third World radicals.[20] Specifically, he singled out those leaders who, scorning the multi-faceted nature of national or revolutionary democracy, had reduced socialist orientation to a single variant – that of the dictatorship of the proletariat.

This advocacy of greater political pluralism was adumbrated with the familiar arguments about non-capitalist development being a long, transitional stage requiring adaptation to what was feasible. But there was also a novel warning: given President Reagan's crusades, transgressing the feasible could threaten world peace.

Coming at a time when several radical regimes face serious counter-insurgencies, as in Nicaragua and Angola, Uli'anovskii's article could well signify that some leading figures in the USSR are not averse to seeing the radical leaders share power with other political forces in order to build greater support at home and to gain wider acceptance abroad. Political pluralism was certainly not envisioned in earlier Soviet discussions of the vanguard parties.

ECONOMIC POLICIES—FOREIGN

Current Soviet views on the LDCs' foreign economic policies indicate that here too an awareness of the gap between ideological formulas and harsh realities has led to important revisions. It is now acknowledged that radical states remain tied to the capitalist markets. Indeed, their adherence to the old economic order even while they set off in a new political direction is considered to be one of the new trends in the world revolutionary experience. Thus, recent scholarly monographs argue that the socialist oriented states should adjust their development plans and expectations to an efficient and effective utilization of the international division of labor.[21]

These views constitute a significant modification of notions prevalent in the early 1970s, which held that it was desirable and possible for the LDCs to distance themselves from capitalist markets and to start forming an alternative economic order – a socialist international division of labor with the Soviet Bloc countries. Unable to form an alternative system, the Soviets have been forced to concede the inescapable condition of global interdependence.

This recognition, in turn, has made Soviet experts become critical of the radical Third World economists. Until about 1976, Soviet specialized writings supported the LDCs economic claims against the West. It was simply assumed that LDC views dovetailed with Soviet theories about the operations of imperialism. (In part, the Soviet outlook stemmed from ignorance, for there were no detailed studies by Latin American and other radical economists; in part, these views did not really affect international relations until the formation of the Group of 77.) But when in the 1970s the LDCs became an articulate and effective pressure group, Soviet scholars began to pay attention to Third World economic thinking.

The first studies were largely descriptive, and such critical observations as they contained were directed at discrete issues and topics. For example, one book criticized Samir Amin's proposals for a substantial upward revision of raw material prices. Whereas Amin considered the issue a simple matter of political will, the Soviet economist argued that "price formation [was] part of an international economic mechanism and subject to its objective laws."[22]

By 1982, B. Slavnyi's study analyzed Amin's theories and the entire dependency school in terms not of committing partial deviations but of being wholly juxtaposed to Marxism.[23] Moreover, Slavnyi found radical Third World economists deficient because they were "outdated." "[They] did not take into account the most recent trends [in international economics] which seem to demonstrate that as the process of internationalization progresses the developing world will attain technological independence and the external factors [making for underdevelopment] will cease to prevail over the domestic factors."[24]

Revealingly, the book's concluding chapter summarized the arguments of various Western economists who reject the "extremism" of the dependence school with its contention that interaction with the advanced capitalist states results in nothing but "plunder." It also drew attention to Western interpretations of the role of monopolies as the consequence of the emergence of supra-nation-state processes and a world-wide economic system.

The USSR's responses in the debates on the New International Economic Order (NIEO) show an evolution that parallels the novel thinking in the community of specialists. When one looks behind the customary rhetoric, it is evident that the substantive portions of Soviet proposals at the UN no longer treat the international market as an imperialist cabal to safeguard capitalist exploitation but as an evolving network of dependencies.[25] Thus, the Bloc's declaration to the 5th United Nations Conference on Trade and Development (UNCTADV) in 1979 held that it was possible to "democratize" international economic relations even before the "inherent defects of capitalism" had been eliminated from the operations of the world economy.[26] The aim of Soviet policy in international trade is to eliminate "discrimination" against *all* nations (a neutral, universalistic term) and not merely "exploitation" of the developing countries (a particular, systematic notion). As was stated by A. Mandzhulo, Deputy Foreign Trade Minister, on the eve of UNCTAD VI: the USSR "always believed . . . that all trade flows are in one way or another interconnected." Therefore, he proposed that UNCTAD should establish universally observed procedures for conducting trade, and that the LDC demands should be discussed in the context of a general review of all the principles, rules and norms of international trade.[27]

Criticism of the LDCs' "local" or "parochial" policies for the NIEO is the obverse of Soviet advocacy of universal principles in international trade. Among various comments on the results of UNCTAD VI, objections to the demands for preferential or concessional treatment of the developing countries ranked high.[28] Soviet specialists criticized the notion of an automatic distribution of income from the developed to the developing countries, for this contradicted all the laws of international trade as well as theoretical principles of economics. Similarly, there was no endorsement of the advocacy to develop South–South cooperation or self-reliance to the extent that such undertakings create barriers to a free flow of trade.

The changing Soviet views on exploitation in international trade naturally touch upon ideological principles. It is interesting to note that new formulations on the nature of imperialism are on the agenda of the discussions related to the new edition of the Party program (as adopted in 1986). Against the traditional interpretation, one revision suggests that the capacity to innovate and adapt, and not the exploitation of the LDCs, sustains the imperialist system.[29]

ECONOMIC POLICIES–DOMESTIC

On the domestic situation of the LDCs, Soviet experts have also come to terms with various aspects of the once-reviled operations of capitalism. Capitalist institutions, it is now acknowledged, are a necessary prerequisite for development and growth; capitalist forms of ownership, labor discipline and work habits, too, for that matter, fulfil economically valid functions.[30]

Well before the Soviets became visibly concerned about economic performance in states of socialist orientation, they had come to accept the need for the LDCs in general to pursue pragmatic rather than strictly systemic (i.e., anti-capitalist or anti-imperialist) policies. But economic rationality was not as readily prescribed for the radical states. By and large, most writers advocated or condoned a more or less speedy elimination of the multinationals and other foreign capital, of the local big business and feudal elements. At present, such policies are criticized as harmful "leftist" excesses that endanger not only the future of a national economy but also the socialist perspective as well. Instead, Soviet specialists in effect endorse a long period of coexistence with capitalist structures.

It is now recognized that the states of socialist orientation should come to terms with foreign investment. Most recent books maintain that it is necessary to attract foreign capital in order to stimulate economic development, to increase employment, and to satisfy the consumer. The ideal means, it seems, is through mixed companies that combine partial foreign private investment with local state investment.[31]

A similar tolerance toward private capital has also emerged in Soviet specialized literature. At first, petty traders and small-scale private enterprise were tolerated as consistent with socialist orientation, largely because of persisting local traditions and the needs of the service sector. By now large, modern capitalist enterprise is also tolerated by some authors on the grounds that its operations are essential for genuine economic development.[32]

What about the state sector, whose size alone used to be considered the indicator of how close a country was getting to socialism? At present, its economic performance, not its extent, is of primary interest. Hence, Soviet specialists write that it is only the few, more advanced states like Egypt (before 1973) and Algeria that can have an efficient and effective public sector. The far more numerous backward states cannot afford that political luxury – for them a large state sector entails deficit operations that can eat up whatever private enterprise manages to accumulate. Similar strictures are now applied to such other government controls as state planning. The less developed a country, the less rigorous the direct state interference it can afford to sustain.[33]

Most of the radical states are agrarian countries where the over-whelming majority of the population lives off land. Here there has also been a change in Soviet attitude toward private ownership. Much was written in the past about the need of progressive states to move to the more advanced form of cooperative farming prior to full collectiviz-ation. Some recent publications concede that this is not the optimal solution and that for a long time to come a highly differentiated structure of ownership will have to remain.[34] This means countenancing not only small but also large-scale private farming before conditions are ripe for the cooperativization of the peasantry. For the present and the immediate future, it has to be recognized that cooperative labor cannot be truly productive. Therefore, "a policy oriented at the decisive role of private factors in production and stimulating the individual labor of the peasantry," is recommended by one specialist.[35]

EASTERN TRADITION AND CIVILIZATION

Some scholars in the mid-1970s started to question the optimistic scenario of a revolutionary future in the Third World by calling attention to the uniqueness of the socio-economic processes in the LDCs.[36] These experts, however, represented a minority view in conflict with the mainstream opinion in academic and political quarters. Accordingly, their writings were severely criticized for departing from the universal and unilinear Marxist version of historical development.

The situation changed completely after 1979, as a result of the turn of events in Afghanistan and Iran. Unfulfilled revolutionary expectations for both countries produced instead a veritable revolution in Soviet Third World studies, in the sense of proving right the less orthodox scholars. As a result, concepts like the multi-structural (*mnogoukladnyi*) society and economy have gained legitimacy and are freely used even by prominent political figures. Attention now centers on the importance of "tradition," and authors who some half-dozen years earlier had to defend their views against quite vicious attacks from Marxist purists are enjoying vindication. They are key speakers at various symposia, they head new research projects, and they see their innovative studies published. More than that, these monographs are reviewed at length with full exposition of the once controversial and disparaged concepts. The obvious intent of the publicity seems to be to inform and educate the public.

The burgeoning discussion of civilization and its relationship to Marxist "formations" is a fascinating aspect of the sudden Soviet discovery of the interaction of tradition and development. It is symptomatic of the degree to which the deterministic Marxist interpretation of history is being qualified with factors that belie the rigid socio-economic scheme. A book on A. J. Toynbee appeared in 1976 without eliciting much notice; by 1983 there were numerous references to his writings.[37] What interests Soviet scholars in Toynbee are his theories about the essence of civilizations – the role of spiritual values and other non-economic factors – not what he had to say about their cycles.[38]

Two recent books are representative of the less deterministic views on the process of change in the Third World, which are closely tied up with the new-found appreciation for tradition and civilization. *The Developing Countries: Economic Growth and Social Progress*, edited by A. Ia. Elianov and V. L. Sheinis, appeared in late 1983.[39] In the preceding few years, Sheinis had published several articles on the specificity of Third World cultured patterns. But this 650-page volume presents an integrated argument about the complex and distinctive interactions among the economic, social and cultural factors as they shape events in the Third World. It broadens the Soviet framework of development or growth indicators by including the role of non-economic factors. Two lengthy reviews praised the book for enriching Soviet scholarship with an innovative system of analysis. Its thesis that backwardness arises from specific local sources and is not solely the heritage of imperialism, and its argument that resolutions of the most elemental social tasks will require "entire historical epochs," were both commended.[40]

The second book, *Evolution of Eastern Societies: Synthesis of Traditional and Modern Structures*, edited by L. I. Reisner and N. A. Simoniia, appeared in late 1984 – the product of a study group set up by the Oriental Institute after 1979 to investigate the role of tradition.[41] The volume posits three models of capitalist development and the preconditions each creates for a socialist revolution: the "classic" West European, the Soviet, and the Eastern variants. The third, or Eastern, model presents the most difficulties, producing unexpected – and at times crippling – reversals. Because of markedly different socio-cultural conditions, the third model must accommodate unprecedented variables and hence will not retract the path traversed by Western Europe. (Nor, incidentally, could the West European pattern be reproduced in Imperial Russia because of its own peculiar background.)

Both publications are considered groundbreaking in the USSR. They argue well the complex case of how local conditions conspire against expectations that the models devised in the West are more or less automatically applicable to the East. Both books exemplify the current, increasingly vocal and better substantiated pessimism about the future evolution of the Third World toward progressive patterns that would bring it closer to the Soviet Bloc.

Naturally, a changed attitude toward Islam goes hand in hand with the heightened appreciation for the tenacity of traditions. Much has been written in the West on how the initial Soviet interpretation of Islam's revolutionary potential has misread the actual course of domestic and foreign policies in Iran after the Shah's fall. But it should be noted that among Soviet scholars there was divided opinion from the outset. G. Kim, the deputy director of the Oriental Institute, saw nothing but revolutionary promise, while E. Primakov, the Institute's director, stressed the possibility of two variants – the regressive and the revolutionary.[42]

It is instructive to outline the evolution of Kim's interests after his original euphoria. In early 1983, Kim presided over a round table conference on tradition and modernity held at the Oriental Institute.[43] What was striking about the chairman's handling of the proceedings was his eagerness to clarify whether Islam offered a third model. There was no agreement among participants. V. Sheinis gave a detailed description of the Third World offering a new alternate paradigm – one based on the rise of fundamentalism and hence unrelated to the existing socialist or capitalist models. N. Simoniia denied that a third model based on tradition was possible. And V. Khoros argued that the persistence of tradition in the East did not preclude modernization.

In 1984, *Aziia i Afrika segodnia* published two articles on Islam that elaborated on the "third model" theme. As editor-in-chief, Kim was responsible for choosing that type of argumentation to appear in print; hence, the publication of the article can be taken to indicate his interests and concerns. In the May 1984 issue, S. L. Agaev, an Iran specialist from the Institute of the International Workers' Movement, wrote about the essence of the Islamic revolution.[44] He was incensed that a recent Soviet handbook on Islam presented it in terms of "vulgar sociology" or class struggle, and argued that the Islamic revolution was not limited to the overthrow of the Shah and anti-imperialist goals. As a movement steeped in a long history and cultural tradition, it offered a total model (one that embraced all aspects of social life – economy, politics, family relations, etc.). Moreover, it reached far beyond Iran's borders.

The following month, L. Reisner contributed an article on civilization and formation in Western and Eastern societies, which probed the relevance of Marxist tenets to the Third World.[45] Although Reisner noted the conflict between Western and Eastern civilizations, between the "revolutionary" thrust of Marxist formations and the "immobilism" of the East, he did not posit a further growth in cultural isolationism among the LDCs. Resolution lay in the emergence of a new global civilization that was all-inclusive and no longer restricted to the West, thereby accommodating the changing Eastern societies with their distinct cultural and social structures.

It seems significant that simultaneously with a growing concern about the sharp turn in the Third World to economic separatism and politico-cultural fundamentalism, there is also the growing opinion among Soviet scholars that these unforeseen challenges can be defused through a global – not a systemic – approach.

THE NON-ALIGNED MOVEMENT

The long-held assumptions about the anti-imperialist thrust of Third World diplomacy are also being reassessed. The positive, pro-Soviet neutralism of the LDCs has been considered in the USSR an integral part of the common anti-imperialist front it formed with the newly liberated countries. This is still the rhetorical claim heard in many official statements from Moscow. But here, too, specialists have started to express doubts about the course of Third World diplomacy, implying that it is not as predictable and useful a tool for the USSR as it had been in the past.

The first article to raise explicit reservations appeared before the non-aligned summit, held in New Delhi in march 1983. Its author, N. A. Simoniia, elaborated on the 26th CPSU Congress' dictum on the complex differentiation among the LDCs by discussing their variegated domestic and foreign policies.[46] At that time, the article seemed to be part of the general post-Brezhnev stocktaking of the prospects for Soviet interests in the Third World. Simoniia provided a general typology of the foreign policies pursued by LDCs, noting the lack of unity in the non-aligned movement. It was composed of the left, consequently anti-imperialist, wing; the moderate center; and the conservative wing, ready to make important concessions to the West (including some of a strategic nature). The diffusion in Third World anti-imperialism, Simoniia argued, was acquiring special importance at present. In that context, he drew attention to the retrogressive, "medieval" strain (obviously Iranian) whose evolution toward the revolution-ary–democratic (i.e., pro-Soviet) type was by no means a foregone conclusion.

After the New Delhi conference, sober stock-taking gave way to guarded expressions of pessimism and disappointment. Here, the article by Iu. Alizov in *Kommunist* was fairly typical.[47] It did admit that the movement was facing difficulties caused by the renewed Cold War, the Iran–Iraq conflict, the disagreements among the Organization of African Unity (OAU), the Arab countries and OPEC, the debt crisis, and rising trade protectionism. But the weight of the argument blamed the United States for trying to capitalize on these difficulties in order to change the character of the non-aligned movement and convert its position to one of equidistance between the United States and the USSR. In conclusion, the article rather weakly asserted that the USSR, as well as the March 1983 Conference of the Communist and Working-Class Parties, welcomed the New Delhi decisions for having "on the whole" given clear anti-imperialist and anti-militarist answers to current international problems.

Such caution did not mark Karen Brutents' article on non-alignment that appeared a year later.[48] In his opinion the New Delhi proceedings saw the establishment of the equidistant position. In addition to stating the fact openly, Brutents elucidated the reasons for the shift. As in many recent Soviet explanations for other untoward developments in the Third World, the causes were found to be economic. All the LDCs remained part of the capitalist world market, dependent for their survival on the advanced capitalist states. Their economic vulnerability precluded the principled anti-imperialist stand that had characterized the movement in the past.

The article was remarkable for its candor, based on pragmatic analysis. It went beyond the already familiar arguments about the LDCs not pursuing uniformly anti-imperialist policies to demonstrate that these countries promoted their own interests (i.e., those of self-reliance or South–South cooperation), which did not necessarily conform to Soviet interests. In addition, there was the strong implication that the USSR did not have the economic wherewithal to influence the non-aligned movement. By contrast, the article acknowledged that the United States had the power to foster and support the equidistant policies.

Such is the sober analysis of someone who is not merely an academic specialist. Brutents' high position in the Central Committee's International Department (as deputy chief) implies that doubts about the congruence of Soviet and Third World radical foreign policies have some operational significance. Moreover, the 1984 article was in keeping with the tone of his recent writings. Ever since 1979 Brutents has been promoting disengagement from too close an identification with the radical states since their rules do not follow a steadfast course on international issues. Instead, he has been urging that Moscow expand ties with all categories of countries, including those which are firmly in the Western camp.[49]

CONCLUSION

What are the implications of the changing tone and content of the specialists' analysis for the conduct of Soviet foreign policy in general and for likely developments under Gorbachev? The evident pessimism and the attendant scaling-down of the former support for radical solutions indicate a definite change of mood. It can be called the "post-Afghan" syndrome, as I have heard it described in Moscow. If equated with our own "post-Vietnam syndrome," it can be taken as a loss of confidence that in turn qualifies the country's readiness to get involved in risky, far-away interventions or initiatives.

The predisposition to seek disengagement from risky ventures is likely to be reinforced by Gorbachev's goal of concentrating on economic reforms and performance at home. As a matter of fact, there is a certain linkage between the new leader's priorities and those of the innovative experts. Some of the more pertinent questioning about the readiness of backward countries for socialism and about the appeal of the current (economically limping) Soviet model for the Third World have been raised by academics who also advocate far-reaching economic reforms at home.[50] The Program approved at the 27th Party Congress in March 1986 echoed the reassessments of Soviet academics, when it pointed to the revitalized role of neo-colonialism but merely offers general Soviet sympathy for Third World needs and strivings.[51]

Keeping in mind the components of the emergent realization of what accounts for Soviet perceptions of their weakness and/or vulnerability in the Third World (ranging from economic deficiencies, through the unpredictability of radical clients, to the American resolve) permits interpreting Soviet responses or proposals less as atypical or as *ad hoc* acts and more as falling into a pattern. Here, Moscow's acquiescence to Mozambique's *rapprochement* with South Africa in 1984 is a highly significant development. The caution that the USSR is exercising in its relations with Nicaragua is equally indicative. More recently, Gorbachev's proposal that every permanent member of the Security Council undertake "to strictly observe the principle of non-interference, non-use of force or threat of force in relations with countries [of Asia, Africa and Latin America] and not to draw them into military blocs" could be weighed as more than mere rhetoric. Significantly, Gorbachev's code of conduct omitted the customary reference to the inalienable right of the developing states to pursue anti-imperialist policies.[52]

The new mood affects more than the USSR's willingness to indulge in high-risk behavior in the Third World. It also spells out some positive promise for Soviet–American relations. The less systemic (i.e., less ideologized) analysis of various processes in the LDCs will not necessarily reduce Moscow's presence in the Third World. The USSR is there for reasons other than ideology. But the new look might well influence the modalities with which Soviet policy is conducted and justified – i.e., less in terms of exclusive and elusive ideology (which is subversive in US eyes) – and more in terms of generally accepted (and hence negotiable) standards of national interest.

Here again the experts' writings are an indicator of what the less ideologically charged components of Soviet–American consultations or negotiations could be. Many of the more moderate, less ideologically confrontational, concepts – such as global interdependence; the complex multisectoral nature of Third World societies; and the rules of conduct that constrain the superpowers from projecting their interests unilaterally – were first formulated by academic experts before they appeared in official speeches or proposals. Specialized publications also explain more fully the new reasoning behind the new formulas.

To be sure, Western negotiators can never be certain which set of principles – the old ideological or the new pragmatic – will prevail in a given case. Still, there exists in the USSR a novel, alternate way of looking at the Third World situation – in generally understood categories and not merely in terms of Marxist revolution. And this should alert American analysts and policy makers to a wider range of possibilities for conducting a reasonable dialogue.

To cite one example: Soviet academic experts have written that the situation in Afghanistan in the fall of 1979 presented a security threat to the USSR. This could be grounds to entertain the idea that the Soviet Union might view our concern with Central America in a similar light, i.e., in terms of legitimate interests or spheres of influence.

The knowledge that universally recognized terms have gained currency and recognition in the writings of many Soviet foreign policy specialists gives us clues about the changing Soviet perceptions of international relations and behavior.

NOTES

1 "The Theory and Practice of the Non-Capitalist Development," *International Affairs*, no. 11 (November 1970), p. 13.
2 A. Kiva, *Strany sotsialisticheskoi orientatsii* [Countries of Socialist Orientation]. (Moscow: Nauka, 1978), p. 28.
3 K. Brutents *et al.*, *Sotsialisticheskaia orientatsiia osvobodivshikhsia stran. Nekotorye voprosy teorii i praktiki* [Socialist Orientation in the Developing Countries: Some Problems of Theory and Practice] (Moscow: Mysl', 1982).
4 See, for example, references to this volume in a collective review. *Kommunist*, no. 1 (January 1985), pp. 115–25.
5 *Sotsialisticheskaia orientatsiia*, pp. 33–35.
6 *Ibid.*, p. 91.
7 *Ibid.*, pp. 36–37.
8 Another important collective volume, *Vostok: rubezh 80-kh godov* [The East: the Threshold of the 80s]. (Moscow: Nauka, 1983), by E. Primakov, G. Kim, G. Shirokov, N. Simoniia, V. Li and other members of the Oriental Institute, gives a

similar list of obstacles in its chapter on socialist orientation. But it does not define the relationship of these states to the USSR.

9 Text of Ponomarev's speech was reprinted in *Kommunist*, no. 16 (November 1980), pp. 30–44.

10 In October 1980, B. Ponomarev, for example, enjoined scholars at the Oriental Institute to explore causes for the setbacks suffered by various radical regimes. Text of speech in *Aziia i Afrika segodnia*, no. 12 (December 1980), pp. 2–5.

11 A. V. Kiva, P. M. Shastitko, "Istoricheskii opyt bol'shevizma i revoliutsionnaia–demokratiia afro-aziatskikh stran" [The Historical Experience of Bolshevism and the Revolutionary Democracy of Afro-Asian Countries], *Narody Azii i Afriki*, no. 6 (November–December 1983), 11. See also, V. Maksimenko, "Leninskaia kontseptsiia politicheskikh partii i osvobodivshiesia strany" [Lenin's Concepts of Political Parties and the Liberated Countries], *Aziva i Afrika segodnia*, no. 8 (August 1983), pp. 2–5.

12 *Sotsialisticheskaia orientatsiia*, p. 124. Or, as *Vostok: rubezh 80* put it, the revolutionary goals outdistance the class content, pp. 177–78.

13 "Problemy formirovaniia rabochogo klassa osvobodivshikhsia stran" [Problems of Class Formation in the Liberated Countries], *Rabochii klass i sovremennyi mir*, no. 6 (November–December 1983), pp. 162–65.

14 In this connection, it is noted that the Labor Party of the People's Republic of the Congo is ridden with tribal factionalism. *Sotsialisticheskaia orientatsiia*, pp. 124–25.

15 *Ibid.*, pp. 134–37.

16 *Vostok: rubezh 80*, pp. 192–93.

17 A. Butenko's, "Nekotorye teoreticheskie problemy perekhoda k sotsializmu stran s nerazvitoi ekonomiki" [Some Theoretical Problems of the Transition to Socialism by Countries with Underdeveloped Economies], *Narody Azii i Afriki*, no. 5 (September–October 1982), pp. 70–79, is probably the most forthright statement about the various problems posed by backward social conditions to radical transformation. For an even more outspoken article by a Hungarian expert, see Barna Talas, "Specific Prerequisites for the Transition to Socialism in the Socio-economically Underdeveloped Countries," *Development and Peace* (Budapest), no. 4 (Autumn 1983), pp. 208–20.

18 *Sotsialisticheskaia orientatsiia*, p. 125.

19 V. Li, *Sotsial'naia revoliutsiia i vlast' v stranakh Vostoka* [Social Revolution and Power in the Countries of the East] (Moscow: Nauka, 1984). A clearer argument is presented by Li in "The Formation and Evolution of Bureaucracy in Developing Countries of the East," *Development and Peace*, no. 3 (Autumn 1982), pp. 32–45.

20 R. Ul'ianovskii, "O natsional'noi i revoliutsionnoi demokratii: puti evoliutsii" [On National and Revolutionary Democracy: Paths of Evolution], *Narody Azii i Afriki*, no. 2 (March–April 1984), pp. 9–18. It is instructive to compare these 1984 arguments with those Ul'ianovskii expressed in 1971: "The important thing is not so much the fact that the national democracy is still a non-Marxist trend as its actual fight against imperialism [and] capitalism as a social system, and the revolutionary democrats' constructive effort to build a new society." *World Marxist Review*, no. 9 (September 1971), 125.

21 *Sotsialisticheskaia orientatsiia*, pp. 35–36; *Vostok: rubezh 80*, pp. 195–6.

22 *Zarubezhnye kontseptsii ekonomicheskogo razvitiia stran Afriki* [Foreign Concepts of the Economic Development of African Countries], (Moscow: Nauka 1980), p. 153.

23 B. Slavnyi, *Nemarksistskaia politekonomiia o problemakh otstalosti i zavisimosti v razvivayushchemsia mire* [Non-Marxist Political Economy on the Problems of Backwardness and Dependence in the Developing World] (Moscow: Nauka, 1982).

The book's "original" contents were subject to favorable commentaries in *Narody Azii i Afriki*, no. 6 (November–December 1984), pp. 141–66.

24 *Ibid.*, p. 195.

25 The shift in Soviet policy was undoubtedly related to the change in the LDCs' behavior. Beginning with the UNCTAD IV in May 1976, they stopped differentiating between the capitalist West and the socialist East, presenting the same set of demands on all the advanced states.

26 "Evaluation of the world trade and economic situation and consideration of issues, policies and appropriate measures to facilitate structural changes in the international economy," UNCTAD, TA/249 (19 April 1979), point 22.

27 A. Manozhulo, *Vneshaniaia torgovlia*, no. 4 (April 1983), pp. 15–20.

28 E. Obminsky, "Proponents and Opponents of Restructuring International Economic Relations," *International Affairs*, no. 7 (July 1984), pp. 81–88; "Bor'ba za mezhdunarodnyi ekonomicheskii poriadok: itogi desiatiletiia" [Struggle for the international economic order: results of a decade], *Mirovaia ekonomika i mezhdunarodnye otnosheniia* (hereafter cited as *MEMO*), no. 7 (July 1984), pp. 101–16; I. Karpov, "Razvivayushchiesia strany i demokratizatsiia mezhdunarodnykh ekonomicheskikh otnoshenii" [The Developing Countries and Democratization of International Economic Relations], *Vneshniaia torgovlia*, no. 11 (November 1984), pp. 46–50.

29 L. Abalkin, "Leniniskaia teoriia imperializma v svete sovremennoi real'nosti" [Lenin's Theory of Imperialism in the Light of Current Day Realities], *MEMO*, no. 5 (May 1985), 61–73. For a conservative reiteration of the old verities, see the *Kommunist* editorial in no. 8 (May 1984), pp. 3–13.

30 For a good example of the present day disposition not to absolutize socialist institutions, see the roundtable discussion on the future of capitalism in the LDCs, *MEMO*, no. 1 (January 1985), pp. 81–94.

31 *Vostok: rubezh 80*, pp. 194–95. There have been no charges in Soviet writings of independent Angola being exploited by the international oil cartel operating in Cabinda. This would indicate acceptance of the benefits accruing to a socialist-oriented state from participating in capitalist international enterprise. Moreover, the USSR is not averse to doing business with the multinationals in the radical states. The biggest Soviet aid project in Angola – the Cuanza river development – is a trilateral venture in which Portuguese capital participates.

32 E. Primakov, "Strany sotsialisticheskoi orientatsii: trudnyi no real'nyi put' perakhoda k sotsializmu" [States of Socialist Orientation: a Difficult but Workable Path for Transition to Socialism], *MEMO*, no. 7 (July 1981), p. 16.

33 *Sotsialisticheskaia orientatsiia*, 178–9; *Vostok: rubezh 80*, pp. 177–9.

34 *Vostok: rubezh 80*, p. 198.

35 A. Butenko, *Narody Azii i Afriki* (n. 14), p. 76.

36 N. Simoniia, *Strany Vostoka: puti razvitiia* [Countries of the East: Paths of Development] (Moscow: Nauka, 1975).

37 Evgenii Pashkovskii, *Vostokovednaia problematika v kul'turnoistoricheskoi kontseptsii A. Dzh. Toinbi* [Oriental Problems in A. J. Toynbee's Concepts of History and Culture]. (Moscow: Nauka, 1976).

38 See "Kruglyi stol: o sootnoshenii poniatii 'tsivilizatsiya' i 'kul'tura" [Round Table: On the Relationship between "Civilization" and "Culture"]. *Novaia i novieishaia istoriia*, no. 4 (July–August 1983), pp. 68–89.

39 *Razvivayushchiesia strany: ekonomicheskii rost' i sotsial'nyi progress*, (Moscow: Nauka, 1983).

40 See the two lengthy reviews in *MEMO*, no. 5 (May 1985), pp. 115–33. The volume was also included in a composite review of important publications in the January 1985 *Kommunist* (no. 1, pp. 115–25).
41 *Evoliutsiia vostochnykh obshchestv: sintez traditsionnykh i sovremennykh struktur* (Moscow: Nauka, 1984).
42 G. Kim, "Social Development and Ideological Struggle in the Developing Countries," *International Affairs*, no. 4 (April 1980), pp. 65–75; E. Primakov, "Islam i protsessy obshchestvennogo razvitiia zarubezhnogo Vostoka" [Islam and the Processes of Social Development in Eastern Countries Abroad], *Voprosy filosofii*, no. 8 (August 1980), pp. 60–71.
43 Proceedings in *Aziia i Afrika segodnia*, no. 7 (July 1983), 33–41.
44 S. L. Agoev, "O poniatii i sushchnosti 'islamskoi revoliutsii'" [On the Concept and Essence of "Islamic Revolution"], *ibid.*, no. 5 (May 1984), pp. 27–31. See also Agaev's review of L. P. Polonskaia and A. Kh. Vafa, eds., *Vostok: ideii i ideologiia* [The East: Ideas and Ideology]. (Moscow: Nauka, 1982) for similar arguments about the *sui generis* nature of Islam. *Rabochii klass i sovremennyi mir* no. 6 (November–December 1983), 177–80.
45 L. Reisher, "'Tsivilizatsiia' i 'formatsiia' v obshchestvakh Vostoka i Zapada," *Aziia i Afrika segodnia*, no. 6 (June 1984), 22–25.
46 K. A. Simoniia, "Natsional'no–gosudartsvennaia konsolidatsiiia i politicheskaia differentsiatsiia razvivaiuschchikhsia stran" [National-State Consolidation and the Political Differentiation among Developing Countries], *MEMO*, no. 1 (January 1983), pp. 84–96.
47 Iu. Alizov, "Dvizhenie neprisoedineniia na vazhnom rubezhe" [The Non-Aligned Movement at a Significant Juncture], *Kommunist*, no. 7 (May 1983), pp. 99–110.
48 K. Brutents, "Dvizhenie neprisoedineniia v sovremennom mire" [The Non-Aligned Movement in the Contemporary World], *MEMO*, no. 5 (May 1984), pp. 26–41.
49 See, for instance, his *Osvobodivshiesia strany v 70-e gody* [The Liberated Countries in the 70s] (Moscow: Izd. Politicheskoi literatury, 1979) and "Sovetskii Soyuz i osvobodivshiesia strany," *Pravda*, 2 February 1982, pp. 4–5.
50 See, for example, A. Butenko's article in *Narody Azii i Afriki* (n. 14) and Yu. Novopashin, "Vozdeistvie real'nogo sotsializma na mirovoi revoliutsionnyi protsess" [The Influence of Genuine Socialism on the World Revolutionary Process], *Voprosy filosofii*, no. 8 (August 1982), pp. 3–16.
51 "Programma Kommunisticheskoi partii Sovetskogo Souiza. Novaia Redaktsiia," *Pravda*, 7 March 1986, p. 7.
52 *Pravda*, 22 May 1985, p. 2. Gorbachev's "code of conduct" was significantly different from the one offered by Brezhnev. It omitted the following points: "Full recognition of these states' sovereignty over their natural resources . . . [and] support of their efforts to eliminate remnants of colonialism, to uproot racism and apartheid." *Pravda*, 28 April 1981, p. 2.

3

Anti-Soviet insurgencies: growing trend or passing phase?

MARK N. KATZ*

Since the end of The Second World War there have been a number of insurgencies in which Marxist forces have fought against pro-Western governments. In some cases the Marxists have come to power, as in Vietnam, Cuba, Kampuchea, Laos, Angola, Mozambique, Ethiopia, South Yemen, and Nicaragua. In others the Marxists have been defeated, as in Greece, Malaya, and Oman. But whether they have won or lost, the West has seen itself on the defensive against the Marxists. Since the mid-1970s, though, a new phenomenon has taken place. Pro-Soviet Marxist Third World governments have had to fight armed internal opponents in Afghanistan, Kampuchea, Angola, Mozambique, Ethiopia, and Nicaragua. Further, these Marxist governments have been unable to defeat their opponents even after many years of fighting.

The term "anti-Soviet insurgency" is not really the most accurate description of these conflicts. For the most part, the forces opposing pro-Soviet governments are not primarily motivated by anti-Soviet or even anti-communist concerns, but by local factors. The term "anti-Soviet insurgency" is nevertheless a useful one, for it points out a larger problem faced by Soviet foreign policy. No matter what the cause of each of these insurrections might have been, they demonstrate that the rule of pro-Soviet Marxist–Leninist governments in the Third World is not especially secure. Although none of these pro-Soviet Marxist–Leninist governments has yet been overthrown by guerrilla forces,[1] neither have Marxist governments been able to defeat the guerrillas. This is especially striking in those cases where the guerrillas have managed to survive even where forces from established socialist states have fought against them, as have the Cubans in Angola, the Vietnamese in Kampuchea, and the Soviets in Afghanistan. Now that these conflicts have been going on for several years, the Soviets must be

* A slightly different version of this article was published in *Orbis*, 30 (1986), 365–91.

extremely concerned whether the anti-Soviet insurgents can be defeated, whether more conflicts will erupt in other nations allied to the USSR, and whether guerrillas might ever succeed in overthrowing a pro-Soviet Marxist–Leninist government.

Are these Soviet difficulties potential opportunities for the West? The US government would undoubtedly consider the overthrow of a pro-Soviet Marxist government by internal forces to be a foreign policy victory. The Reagan Administration has given military aid to the Nicaraguan *contras*, the Afghan *mujahideen*, and most recently, the Union for the Total Independence of Angola (UNITA). But is it really possible for the West to bring about the overthrow of a pro-Soviet Third World government or prevent the USSR and its allies from eventually defeating the anti-Soviet guerillas? After all, there have been anti-Soviet insurgencies before, and all of them have been defeated. From the Russian Revolution until the mid-1930s, Moslems in Soviet Central Asia fought against Bolshevik rule. Although the insurgents, whom the Soviets called *basmachi*, or bandits, held out for many years, Moscow was victorious over them in the end. There was also an insurgency in the Ukraine that lasted for several years after the Second World War with similar results.

While it might not be surprising that the Soviets were able to defeat insurgencies in their own country, there have also been two previous attempts to overthrow pro-Soviet regimes distant from the USSR. The first was the Bay of Pigs invasion in 1961. This is commonly remembered as a CIA-sponsored action, but the military operation itself was carried out primarily by Cuban exiles. In addition, after a Marxist government came to power in South Yemen in 1967, several South Yemeni exile groups based in both Saudi Arabia and North Yemen tried on many occasions from 1967 to 1973 either to overthrow the radical government or to make the eastern part of the country independent. Both in Cuba and South Yemen these attempts at counterrevolution failed.

Are anti-Soviet insurgencies likely to be a long-term problem for Soviet foreign policy, or are they merely a passing phase in the consolidation of pro-Soviet Third World regimes? Can any of them realistically be expected to succeed in overthrowing the Marxist governments against which they are fighting? What has Moscow's response been to the phenomenon of anti-Soviet insurgencies and what policy choices does it face? What are the opportunities and the dangers that this phenomenon presents for American foreign policy? In seeking to answer these questions, it is first necessary to examine the particular circumstances of each of the six anti-Soviet insurgencies.

THE SIX ANTI-SOVIET INSURGENCIES

One feature that all six of the ongoing anti-Soviet insurgencies have in common is that they each began immediately upon or soon after the establishment of the pro-Soviet Marxist–Leninist government at which they are directed. In one case, Ethiopia, the regional insurgency in Eritrea actually predated the Marxist revolution. None of these Marxist governments had been firmly settled in power for a long period of time before these conflicts broke out. In addition, in each of these conflicts, there is an element of indigenous support for the guerillas as well as an element of foreign support, though the relative mix of each varies widely among the six conflicts. Further, the degree of internal support for the Marxist regime varies quite widely, from very little in Afghanistan to fairly substantial in Nicaragua. Finally, the degree of military involvement on the part of established socialist states also varies widely, from extremely heavy in Afghanistan and Kampuchea to limited in Nicaragua and Mozambique.

Angola. At the time of the 1974 left-wing military coup that ousted the conservative Portuguese dictatorship, there were three main rebel groups in Angola based roughly on Angola's main tribal divisions. The Front for the National Liberation of Angola (FNLA), led by Holden Roberto, was backed by the Bakongo in the North; the Popular Movement for the Liberation of Angola (MPLA), led by Agostinho Neto, was backed by the Mbundu in the center; and UNITA, led by Jonas Savimbi, was supported by the Ovimbundu in the South. The Marxist MPLA was strong in the capital, Luanda, and had the support of many leftist Portuguese and *mesticos* there.

In early 1976 the Soviet and Cuban-backed MPLA rallied and drove the FNLA into Zaire and South African forces back into Namibia.[2] The FNLA was completely defeated and has never recovered its strength. It appeared that UNITA was also defeated, but this proved not to be the case. The MPLA was never able to assert its authority in the Ovimbundu heartland. UNITA was not only able to stave off defeat, but also to consolidate its hold in the south and expand its influence northward. By the summer of 1985, it was estimated that UNITA controlled approximately 55 per cent of Angola and was able to mount operations in other parts of the country, including the capital, despite the presence of Cuban troops. In September 1985, however, MPLA forces launched an offensive against UNITA with Cuban and Soviet support and succeeded in driving the latter southward. The MPLA offensive ceased by early October 1985 some 150 miles north of Jamba, UNITA's capital.[3]

UNITA's main strength is derived from its solid base of internal support among the Ovimbundu. This has allowed UNITA to develop a firm territorial base inside the country from which to operate. According to the International Institute for Strategic Studies, Savimbi controlled some 18,000 "regular" fighters and a militia force of 23,000 in 1985.[4] The United States did not provide UNITA with any military aid from the passage of the Clark Amendment in 1976 until its repeal in 1985, but South Africa has given it a substantial amount of assistance over the years. South Africa has also conducted military operations in southern Angola in order to weaken the South West Africa Peoples Organizations (SWAPO), which is trying to win independence for Namibia. Savimbi's willingness to cooperate with South Africa has made it difficult for the West, China, and black African states to support him, but in March 1986 the Reagan Administration began sending Stinger shoulder-fired anti-aircraft missiles to Savimbi's forces.[5] UNITA's strength among the Ovimbundu might ultimately limit its popular appeal in Angola, especially among the Mbundu who prefer to be ruled by their own tribesmen in the MPLA.

The MPLA government has been strongly supported by Cuba and the USSR since 1975. In 1975–6, Cuban forces in Angola reached a high of 36,000, according to Fidel Castro, then fell to about 12,000, but rose again to their current level of 25–35,000 when UNITA and South African military operations grew more threatening. The USSR, which signed a treaty of friendship and cooperation with Angola in October 1976, has provided most of Angola's weaponry and maintains about 500 military advisers there.[6]

A rough rule of thumb that is often cited with regard to insurgencies is that counterinsurgency forces need to have a 10-to-1 advantage over the insurgents in order to defeat them.[7] The MPLA's regular armed forces consist of 49,500 troops. Together with 25–35,000 Cubans, 500 Soviets, and 500 East Germans, the MPLA has some 75–85,000 regulars at its disposal, as compared to 18,000 UNITA regulars.[8] This means that the MPLA only has a 4-to-1 advantage, and thus is not likely to be able to defeat UNITA.

The United States has called for Cuba's departure from Angola in return for Namibian independence accompanied by a complete South African military withdrawal.[9] If the Cubans depart, UNITA might find itself in a better position, but the MPLA would still have an almost 3-to-1 advantage in regular forces. And if South Africa withdrew from Namibia, UNITA would not receive as effective military assistance from Pretoria as it does now. Thus the prospects for UNITA's survival are very good, but it is much less likely that UNITA will be able to defeat the MPLA or force it into a power-sharing agreement – a formula called for by Savimbi but rejected by Luanda.

Mozambique. The Front for the Liberation of Mozambique (FRELIMO) was formed in 1964, and by 1969 was dominated by Marxist–Leninists. Its operations were at first largely confined to north Mozambique, where FRELIMO benefited from sanctuaries in Tanzania. FRELIMO's influence grew rapidly after June 1974, when the new Portuguese government announced it would withdraw from Africa the following year. When Mozambique became independent, FRELIMO assumed power without having to fight serious rivals as the MPLA did in Angola.[10]

The new FRELIMO government openly allowed Robert Mugabe's guerrillas to use bases inside Mozambique to launch attacks against the forces of white-ruled Rhodesia. The Ian Smith government in Rhodesia responded by sponsoring the Mozambican National Resistance (MNR) to fight against the Marxist government in Maputo, the Mozambican capital. When Rhodesia became Zimbabwe, the MNR transferred its headquarters to South Africa. At first, the MNR made little impression in Mozambique, and by 1979 it had only about 1,000 guerrillas under arms.[11] But worsening economic conditions combined with the unpopular policies of the government gave rise to popular dissatisfaction with FRELIMO.[12] This has allowed the MNR to develop a basis of internal support within Mozambique in addition to its backing from South Africa. Certain ex-FRELIMO members also joined the MNR, including Afonso Dhlakama, who is the current leader of the MNR.

The MNR has expanded its military operations to all ten of Mozambique's provinces, especially those in the central region of the country. As other black African nations, Mozambique is not free of tribal cleavages, and the MNR has been able to take advantage of this to gain support from some of the Manica, Nbau, Makonde, and Makusas.[13]

The MNR claims to have 16,000 guerrillas under arms, while FRELIMO puts MNR strength at 10,000. Others estimate the figure as being lower still. The International Institute for Strategic Studies has said that there are 6,000 trained guerrillas and 3,000 MNR reservists. Mozambique's army has about 14,000 troops, but approximately 75 per cent are conscript whose reliability is doubtful.[14] FRELIMO, then, does not come anywhere near having a 10-to-1 advantage over the MNR, and indeed might not even have a 2-to-1 advantage.

FRELIMO has received military assistance from the Soviet bloc. In March 1977, Maputo and Moscow signed a treaty of friendship and cooperation. The USSR has also provided some military equipment, and Soviet naval vessels have visited Mozambique. There are also about 750 military advisers from Cuba, 100 from East Germany, and 300 from the USSR in the country.[15] Yet, despite the obvious threat that the MNR poses to FRELIMO – arguably a greater one than UNITA poses to the MPLA – the Soviet bloc has either been unable or unwilling to make the same sort of large-scale military commitment to Maputo that it has to Luanda.

In order to defend itself, the FRELIMO government has chosen to turn more and more toward the West. At the end of 1981, Mozambique and Portugal announced plans for joint military cooperation. In April 1982, the two signed an agreement whereby Portuguese military instructors would provide training in counterinsurgency warfare to the Mozambicans.[16] In April 1984, Mozambique and South Africa signed the Nkomati Accord in which the former agreed to stop supporting the African National Congress (ANC) and the latter agreed to cease aiding the MNR. The willingness of FRELIMO's late leader, Samora Machel, to sign this agreement with South Africa only shows how threatened he was by the MNR. His government previously gave much assistance to Zimbabwean rebels and was one of the strongest critics of the white regime in Pretoria.

When the accord with South Africa was signed, FRELIMO indeed stopped supporting the ANC, but MNR activities continued. In 1985, the South African government admitted that it had continued to support the MNR even after the agreement was signed.[17] Thus the Nkomati Accord does little to help FRELIMO defeat the MNR.

The MNR has benefited from the absence of a large-scale Soviet-Cuban military presence. Yet the MNR's prospects for overthrowing FRELIMO are doubtful. Observers note that, aside from anti-communism, the MNR has yet to articulate a political program that would appeal to the Mozambican people as a whole. Nor has it made much effort to set up an alternative government. Rather, it has concentrated on attacking FRELIMO positions and then withdrawing. In addition, there are over 7,000 Zimbabwean troops in Mozambique helping FRELIMO. FRELIMO and Zimbabwean troops launched an offensive in August 1985 that succeeded in capturing the MNR's headquarters in central Mozambique, but in February 1986 the MNR recaptured it.[18] Finally, it is not clear whether South Africa really wants the MNR to come to power. Pretoria might prefer a weak Marxist government that is increasingly willing to cooperate with it instead of a strong non-communist government that is not willing to do so, or a weak non-communist government that South Africa might have difficulty keeping in power. It is much easier for South Africa to support the MNR in its effort to weaken FRELIMO than it would be to help it stay in power as a government that might in turn face armed opposition. Nevertheless, FRELIMO is one of the pro-Soviet Marxist–Leninist governments most seriously threatened by anti-Soviet insurgents.

Ethiopia. After the 1974 Marxist coup in Ethiopia, the Somali attack to regain the Ogaden in 1977, and the expulsion of the Soviets and Cubans from Somalia, the Ethiopians, with the aid of 1,500 Soviet advisers and 12–15,000 Cuban troops, were able to drive the Somalis out of the Ogaden by March 1978.[19] But this was not the end of the regime's problems, as it was also faced with growing insurgencies in other parts of the country, especially Eritrea.

In the late nineteenth century the Italians failed in their attempt to colonize Ethiopia, but occupied Eritrea. Except for the brief period when Mussolini occupied Ethiopia, Eritrea was ruled separately until the end of the Second World War. The British then occupied Eritrea, but the United Nations decided after the Second World War that it should be ruled as an autonomous region by Haile Selassie. In 1962 he annexed Eritrea, and an insurgency soon arose there. Since the 1974 revolution several other regional revolts, including rebellions in Tigray, Afars, and Oromo, have flared up.[20]

The new Ethiopian regime was just as determined to assert its authority over the rebellious Eritreans as the old regime had been. After driving the Somalis out of the Ogaden, Addis Ababa launched an offensive against the Eritrean rebels. Although the Soviets had helped the Eritrean Marxists for years, Moscow quickly switched to helping the Ethiopian Marxists in their attempt to suppress the Eritreans. The Cubans, however, refused to do so. After aiding the Eritreans for so long, Castro would not send Cuban soldiers to fight against them. Instead, he urged a political solution to the Eritrean conflict.[21]

The several attempts that Addis Ababa has made to crush the Eritreans have all failed. In 1982, for example, the Ethiopians launched a major offensive against an Eritrean stronghold in Nakfa, but this failed partly because rebels in Tigray kept attacking Ethiopian supply lines. In 1983 Addis Ababa tried to defeat the rebels in Tigray, but again was unsuccessful.[22]

Ethiopia's armed forces, including the regular army and the People's Militia, total 217,000 troops. Addis Ababa signed a treaty of friendship and cooperation with Moscow in November 1978 and has received modern Soviet weapons. There are also some 1,500 Soviet and 550 East German military advisers in Ethiopia. Cuba once had as many as 17,000 soldiers in Ethiopia, but this number has fallen to 5,000, due in part to the expectation that Somalia will not attack again and in part to Ethiopia's unwillingness or inability to continue paying for such a large Cuban presence. There are about 28,500 Eritrean, 5,000 Tigrayan, and 600 Oromo rebels.[23] Although they apparently do not receive aid from the West, conservative Arab states assist them.

The Ethiopian government has a better than 6-to-1 force advantage over the guerrillas. However, it is believed that Addis Ababa keeps only 100,000 troops in Eritrea.[24] It therefore only has an actual advantage of 3.5-to-1 in that rebellious province. Ethiopia has not sent more troops into Eritrea partly because it must deploy a share of its forces in the Ogaden region and keep a large number in the Ethiopian heartland to maintain internal security. As long as this remains the case, the Ethiopian government will find it difficult to defeat the guerrillas.

While Addis Ababa might be unable to crush the rebels, the continuing insurgency does not threaten the Ethiopian government in the same way that UNITA threatens the MPLA or the MNR threatens FRELIMO. It is not the aim of the various Ethiopian rebel groups to overthrow the Marxist government in Addis Ababa, but to gain independence, or perhaps just autonomy.

Another factor hindering the guerrillas in Eritrea is that they are divided into four separate groups and have spent as much time fighting each other as they have Ethiopian government forces.[25] This of course helps Addis Ababa to maintain its presence in the province. As a result of internal divisions and the smaller size of their forces as compared to Addis Ababa's, the Eritreans are not likely to obtain independence by militarily defeating the Ethiopian army. As long as Eritrea cannot win its independence, the more united but numerically much smaller Tigray People's Liberation Front has no real hope of winning independence for its province either. Perhaps the best they can both hope for is that Addis Ababa will get tired of fighting and will be willing to negotiate a political settlement granting them some form of political autonomy.

Kampuchea. In 1975 the Khmer Rouge came to power in Kampuchea at the same time that South Vietnam fell to Hanoi's forces. Although Marxist, the Khmer Rouge was bitterly opposed to the Hanoi government because it feared the Vietnamese sought to dominate Kampuchea. The Chinese backed the Khmer Rouge leader Pol Pot in his independent stand *vis-à-vis* Vietnam – a policy that did much to sour Sino-Vietnamese relations from 1975 onward. Tensions grew along the Vietnam–Kampuchea border as the Pol Pot government reasserted claims to territory in Vietnam that was formerly Kampuchean. At the end of December 1978 Vietnamese forces invaded Kampuchea and quickly overwhelmed the Khmer Rouge. Hanoi established a new government in Phnom Penh led by the Kampuchean Marxist, Heng Samrin, who had earlier broken with Pol Pot. The new Vietnamese-backed government was recognized by the USSR and its allies, but through the efforts of China and the Association of South East Asian Nations (ASEAN), the Pol Pot regime continued to hold Kampuchea's seat at the United Nations.[26]

Although the Vietnamese succeeded in sweeping through most of Kampuchea, they did not completely destroy the Khmer Rouge. The Khmer Rouge was able to remain in parts of western and northwestern Kampuchea as well as to conduct guerrilla operations elsewhere. Both China and ASEAN funneled military aid to the Khmer Rouge via Thailand. A pattern emerged in which, during the dry season of every year (January through April), the Vietnamese would launch an offensive against the resistance that would make substantial progress, but during the wet season resistance activity would resume. Vietnamese forces have on several occasions pursued the Kampuchean rebels across the border into Thailand, and this has led to several clashes between Vietnamese and Thai forces.[27]

The Khmer Rouge is not the only Kampuchean group resisting the Vietnamese; there are also two non-communist groups. One is led by Prince Norodom Sihanouk – the neutralist leader of Kampuchea until he was overthrown in 1970 by Lon Nol – and another is led by former Prime Minister, Son Sann. In 1982 the Khmer Rouge joined a "coalition government" with the two non-communist resistance movements in order to reduce the risk of losing its UN seat because of Pol Pot's past activities. The Khmer Rouge, however, remains the most important element in the coalition. In 1985 the Khmer Rouge had a guerrilla force of 35,000, while Son Sann had some 18,000 fighters and Prince Sihanouk had only 7,000. The Heng Samrin government has a conscript army of about 35,000, and the Vietnamese have a force of 160,000 troops in Kampuchea.[28]

The Vietnamese and the Heng Samrin government only have a force advantage that is somewhat greater than 3-to-1. This shows that having a 10-to-1 force advantage over insurgent forces is not always necessary for counterinsurgency warfare to succeed. The Vietnamese, however, are much better equipped than the Kampuchean resistance. In addition, much of the Kampuchean resistance is based in Thailand.

Although united in a coalition, for the most part the three resistance forces operate independently. In their 1985 dry season offensive the Vietnamese for the first time were able to drive virtually all the resistance forces out of Kampuchea into Thailand. The Kampuchean resistance groups, especially the Khmer Rouge, succeeded in moving their forces back into the country during the subsequent wet season, but their operations were reduced.[29]

Unlike the rebels in Angola and Mozambique, the Kampuchean resistance forces do not appear to have any chance of ousting the Heng Samrin government so long as Vietnamese forces remain in the country. Prince Sihanouk once said that he was fighting in order to get the Vietnamese to enter negotiations, not to defeat them, as he did not see this as possible. But although the Kampuchean rebels have little chance of succeeding and even their ability to continue operating in Kampuchea is doubtful, the Heng Samrin government is unable to survive without Vietnamese help.[30] Thus Vietnam must continue to maintain large numbers of troops in Kampuchea in order to keep its protégé in power.

Afghanistan. A coup in April 1978 brought a Marxist government to power in the Afghan capital, Kabul, and its radical policies quickly led to the growth of internal opposition. Exacerbating the situation was the fact that the Afghan Marxists were divided into two opposing factions, the Khalq and the Parcham. Both were pro-Soviet, though the Parcham was more so. The first two Marxist rulers, Noor Mohammad Taraki and Hafizullah Amin, were Khalqis. By December 1979, internal opposition had become so strong that the Soviets invaded with 80,000 troops in order to preserve Marxist rule. The Soviets immediately executed Amin and replaced him with a Parchami, Babrak Karmal. But if the Soviets had been under the impression that invading and pacifying Afghanistan would be as easy as subduing Hungary and Czechoslovakia, they were quickly disabused of this notion.[31]

At present, the Soviets have about 115,000 troops in Afghanistan, and the Kabul regime has an army of about 30–40,000. The Afghan army is not an especially effective force, and its numbers are considerably smaller than they were prior to the Soviet invasion because of large-scale defections to the rebels. Defections still take place at a high rate, and the Kabul regime has had to resort to press-gang techniques to keep the army at its current size, but these soldiers are not reliable. The Afghan rebels are believed to have a force of anywhere from 75,000 to 100,000 guerrillas, along with the sympathy and support of most of the population and 2 million to 3 million refugees in Pakistan.[32] Thus even including the Kabul regime's forces, the Soviets at best have only a 2-to-1 advantage over the guerrillas.

The guerrillas hold most of the countryside while the Soviets hold the main cities and roads, but the rebels often successfully attack these too. The Soviets have launched several offensives against the rebels, and these have usually done well as long as Soviet forces have been concentrated on the attack. However, after the Soviets withdraw the bulk of their forces, the rebels are usually able to reclaim lost areas. As the Soviets have not succeeded in making the Marxist government at all popular, the regime would be quickly overthrown without the presence of Soviet troops.[33]

The Afghan rebels, however, suffer from several disadvantages. Instead of being united, they are divided into seven separate groups – three traditionalist and four Islamic fundamentalist. They have often fought each other as well as the Soviets. Efforts have been made to join them together, but the largest rebel group, the fundamentalist Hizb-i-Islami, refuses to cooperate.[34] In addition, the Soviets have resorted to increasingly brutal tactics. One French observer noted that, because the Soviets understand that the guerrillas are supported by the population, they have undertaken campaigns to destroy agricultural areas in order to drive as much of the population either into Pakistan or into the main cities where the Soviets have more control.[35]

Thus far the Soviets have been unable to defeat the Afghan rebels, and it does not seem likely that they will be able to do so in the near future. On the other hand, the Afghan rebels do not have any real possibility of driving the Soviets out of their country. The rebels have obtained most of their arms by capturing them from the Soviets, but they have also received some weapons via Pakistan. The rebels would like to receive more sophisticated Western arms, especially surface-to-air missiles capable of shooting down Soviet aircraft and helicopters. The United States and other nations have given a substantial amount of aid to the Afghan *mujahideen*, but Pakistan is understandably reluctant to allow too much aid to be transferred to the rebels for fear of Soviet retaliation. In March 1986, though, it was announced that the Reagan Administration had begun sending Stinger shoulder-fired anti-aircraft missiles to the Afghan guerrillas.[36] At best, the Afghan rebels can hope to maintain or even expand control over as much of their country as possible, but they cannot defeat the Soviets, and fighting is likely to continue for a long time to come.

Nicaragua. In 1979, a pro-American regime headed by Anastasio Somoza and based on the Nicaraguan National Guard was driven from power by the Sandinistas.[37] Although predominantly Marxist, the Sandinistas were supported in their effort to oust Somoza by a broad range of Nicaraguan society, including the Chamber of Commerce. In their final battles with the National Guard, they apparently received some Cuban military assistance, though exactly how much is uncertain.

The reaction of the Carter Administration to the new regime was to give it economic assistance in the hope that the Sandinistas would not become strongly pro-Soviet and would eventually allow free elections.

Citing Sandinista assistance to the Marxist rebels in El Salvador, the Reagan Administration ended economic assistance to Managua soon after coming to office and by the end of 1981 had begun a program of covert assistance to the *contras* fighting against the Sandinistas.[38]

The Sandinistas claim that the United States is completely responsible for the *contras*, but their own policies have also given rise to internal discontent. Like many other radical regimes when they first come to power, the Sandinistas tried to socialize the economy too quickly and economic chaos resulted. They have imposed press censorship and have periodically closed down the independent newspaper *La Prensa*, which supported them before Somoza's overthrow. In addition, the Sandinistas did not allow opposition candidates much freedom to campaign in the 1983 elections, and their imposition of conscription was highly unpopular.[39]

There have been four separate opposition movements in Nicaragua. By far the largest is the Nicaraguan Democratic Front (NDF), composed of about 15,000 guerrillas. This group has bases in Honduras and operates in northern Nicaragua. The CIA gave the NDF approximately $80 million in covert aid from 1981 until June 1984, when Congress cut off funding. It is led by ex-officers of Somoza's National Guard, and this fact alone seems to limit the NDF's appeal inside Nicaragua. Another group, the Democratic Revolutionary Alliance (ARDE) was led by the former Sandinista guerrilla leader Eden Pastora ("Commander Zero"). It had about 2,000 to 3,000 fighters and operated out of Costa Rica. In the spring of 1986 most ARDE fighters joined the NDF and Pastora gave up the struggle. Finally, there are two resistance groups among the Miskito and other Indians of Eastern Nicaragua, whom the Sandinistas have treated particularly badly. Together these two groups are said to have anywhere from 1,000 to 6,000 guerrillas under arms. The two groups agreed to form an alliance in June 1985.[40]

The Sandinista army has 60,000 troops. The Reagan Administration estimates the total number of *contras* at 15,000, meaning that Managua has a 4-to-1 force advantage over the guerrillas. With this ratio, the White House expects that the Sandinistas do not have enough troops to defeat the *contras*. Assisting the Nicaraguans are 50 Soviet and 3,000 Cuban military advisers.[41]

Should the *contras* ever be in a position seriously to threaten the Sandinistas, the Soviets are not in a geographically advantageous position to help them. Despite the claims of the Reagan administration, the Soviets have not provided Managua with much military assistance and do not seem to be willing to do so. Indeed, Castro was reportedly annoyed with Moscow in 1985 for not increasing its aid to Managua.[42]

It is doubtful that the *contras* will soon be in a position actually to overthrow the Sandinistas. The NDF's leadership has not come up with a political program beyond overthrowing the Marxists. Many fear that they seek to restore the old order, including reclaiming land taken from large landholders. Pastora was not tainted with the Somoza connection and was committed to building a republican democracy. His forces, however, were able to accomplish little. The Indian groups' appeal is strong among the Indians, but not among the rest of the population, and thus they cannot be expected to grow into a national movement. Therefore, while it is not impossible for the *contras* to overthrow the Sandinistas, they will probably have to become much stronger, especially in terms of internal support within Nicaragua, in order to oust the Marxists.

THE SOVIET RESPONSE

For the most part Soviet writers have not seen the phenomenon of anti-Soviet insurgencies as a permanent or growing problem faced by the USSR. Instead, they have tended to discuss these conflicts as problems in the consolidation of socialism in the Third World. The blame for them is placed firmly on Western "imperialists" as well as their Chinese and reactionary Third World allies. The internal causes of these conflicts are usually overlooked. Whether they really believe it or not, the Soviets portray these conflicts as only temporary and appear to have no doubt that the pro-Soviet Marxist regimes will eventually prevail.

One of the premier Soviet military theorists, Colonel E. Rybkin, discussed the existence of anti-Soviet insurgencies as early as 1978. In an article attempting to classify all the various conflicts occurring in the world into specific types, Rybkin took note that there were several of these insurrections taking place. Instead of calling them anti-Soviet insurgencies, he termed them "wars of nations on the path of socialist development in defense of socialism." In other words, these are conflicts in which pro-Soviet Marxist governments in the Third World are defending themselves against armed opposition. The USSR does not have, nor perhaps does not desire to have, full-fledged defense commitments to these governments such as those it maintains with its East European allies. Rybkin did not acknowledge that the opposition to these governments could be widespread or result from such a government being unpopular in a given nation. Instead, external forces were seen as the cause of armed opposition.[43]

This refusal to acknowledge the internal causes of revolt against Marxist Third World dictatorships is in sharp contrast to Rybkin's earlier writing about revolts against conservative Third World dictatorships. In these, he saw the entire basis for such conflicts not in the overall East–West competition, but in strictly local terms. He also made distinctions within the opposition to conservative dictatorships, seeing it contain both communist and non-communist elements.[44]

This was rather more sophisticated than the American view of such conflicts, which portrayed non-communist governments facing externally-backed communist opposition movements. But all this sophistication disappeared when Rybkin discussed revolts against Marxist dictatorships. Such conflicts are also seen strictly in terms of communist versus anti-communist, though the actors are reversed.

How the USSR should respond to these anti-Soviet insurgencies appears to be a matter of some debate among Soviet writers. Several Soviet military writers, who probably reflect the ideas of the military leadership, have concluded that intervention in local wars can be successful. There has been a marked evolution in Soviet military thinking about the utility of external intervention in Third World insurgencies. During the Vietnam War, the standard Soviet military judgment about US involvement was that while American forces were militarily superior to the Vietnamese communists, the Americans were "doomed to failure" because their fight was morally unjust.[45] After the war, however, Soviet military writers began to see the American failure as resulting less from moral factors than from the poor use of military force. In the late 1970s some Soviet military writers began to see certain American military actions in Vietnam, such as the use of helicopters in mountainous countryside for counterinsurgency operations, as having been effective. While they did not favor Israel in either the 1967 or 1973 Middle East wars, they saw Israeli strategy and tactics as extremely effective and that this military effectiveness led them to victory.[46] Since late 1983 one of the most important Soviet military journals, *Voenno-istoricheskii zhurnal*, has published many articles under the general heading "local wars." These articles have not been general, theoretical treatments of local wars or propaganda blasts at the US role in such wars, as were many past articles on this subject, though these types of articles have not disappeared. Rather, they deal with very specific tactical questions with regard to local warfare. Almost all the discussion focuses on the success or failure of Western tactics in local conflicts. Occasionally, the success or failure of present or former Soviet allies such as Syria and Egypt are examined, but the military operations of the USSR or its socialist allies are not.

These articles discuss subjects such as air defense, air tactics against air defense, air tactics against enemy aircraft, air tactics against airfields, armed forces organization in local wars, the use of helicopters in local wars, naval attacks against shore positions, and others. Detailed conclusions regarding the specific lessons that the Soviet military should learn in planning its own tactics and weapons procurement are not spelled out, but the overall conclusion in most articles is clear. Such tactics can be used successfully by intervening forces in local wars.[47] As many of these articles discuss intervention against insurgents, it is evident that several Soviet military writers believe that the USSR and its allies can successfully use these tactics in anti-Soviet insurgencies.

In a major study edited by General I. Shavrov, Commandant of the General Staff Academy, lip service is given to the importance of moral factors in war, but the bulk of the book examines several case studies of local conflicts and looks carefully at the question of why the United States or its allies were or were not successful. [48] Another study by civilian scholars closely examines the Soviet experience with the Moslem insurgencies that took place in Soviet Central Asia in the 1920s and 1930s. The authors openly state that this experience has relevance to Afghanistan. They note that Moslem insurgents were defeated then and imply that they can be defeated again.[49]

There are other Soviet writers, especially in the international institutes of the Academy of Sciences of the USSR, who seem to be wary about the USSR becoming too involved militarily in Third World insurgencies. One wrote an article emphasizing the theme, "the revolution must defend itself," indicating that Marxist Third World governments should bear the brunt of any fighting necessary to put down armed opponents.[50] The established socialist states could not be expected to do this for them. There are even signs that some in the Soviet military think this way. For example, in an interview in the British publication *Détente*, a Soviet officer identified only as "Colonel X" admitted that Moscow's military intervention in Afghanistan "does not serve our interests." He proposed that "non-alignment pacts" should be signed in countries where conflicts are occurring and that the great powers exert pressure on their clients to form coalition governments with insurgent forces. The superpowers should then work to halt all outside assistance to any insurgent forces that refuse to join the coalition, and should give economic assistance to the new government. That he mainly thought of this arragement for anti-Soviet insurgencies was evident when he stated, "Instead of paying these hooligans to make war, let us pay them to keep the peace" – not the sort of language the Soviets use to describe pro-Soviet forces of "national and social liberation."[51]

A conclusion that could be drawn from this argument is that the USSR would welcome the opportunity to withdraw Soviet, Vietnamese, or Cuban forces from various Third World conflicts and see Marxist rule somewhat diluted by giving the insurgents a share of power. If they did this, of course, the Soviets would not be in a position to prevent the insurgents from seizing full power, except through renewed intervention by one of the established socialist states. It is not at all clear that the Soviets are willing to take this risk. In the one nation that "Colonel X" discussed what a "non-alignment pact" would look like – Afghanistan – he called for a coalition government composed of both the insurgents and government, but insisted that, first, a non-alignment pact should be concluded with Pakistan to ensure that aid to the insurgents could no longer be channeled through it.[52] In other words, strict guarantees against the West helping the insurgents must be in place before the Soviets would agree to stop backing the Marxist government. Thus, the Marxists would remain in power along with a few ex-guerrillas. What those Soviets who do not want continued large-scale Soviet military intervention in Afghanistan really desire is to be able to withdraw while keeping their allies in power, preferably with Western consent.

The Soviets' response to anti-Soviet insurgencies has been varied, not only in their writing, but also in terms of their foreign and military policies. At one extreme the USSR has sent 115,000 troops to battle the *mujahideen* in Afghanistan and it supports both the Vietnamese invasion of Kampuchea and the Cuban intervention in Angola. At the other extreme, none of the established socialist states has sent nearly as many advisers to either Nicaragua or Mozambique, and the Soviets have only sent relatively limited military assistance.

The USSR can obviously project force into a nation on its borders more easily than into one that is far away. The same is true of Vietnam in Kampuchea. But distance is not necessarily a barrier to military force projection, as Cuban intervention in Angola and Ethiopia has shown. It is not surprising that Cuban and Soviet involvement in Nicaragua has been limited, as Nicaragua is close to the United States and very far from the USSR. Nicaragua is of course clost to Cuba, but if large numbers of Cuban forces entered Nicaragua and the United States responded by intervening, there is little that the Soviets could do to help their allies. What seems unusual is the relatively limited amount of Soviet and Cuban military assistance given to Mozambique as compared to Angola and Ethiopia. Instead, Zimbabwe sent troops, thus relieving the established socialist states of the need to do so.

In addition to geographic accessibility and the likely resonse of the United States, the degree to which insurgents threaten pro-Soviet Marxist governments must be an important factor in deciding what degree of military support from the established socialist states is necessary. In Afghanistan the guerrillas would quickly overthrow the Marxist government were it not for the presence of Soviet forces. In Kampuchea the Heng Samrin government only came to power because of the Vietnamese and could not be expected to survive long is they withdrew. There is a strong, though less certain, probability that the MPLA would be ousted by UNITA if the Cubans left Angola. In Ethiopia the insurgents do not actually threaten the government, and so a considerably smaller military presence from outside is needed. Perhaps the reason why more help has not been given to Mozambique is that the Soviets and Cubans judge that, while the MNR is a nuisance, it does not really threaten FRELIMO's rule. Thus far the Sandinistas have been able to hold the *contras* at bay without much Soviet and Cuban assistance.

At present none of the six anti-Soviet insurgencies seems about to succeed in toppling a pro-Soviet Marxist government. This is true not only in those countries where the established socialist nations have a heavy military presence, as in Afghanistan and Kampuchea, but even in those where there is a moderate presence, as in Angola and Ethiopia, or a light presence, as in Mozambique and Nicaragua. But what would the USSR and its allies do if the insurgents in countries where they do not have a strong military presence suddenly grew more powerful? What would they do if anti-Soviet insurgencies broke out in other countries, such as might have happened in South Yemen if the fighting that erupted between the Marxist factions there had been prolonged or non-Marxist forces seized the opportunity to rebel? The USSR and its allies could undertake a large-scale military intervention that would risk alienating Third World countries and induce America's traditional allies to cooperate more closely with the United States, but without giving them any more guarantee of being able to crush the rebels than the Soviets have had in Afghanistan. Or they could choose the option of giving only so much military aid and no more to the besieged Marxist government and risking that it be overthrown. The latter scenario would be especially unwelcome to the Soviets because, if a pro-Soviet Marxist government were actually overthrown by its internal opposition rather than simply by an external power as was the government of Grenada, not only would a Soviet ally be lost, but anti-Soviet guerrillas in other countries might be greatly encouraged. They might redouble their efforts to overthrow their Marxist adversaries once they saw that it had been done successfully elsewhere.

These are developments that would be most unwelcome to Moscow. Thus, if confronted with a stronger or a new anti-Soviet insurgency, the USSR is most likely to react by seeking to help Third World Marxist governments militarily defeat rebel insurgencies. However, if this could not be done with arms transfers or a relatively small number of military advisers and required another large-scale military intervention, the Soviets could be faced with a serious problem. The intervening forces would have to come from somewhere. The Vietnamese are probably not willing to become involved in operations outside Southeast Asia. Their forces already have major commitments in maintaining internal security in Vietnam, occupying Laos and Kampuchea, and being prepared to defend against another Chinese attack.

Soviet forces remain in Afghanistan, but Moscow has never before attempted a large-scale overseas military intervention. This would be much more difficult for the Soviets than launching an invasion across its own border. An overseas Soviet military intervention would be regarded as extremely threatening by the West and could severely jeopardize the Soviet goals of achieving arms control agreements and keeping Western defense expenditures and cooperation from growing rapidly. Finally, the Soviets do not want to risk a military confrontation with the United States that an overseas military intervention by Soviet forces could lead to.

The one nation that has the capability of intervening militarily in anti-Soviet insurgencies is Cuba. Castro did not anticipate that once the MPLA had driven UNITA, the FNLA, and South Africa away from Luanda in 1975–76 that Cuban forces would still be there a decade later on the defensive against UNITA. Cuba intervened in the Horn of Africa to help the Ethiopians fend off a Somali attack, but Castro refused to become heavily involved in fighting the Eritrean guerrillas. Even if Castro is willing to send forces elsewhere, there is a limit to the number of counterinsurgency struggles Cuba can intervene in at any one time. Cuba, after all, is a nation of only 10 million people, and its armed forces number 161,500, of whom 99,500 are conscripts. Finally, Moscow can hope that other leftist but not fully Marxist–Leninist governments might use their troops to help a neighboring pro-Soviet regime, but as Zimbabwe's faltering commitment to Maputo shows, this is not something on which Moscow can rely.

Should any of the present anti-Soviet insurgencies intensify or more break out, the Soviets will face very difficult choices. Their decision whether or not to intervene or support an ally such as Cuba in doing so will depend on geographical proximity to the USSR, proximity to any other socialist or socialist-oriented country, the seriousness of the internal opposition, the amount of outside support the opposition receives, proximity to the United States, the likely American response to socialist intervention in a given nation, and in some cases the willingness of Moscow's allies to undertake military intervention at the Kremlin's behest.

Of course, it is the Soviet goal not just to prevent pro-Soviet Marxist regimes from being overthrown, but also completely to defeat the guerrillas attempting to do so even when these guerrillas cannot succeed because of a strong socialist military presence such as in Afghanistan. When, in March 1985, President Zia al-Haq of Pakistan went to Moscow for Chernenko's funeral and met with General Secretary Gorbachev, Gorbachev threatened to give aid to Pakistani rebels unless Pakistan stopped aiding the Afghan rebels. Further, the Soviets threatened to aid Pakistani rebels if the United States continued to assist the Nicaraguan rebels.[53] It is probably not coincidental that government forces launched offensive against the rebels in Afghanistan, Angola, Ethiopia, and Mozambique during the summer of 1985. This could be an ominous sign that Gorbachev is much more willing than his predecessors to undertake confrontational measures in order to protect Moscow's weak allies in the Third World.

How far the Soviets will actually follow through on their threat to Pakistan is not yet clear. What is dangerous, though, is the implication in the threat that the Soviet leadership believes its own propaganda about the anti-Soviet insurgents in Afghanistan and elsewhere being supported mainly by external and not internal forces. In Afghanistan, the rebels are supported by the Afghan people. But, if the Soviets insist on blaming Pakistan for their actions, Moscow might be tempted to take some form of military action against Pakistan and thus widen the war. Such an action might be similar to Nixon's widening of the Vietnam War, when the United States attacked communist sanctuaries in Laos and Kampuchea. Another example of this tendency is Vietnam's attacks on Thai territory where Kampuchean rebels have their camps.[54]

US POLICY OPTIONS

One crucial element in determining the ability of anti-Soviet insurgents to succeed, or merely to avoid defeat, is the level of external military assistance they receive. To what extent should the United States become involved in aiding them?

As anti-Soviet insurgencies are a problem for Moscow's foreign policy, so they are an opportunity for that of Washington. The United States would benefit if indigenous forces in a Third World nation overthrew a pro-Soviet Marxist–Leninist regime for several reasons. First, the USSR would lose an an ally in the government that was overthrown and the United States would probably gain one in the new government. Second, unlike Egypt, Somalia, or other not fully Marxist Third World governments that have asked the USSR to leave, the overthrow of a strongly pro-Soviet Marxist–Leninist government by indigenous forces would be a serious ideological loss for the Soviets. In the Soviet view, once a Marxist revolution occurs, it is not supposed to be subject to reversal. If, as in Grenada, the Marxists are overthrown by the United States, the Soviets would consider it a loss, but an understandable one due to overwhelming "imperialist" force. But for a Marxist government to be overthrown by indigenous forces is simply not supposed to happen. If such an event actually occurred, it would show that even though the USSR is now stronger than ever before, Marxism is not irreversible. This could have two concrete benefits. Third World leaders, attracted to the USSR and Marxism–Leninism because the Soviets have a better record of helping their Third World allies stay in power than the United States, will have to question just how worthwhile the USSR actually is in this regard. Further, the overthrow of one pro-Soviet Marxist–Leninist regime might encourage anti-Soviet insurgents elsewhere to improve and expand their own efforts and, perhaps, eventually to succeed.

There is no guarantee that, other than the blow of losing an ally, the overthrow of a pro-Soviet Marxist Third World regime would lead to additional problems for Moscow. But the prospect of the Soviets losing an ally and suffering other adverse consequences provides an incentive for the United States to support anti-Soviet guerrillas in their attempts to overthrow Marxist–Leninist regimes. At this time the guerrillas in Mozambique, Angola, and Nicaragua only have an uncertain chance of victory. They cannot win in Afghanistan, Kampuchea, and perhaps not in Ethiopia either. Yet supporting anti-Soviet guerrillas even where they cannot win might be seen as in the interest of the United States because the continuation of these struggles demonstrates that Marxist governments are not popular. If the USSR and its allies are going to be active militarily in the Third World, the United States is better off if they have to struggle just to remain in the nations where they already are, instead of concentrating all their efforts on expanding their influence elsewhere in the Third World at the expense of the United States. But besides such great power motivations for supporting anti-Soviet insurgents, there is also a moral dimension. If the United States is really committed to helping other nations to become independent and determine their own system of government, then it should give help to people such as the Afghans who have demonstrated that they do not want either Soviet troops or a Marxist government in their country by fighting against both for many years.

Yet while, for the United States, giving aid to anti-Soviet insurgents might appear an easy way to bring about a foreign policy failure for the USSR, or at the minimum discomfit Moscow by making it more difficult for the USSR to protect its weak Marxist allies, there are several dangers for the United States that could arise from this policy. One of the foremost is that, if the United States gives large quantities of arms or sends military advisers to insurgent forces and the Soviets greatly increase their military assistance to their clients, there is the possibility that such conflicts could widen and that the superpowers themselves might be drawn into them. Obviously both the United States and the USSR want to avoid this. This consideration will serve to limit the type of assistance that the United States will be willing to provide the insurgents. In the past when one superpower has sent its own forces to fight in a Third World conflict, the other has limited its involvement. Thus, the United States will not undertake actions, such as sending advisers to Afghanistan, that could lead to a wider conflict. The type of assistance that the United States is ordinarily limited to in order to avoid the risk of provoking a wider conflict are arms transfers, funding, and training in either the United States or third nations.

But there are problems for the United States in undertaking these forms of aid. US aid to the *contras* in mining Nicaraguan ports led to a public outcry in the United States and the world that significantly contributed to Congress cutting off funds to the rebels. The sort of US military assistance to anti-Soviet guerrillas that might be acceptable to Congress and the American public in general might be so limited that it is insufficient to help rebel forces overcome Marxist–Leninist governments, or even to avoid being defeated.

Yet, even if American public opinion changed and decided that these groups should be supported, there is another problem. As the Soviets have already learned, it often takes guerrillas a long time actually to succeed, even when they receive external military assistance. The Vietnamese communists fought the French from 1945 until 1954 before ousting them, and then they only won North Vietnam. They needed another twenty-one years to gain the South. Guerrilla forces in Angola and Mozambique began their operations in the early 1960s, but accomplished little until the 1974 Portuguese coup brought to power a government that declared it would pull out of Africa the following year. The Sandinistas came to power in 1979 after a relatively short struggle, but the Somoza regime they replaced had been in office for over forty years. In addition, some insurgencies failed even though they might have lasted for many years. Marxist guerrillas were defeated in Greece (1944–48), Malaya (1948–61), Oman (1965–75), North Yemen

(1978–82), and elsewhere. The United States should not expect that by simply initiating or increasing military aid programs, anti-Soviet insurgents will be able to seize power quickly. Supporting insurgents is a long-term policy that can take several years ultimately to succeed, if at all.

Finally, should insurgent forces ever succeed in toppling a pro-Soviet Marxist-Leninist Third World government, a strategy of backing anti-Soviet guerrillas could not be regarded as successful until a stable, domestically popular regime emerged. Should the policies of the former insurgents prove unpopular or even brutal, the world might judge that the United States is not interested in helping nations free themselves of a government or foreign influence that the local populace does not want, but in merely seeing left-wing dictatorships replaced by right-wing ones. The worst result of all would be if anti-Soviet insurgents succeed in ousting a Marxist government but the new American-backed government became so unpopular that the former Marxist rulers were able to rally the populace against the anti-Soviet regime and return to power. This is a situation that the United States should take care to avoid because, if it ever occurred, the Soviets and their allies would be able to argue that no matter what sort of "mistakes' the Marxists might have made, they had proved they were better than the non-Marxists. In addition, domestic and international support for further US efforts to aid anti-Soviet insurgents would probably be greatly reduced, perhaps making it impossible for the United States to help other such groups.

Thus, while the phenomenon of anti-Soviet insurgencies provides an opportunity for US foreign policy, it also poses serious dangers that could result from a poorly conceived policy of aiding anti-Soviet guerrillas. How, then, can the United States take advantage of Moscow's problems most effectively? Based on the above discussion, several guidelines seem appropriate.

First, direct US military involvement or sending US military advisers to aid anti-Soviet insurgents should not be undertaken in order to avoid escalating or expanding the conflict, to stave off potential domestic opposition in the United States and among its allies that might force a withdrawal before the goal was achieved, and to make certain that the United States is not legitimizing a Marxist regime by allowing it to claim that, rather than fighting against domestic opponents, it is defending itself against foreign aggression, thus allowing it to gain more appeal among the populace than it had before.

Second, the United States should only support those insurgent groups that have a strong basis of internal support inside the country where they are fighting. Washington should not support those forces associated with a foreign power or an unpopular right-wing dictatorship that has been ousted, as these are not likely to command internal support, and hence are not likely to come to power even if they receive a great deal of aid.

Third, the United States should consider sending arms and perhaps even giving training in the United States or third countries to popularly supported anti-Soviet insurgents. The United States should not, however, attempt to organize and lead the rebel movement, as this will only allow the regime it is fighting to claim that the rebels are US puppets. Nor should the United States expect anti-Soviet insurgents to be able to succeed rapidly. It should expect that even under advantageous circumstances guerrillas will take a long time to triumph. Even if they do not seem likely to win but are popularly supported as in Afghanistan, the United States should consider sending them arms in order for them to expand and maintain control over as much of their country's territory as possible.

Fourth, US policymakers should realize that any covert aid that they give to anti-Soviet groups is probably going to become public knowledge sooner or later. Indeed, it is virtually impossible to keep knowledge of a sizable military operation secret because the target government has every incentive to publicize the fact that its opponents are receiving US assistance. If American policymakers would judge the desirability of all aid to guerrillas as if it were overt, perhaps highly damaging incidents such as support for the mining of Nicaragua's harbors, which led to Congressional restrictions on US aid to the *contras* and the cancellation of the operation itself, would be avoided.

Fifth, Washington should keep in mind that the overthrow of a pro-Soviet government is not the only possible benefit that can result from an anti-Soviet insurgency. Another is that if the Marxist government is at all independent of the USSR, it might modify its internal policies to become more popular or cease supporting Marxist insurgents in neighboring countries if it is doing so. The United States should be open to friendly relations with Marxist Third World governments and be prepared to exploit differences between such governments and Moscow, especially where guerrilla forces do not appear to have domestic support. To support a guerrilla movement that is not domestically popular is unproductive because the guerrillas are not likely to succeed, and the government they are fighting against is likely to move closer to the USSR in the face of American hostility.

What has the American record been thus far? The United States was prevented from aiding UNITA by the Clark Amendment, but after its repeal in July 1985, the United States began sending UNITA some aid in the spring of 1986. The United States has not aided rebels in Ethiopia or Mozambique, nor do there appear to be any plans to do so. In Ethiopia, the United States did not support the Eritrean rebels before the revolution, and because the main Eritrean rebel group is Marxist, America did not support it after the revolution. This restraint, however, has not aided the United States in improving ties with Addis Ababa or prevented the latter from moving even closer to the USSR. American relations with Maputo have improved in recent years. The Reagan Administration has even proposed giving some military aid to FRELIMO, and the former president of Mozambique, Samora Machel, was received at the White House in September 1985. In Afghanistan the United States has given about $400 million in military aid to the *mujahideen* since 1979, and in late 1985 the Administration and Congress agreed to increase the level of US support greatly. The Afghan rebels are not tainted by association with a previous government and are fighting a Soviet invasion, and so Congress favors aiding them. There has also been a movement in Congress to provide the non-communist Kampuchean rebels with some assistance, which up until now the United States has not done. In Nicaragua, the United States has given covert aid to the *contras*, but Congress cut this off. The Reagan Administration has attempted to restore this aid, but so far has only persuaded Congress to provide "non-lethal" assistance. In the summer of 1986, both houses of Congress voted to provide the contras with $70 million in military aid as well as $30 million in non-military aid. The Administration has mainly supported the Nicaraguan Democratic Front – the group led by ex-Somoza officers whose popular support in Nicaragua is doubtful.[55] This could well prove to be a mistake, not only because an unpopular guerrilla movement is unlikely to succeed no matter how much aid it is given, but because the possible failure of the NDF might negatively affect the political climate for this Administration or a future Administration to seek Congressional support for an anti-Soviet insurgent group that has domestic internal support. The Reagan Administration might be better off in the long run by not attempting to support the NDF, waiting and seeing if the NDF can build significant internal support for itself within Nicaragua. This is the policy that the USSR pursues before making large contributions to Marxist guerrilla movements.

Whether the phenomenon of anti-Soviet insurgencies is a great historical change signalling the inability of the USSR to maintain pro-Soviet Marxist–Leninist regimes in the Third World, or whether it is only a temporary problem that the USSR and its allies will soon be able to overcome, is not yet certain. A well-planned, effective US strategy for assisting anti-Soviet insurgents can help them be successful, but a poorly planned, ineffective US policy can contribute to their failure.

NOTES

1 Grenada was an exception. The Marxist regime there was not overthrown by local insurgents, but through American military intervention.

2 On the Soviet–Cuban intervention in Angola during 1975–6, see Bruce D. Porter, *The USSR in Third World Conflicts: Soviet Arms and Diplomacy in Local Wars, 1945–1980*. (Cambridge: Cambridge University Press, 1984), ch. 8; and Raymond L. Garthoff, *Détente and Confrontation: American–Soviet Relations from Nixon to Reagan* (Washington, DC: Brookings Institution, 1985), ch. 15.

3 Simon Jenkins, "Destabilisation in Southern Africa," *The Economist*, 16 July 1983, p. 21; and Allister Sparks, "Angolan Forces Fall Back from Site of Heavy Battle," *Washington Post*, 9 October 1985.

4 International Institute for Strategic Studies, *The Military Balance, 1985–1986* (London: IISS, 1985), p. 91.

5 On South Africa's role in Angola after the Angolan revolution, see Jenkins, "Destabilisation in Southern Africa," pp. 20–22; and Kenneth W. Grundy, "Pax Pretoriana: South Africa's Regional Policy," *Current History*, vol. LXXXIV, no. 4 (April 1985), pp. 150–4. On recent US military aid to UNITA, see David B. Ottaway and Patrick E. Tyler, "US sends New Arms to Rebels," *Washington Post*, 1 February 1986.

6 Mark N. Katz, "The Soviet–Cuban Connection," *International Security*, vol. VIII, no. 1 (Summer 1983), pp. 94–5; *The Military Balance, 1985–1986*, pp. 30 and 91; and David B. Ottaway, "Rebel Threatens US Firms in Angola," *Washington Post*, 1 February 1986.

7 This 10-to-1 force advantage was often cited by the Pentagon as necessary for pro-Western forces to defeat Marxist insurgents in Vietnam and more recently in El Salvador. Those who support American aid to anti-Soviet rebels cite this figure in reverse to show that despite numerical inferiority, rebel forces can avoid being defeated. Whether this means they can also be victorious is another question.

8 *The Military Balance, 1985–1986*, p. 91.

9 The United States has attempted to arrange for a simultaneous withdrawal of Cuban forces from Angola and South African forces from both Angola and Namibia. South Africa has announced that it would withdraw its troops from Angola and allow Namibia to become independent, while the Cubans and Angolans have said that Havana would withdraw all but 6–10,000 Cuban troops, which would remain in Luanda and the oil-rich Cabinda enclave. Little progress toward a settlement has actually been made. David B. Ottaway, "US Offers a Timetable for Cuban Withdrawal from Angola," *Washington Post*, 6 April 1985; Allister Sparks, "S. Africa to Remove Troops from Angola," *Washington Post*, 16 April 1985; and David B. Ottaway, "Angolan Says Talks are at Impasse Following Sabotage Attempt," *Washington Post*, 14 June 1985.

10 Robert D'A. Henderson, "Principles and Practice in Mozambique's Foreign Policy," *The World Today*, vol. XXXIV, no. 7 (July 1978), pp. 276–86; and Thomas H. Henriksen, "Mozambique: The Enemy Within," *Current History*, vol. LXXXI, no. 3 (March 1982), pp. 111–14 and 135–36.

11 Michael S. Radu, "Mozambique: Nonalignment or New Dependence?" *Current History*, vol. LXXXI, no. 1 (March 1982), pp. 134.

12 *Ibid.*, pp. 102–3.

13 *Ibid.*, p. 134.

14 *Ibid.*, and *The Military Balance, 1985–1986*, p. 102.
15 *The Military Balance, 1985–86*, pp. 30, 32, 102, and 147.
16 Norman MacQueen, "Mozambique's Widening Foreign Policy," *The World Today*, vol. XL, no. 1 (January 1984), pp. 22–8.
17 Glenn Frankel, "Aid to Mozambican Rebels Said to Continue," *Washington Post*, 23 January 1985; and Brian Pottinger, "Military Up in Arms Over Nkomati," *Sunday Times* (South Africa), 22 September 1985.
18 Jenkins, "Destabilisation in Southern Africa," pp. 23–4; and "Mozambique: A Need to Settle," *The Economist*, 22 March 1986, pp. 38 and 41. According to well-informed sources, FRELIMO and Zimbabwean forces captured MNR headquarters yet again in the spring of 1986.
19 On these events, see Porter, *The USSR in Third World Conflicts*, ch. 9; and Garthoff, *Détente and Confrontation*, pp. 630–53.
20 Mekalh Harnet, "Reflections on the Eritrean Revolution," *Horn of Africa*, vol. VI, no. 3 (1983–84), pp. 3–4; and Paul B. Henze, "Communism and Ethiopia," *Problems of Communism*, XXX, no. 3 (May–June 1981), pp. 65–66.
21 Katz, "The Soviet–Cuban Connection," pp. 95–97.
22 James Myall, "The National Question in the Horn of Africa," *The World Today*, vol. XXXIX, no. 9 (September 1983), p. 338. Another Ethiopian offensive was launched in Eritrea during the summer of 1985. See Paul Vallely, "Relief Workers Moved in After Ethiopian Troops Rout Rebels in the North," *The Times* (London), 1 November 1985.
23 *The Military Balance, 1979–1980*, p. 79; and *The Military Balance, 1985–1986*, pp. 30, 33, 96–97, and 147.
24 Henze, "Communism and Ethiopia," p. 69.
25 For an account of intra-Eritrean disputes, see Harnet, "Reflections on the Eritrean Revolution," pp. 3–15.
26 David P. Chandler, "Kampuchea: End Game or Stalemate?" *Current History*, vol. LXXXII, no. 12 (December 1984), pp. 413–17 and 433–34.
27 Leszek Buszynski, "Vietnam's ASEAN Diplomacy: Incentives for Change," *The World Today*, vol. XL, no. 1 (January 1984), pp. 29–36.
28 *The Military Balance, 1985–1986*, pp. 126 and 137.
29 See Daniel Southerland, "Sihanouk Doubts Cambodia Victory," *Washington Post*, 13 April 1985; and Paul Quinn-Judge, "Vietnam Said to Be Planning Major Offensive in Cambodia," *Christian Science Monitor*, 13 November 1985.
30 On this point, see Kishore Mahbubani, "The Kampuchean Problem: A Southeast Asian Problem," *Foreign Affairs*, vol. LXII, no. 2 (Winter 1983–84), p. 413.
31 Garthoff, *Détente and Confrontation*, pp. 887–937. In May 1986 the ailing Karmal resigned as general Secretary of the ruling party and was replaced by Najibullah, who is also a Parchami.
32 *The Military Balance, 1985–1986*, pp. 30 and 118–19; and Tahir Amin," Afghan Resistance: Past, Present, and Future," *Asian Survey*, vol. XXIV, no. 4 (April 1984), pp. 382–84 and 391.
33 For an assessment of the strengths and weaknesses of Soviet operations in Afghanistan, see Joseph Collins, "Soviet Military Performance in Afghanistan: A Preliminary Assessment," *Comparative Strategy*, vol. IV, no. 2 (1983), pp. 147–68.
34 For an excellent analysis of the strengths and weaknesses of the Afghan resistance, see Amin, "Afghan Resistance," pp. 373–99 and Zalmay Khalilzad, "Moscow's Afghan War," *Problems of Communism*, vol. XXXVI, no. 1, (January–February 1986), pp. 10–13.

68   MARK N. KATZ

35 Claude Malhuret, "Report from Afghanistan," *Foreign Affairs*, vol. LXII, no. 2 (Winter 1983–84), p. 427.
36 Ottaway and Tyler, "US Sends New Arms to Rebels." As of June 1986, though, Afghan rebel leaders claimed that they had not received any Stingers (unlike UNITA which claimed to have received them); David B. Ottaway, "Controversy Grows over Giving Afghan, Angolan Rebels missiles," *Washington Post*, 21 June 1986, p. A8.
37 "Evolution of US Policy," *Congressional Digest*, November 1984, pp. 260–61.
38 *Ibid.*, pp. 261, 288; and "Action in the current Congress," pp. 264–65.
39 For critical accounts of the Sandinistas by two of their former admirers, see Piero Gleijeses, "Resist Romanticism," *Foreign Policy*, no. 54 (Springs 1984), pp. 122–38; and Robert Leiken, "Nicaragua's Untold Stories," *The New Republic*, 8 October 1984, pp. 16–22. For a strong argument that American hostility indeed led to Sandinista intransigence, see Roy Gutman, "America's Diplomatic Charade," *Foreign Policy*, no. 56 (Fall 1984), pp. 3–23.
40 Forrest D. Colburn, "Nicaragua Under Siege," *Current History*, vol. LXXXIV, no. 3 (March 1985), p. 108; *The Military Balance, 1985–1986*, p. 153; Rowland Evans and Rovert Novak, "Commandante Zero," *Washington Post*, 7 June 1985; Bernard Nietschmann, "The Unreported War Against the Sandinastas," *Policy Review*, no. 29 (Summer 1984), pp. 32–39; Joanne Omang, "Nicaraguan Indians Form Alliance," *Washington Post*, 22 June 1985, "CIA Role Reported in Contra's Fall," *New York Times*, 30 May 1986, p. A3.
41 "White House Clarifies Tally of 'Contras,'" *Washington Post*, 21 March 1985.
42 Dusko Doder, "Castro Faults Soviets on Managua Aid," *Washington Post*, 24 March 1985.
43 Colonel E. Rybkin, "XXV s″ezd KPSS i osvoboditel′nie voini sovremennoi epokhi," *Voenno-istoricheskii zhurnal*, no. 11 (November 1978), pp. 11–12.
44 Major General K. Stepanov and Lt. Colonel E. Rybkin, "The Nature and Types of Wars of the Modern Era," *Voennaia mysl′*, no. 2 (February 1968), translated in CIA FB FPD) 0042/69, pp. 76–79; see also Mark N. Katz, *The Third World in Soviet Military Thought* (Baltimore: The Johns Hopkins University Press, 1982), pp. 39–51, 69–79, and 98–102.
45 See Major General V. Matsulenko, "Lokal′nye voiny imperializma (1945–68 gg.)," *Voenno-istoricheskii zhurnal*, no. 9 (September 1968), p. 47; and Lt. Colonel T. Kondratkov, "Organichennaia voina – orudie imperialisticheskoi agressii," *Kommunist vooruzhennykh sil*, no. 8 (April 1969), p. 28.
46 Colonel N. Nikitin, "Nekotorye operativno-takticheskie uroki lokal′nykh voin imperializma," *Voenno-istoricheskii zhurnal*, no. 12 (December 1978), p. 66; and Colonel A. Sinitskii, "Nekotorye takticheskie vybody iz opyta agressivnoi voiny SShA protiv V′etnama," *Voenno-istoricheskii zhurnal*, no. 6 (June 1979), p. 57. See also Katz, *The Third World in Soviet Military Thought*, pp. 29–30, 55–56, 83–84, and 109–113.
47 See, for example, Colonel General G. Dol′nikov, "Razvitie taktiki aviatsii v lokal′nykh voinakh," *Voenno-istoricheskii zhurnal*, no. 12 (December 1983), pp. 34–43; Major General M. Fesenko, "Ognevoe porazhenie nazemnykh sredstv PVO," *Voenno-istoricheskii zhurnal*, no. 5 (May 1984), pp. 66–73; Major General V. Maksimov, "Udary po aerodromam," *Voenno-isroricheskii zhurnal*, no. 6 (June 1984), pp. 79–84; Colonel R. Loskutov and Colonel V. Morozov, "Nekotorye voprosy taktiki vooruzhennogo konflikta v Livane v 1982 godu," *Voenno-istoricheskii zhurnal*, no. 7 (July 1984), pp. 75–80; Admiral P. Navoitsev, "Deistviia

VMS protiv berega," *Voenno-istoricheskii zhurnal*, no. 8 (August 1984), pp. 47–52; and Colonel V. Odintsov, "Tylovoe obespechenie voisk s primeneniem aviatsii po opytu lokal'nykh voin," *Voenno-istoricheskii zhurnal*, no. 2 (February 1985), pp. 81–86.

48 General of the Army I. E. Shavrov, *Lokal'nye voiny: istoriia i sovremennost'* (Moscow: Voenizdat, 1981).

49 A. I. Zevelev, Iu. A. Poliakov, and A. I. Chugunov, *Basmachestvo: Vozniknovenie, suschnost', krakh* (Moscow: Nauka, 1981). See p. 6 where an analogy between the activities of the *basmachi* in the 1920s and 1930s and the Afghan rebels now is explicitly made. See also B. Lunin, ed., *Basmachestvo: sotsial'no-politicheskaia sushchnost'* (Tashkent: Iz. "Fan" Uzbekskoi SSR, 1984), p. 3.

50 P. Shastiko, "Revoliutsiia dolzhna umet' zashchishchat'sia," *Aziia i Afrika segodnia*, no. 1 (1982), pp. 2–5.

51 "Colonel X's Peace Proposals," *Détente*, February 1985, pp. 2–4.

52 *Ibid.*, Soviet statements about the desire to see the Afghan conflict brought to a peaceful political resolution were greeted with skepticism by US officials at the time of the Reagan–Gorbachev summit in November 1985. See Gary Lee, "Soviets Voice Concern over Afghan War," *Washington Post*, 18 November 1985.

53 Dusko Doder, "Gorbachev Warns on Afghan Aid," *Washington Post*, 16 March 1985; and "Zia Confirms Soviet Warning," *Washington Post*, 24 March 1985.

54 In 1983 Soviet deputy Foreign Minister Mikhail Kapitsa reportedly warned the ASEAN nations that Vietnam would begin aiding rebels in Southeast Asian nations if they continued to aid Cambodian rebels. See Justus M. Van der Kroef, "Kampuchea: Protracted Conflict, Suspended Compromise," *Asian Survey*, vol. XXIV, no. 3 (March 1984), pp. 314–34.

55 For a summary of American policy toward each of the anti-Soviet insurgent movements, see Stephen S. Rosenfeld, "The Guns of July," *Foreign Affairs*, vol. LXIV, no. 4 (Spring 1986), pp. 698–714. See also "Text of President Reagan's United Nations Speech," *Washington Post*, 25 October 1985; and Ronald Reagan, "Freedom, Regional Security, and Global Peace," 14 March 1986 (Washington, DC: White House).

4

The Soviet Union and the New World Information Order

PAUL ROTH

The contours of the various models for a New World Information Order (NWIO) or a New World Information and Communication Order (NWICO) became clear only in the course of the debate concerning the issues involved. The fundamental outline, however, had already been established before the term "New World Information Order" emerged in the mid-1970s. The existing or desired communication system of a given developing nation or political system is offered as a model for World Information Order, projected across the globe. Before we turn to a full discussion of the subject, some frequently ignored truisms concerning the role of communications in human affairs must be emphasized:

1 human social life depends on the exchange of information, on communication;
2 throughout history information has not only consisted of messages, but has also constituted a means of exerting influence;
3 no one can report about everything that happens or about everything on which information is available;
4 possessing information is a prerequisite for exerting influence, for power and information are intimately interrelated; and
5 the domestic information and communication policy of a country and its foreign information and communication policy depend on the given political and social system.

SOVIET MEDIA POLICY

If we wish to present the development of the Soviet concept of a NWIO, then we must investigate basic Soviet policy towards the mass media. Since 1917 it has been guided by the three functions Lenin defined for the press: those of collective propagandist, collective agitator, and collective organizer.[1] These functions were extended to all mass media. The statement ascribed to Lenin," Information is agitation through facts," became the guideline for the whole public information sector.[2] In 1972, Ivan Zubkov, chief of the Newspaper Section of the Central Committee Propaganda Division, wrote: "The XXIV Congress of the Communist Party of the USSR has defined information as 'an instrument of guidance, a means of education and control.'"[3] Immediately after the Revolution the annihilation of the non-Bolshevik press was initiated with the "Decree on the Press." The Soviet Union has never since witnessed freedom of information, of opinion, or of the press. Based on Lenin's theory and practice, Stalin created a huge controlled and censored media apparatus. During the CPSU Congress in June 1983, then Central Committee Secretary Chernenko said in his briefing on "Current Issues in the Ideological and Political Work of the Party," that "our whole system of ideological work must function like a smoothly playing orchestra, with each instrument playing its own voice, its part, but with harmony being achieved through skilful directing."[4]

For as long as the Soviets have been in power, the government has shielded its citizens against information and opinions from abroad. Conversely, they have always endeavored to disseminate information and propaganda in foreign countries. The class-related nature of Soviet propaganda is described in the anthology, *Soviet Foreign Propaganda Issues*, edited by the jurist Sanakoev, as follows: "Foreign policy propaganda designed to propagate ideology among the masses inevitably has a class-related and partial nature. Reflecting the interests of a particular class in foreign policy issues, it simultaneously serves as a weapon in the fight against the enemy's ideology."[5] In line with this policy at the beginning of the history of the Soviet state Lenin had appealed for support from workers abroad by addressing telegrams to "all"; later the Comintern, with its auxiliary organizations, served as the main agency to disseminate revolutionary propaganda in the capitalist countries. In November 1929 Moscow initiated what came to be referred to as the "radio war," when it began regular international broadcasting transmissions for foreign countries that were liberally laced with revolutionary propaganda.

SOVIET INFORMATION POLICY AND FOREIGN PROPAGANDA AFTER 1945

After the Second World War the United Nations launched an attempt to improve the global dissemination of information. One of the suggestions proposed was the free collection and dissemination of news all over the world. This view was reflected in article 19 of the UN Declaration of Human Rights in 1948: "Everyone has the right to freedom of opinion and expression; this right includes freedom to hold opinions without interference and to seek, receive and impart information through any media and regardless of frontiers." During the 1948 UN General Assembly voting on this Declaration, eight states abstained from voting, among them the Soviet Union, South Africa and Saudi Arabia.

Simultaneously, Stalin again sealed off his sphere of influence from external media influences. During the Cold War, which was predominately carried out in the ether, the Soviet Union "protected" its citizens by building a chain of jamming transmitters. The point that the Soviets were emphasizing – one that had formed the basis of policy prior to the Second World War – was that national sovereignty would always take priority over the flow of information across national borders.

In 1954 the Soviet Union entered UNESCO as part of the policy shift introduced after Stalin's demise. Although the "thaw" in relations with the West gave Soviet citizens a limited latitude for voicing criticism, the Party never put its monopolization of opinion and information up for discussion. Following Khrushchev's ouster in 1964 the reins were tightened again; the persecution of dissidents was intensified. The Czechoslovak Communist Party's abolition of the monopoly on information and the press in 1968 during the "Prague Spring" constituted a decisive reason for the invasion by Soviet and other Warsaw Pact troops. At this time the Soviet Union reintroduced extensive jamming of broadcast, a practice that had been partially discontinued in 1963. At the same time the Soviets expanded their foreign propaganda broadcasts – especially those targeted at the Third World.

In the late 1950s and the early 1960s the news agency TASS extended its area of operation into Africa. In 1961 the Sovinform office was replaced by the news agency Novosti (APN) for propagating information abroad. The broadcasting service "Peace and Progress," founded in 1964, primarily addressed a Third World audience. Since the late 1960s, the focus of all Soviet broadcasts for foreign countries has shifted more and more to the developing countries.

THE DEVELOPING COUNTRIES' DEMAND AND THE SOVIET UNION

In the early 1970s representatives of developing countries called UNESCO's attention to the unbalanced flow of information, as they noted the degree of control that Western news agencies exercised over the international dissemination of information. In the mid-1970s the developing countries' demand for a "New World Information Order" was placed on the table at UNESCO. Since then the Soviet Union has solemnly assured the developing countries of its solidarity with their position. The major issue in dispute between many developing countries and the West was the issue of "free flow of information" – a concept which many of the former did not accept. On the one hand, authoritarian political systems had evolved in many developing countries; on the other, it is indisputable that the Western international news agencies, especially American television producers, were and still are the major suppliers of news and other programs for most developing countries. The developing countries' demands for a NWIO, and for technological development, prompted the Soviet Union to propose its own model for a NWIO. In the process they linked the North–South problem of an NWIO with the discussion about information across national borders between East and the West. The titles of Soviet pamphlets and books on the topic that appeared during the 1970s illustrate that development and its trends, whose focal point was not the formula "NWIO," but rather the "ideological struggle."[6] They called for the repulsion of the "ideological diversion" practiced by the "capitalist" countries. Although the fundamental problem of a free flow of information was discussed in those books, it always occurred with reference to "inadmissible interference" by the West in the internal affairs of the socialist and the developing countries; the connection between this topic and the NWIO is evident. As far as the relations between North and South or the demands of the developing countries on the industrial countries of the Northern Hemisphere were concerned, Soviet authors said that the Soviet Union was not affected by these demands. It would be prepared to help the developing countries; however, since the USSR had never been a colonial power, no one could make it accountable for the backwardness of the newly founded states.

At the same time the debate on a new international information system offered the Soviets the possibility to fight against the disquieting problem of the free flow of information on, so to speak, foreign territory. S. Beglov, for example has argued:

Attempts to gloss over the fundamental differences between the functions of the mass media in capitalist and socialist countries, arbitrarily to divide the world into "North" and "South," entail the risk that the developing countries will become isolated from their true ally – socialism. Only with the cooperation of all anti-imperialist forces in the developing countries can they be freed once and for all from the chains used – also in the information section – by the common enemy of the forces of progress and democracy, by imperialism, in its attempt to stifle them.[7]

Without doubt the USSR has succeeded in significantly helping to obstruct a reconciliation between the developing countries and the Western industrial countries on the issue of a World Information Order, because the latter perceive a world-wide threat to the free flow of information, not so much in the demands of the developing countries, but primarily in the context of the Soviet Union's position.

Until now the developing countries have not had news agencies and radio stations that can rival the news agencies and radio stations of the industrial nations. East–West relations are characterized by both sides having world-wide news agencies and long-range stations. The difference here, however, is that the socialist countries shield themselves against the flow of information from the Western countries, while they themselves freely disseminate information to the West.

THE 19TH UNESCO GENERAL CONFERENCE (1976)

The International Organization of Journalists (IOJ), a Soviet-orientated front organization, has supported the position of the socialist countries on a NWIO. The president of the IOJ, Finnish Professor K. Nordenstreng, and his fellow countryman, T. Varis, praised the delegates of the developing countries and the socialist countries. They had emphasized at the 1974 UNESCO Conference that "the concept of the free flow of information" is definitely outdated and that from the position of current developments it must be assigned to the last century. This judgment on the doctrine of the "free flow" became possible only "as a consequence of the global change in favor of socialism, only as a result of the indisputable increase in the influence of the international anti-imperialistic movement."[8] During the preparations for the UNESCO General Conference of 1976 in Nairobi, the Soviet Union was involved in drafting the resolution that dealt with the obligations of the mass media and the responsibilities of governments and nations, as well as with the need to fight racism. The term "balanced flow of information" was designed to replace the "free flow of information." The Western countries regarded the draft of the declaration as partially incorporating the principles of Soviet public information policy, and it was shelved. L. Sussman calls the 1976 19th UNESCO General Conference in Nairobi the "dividing line" in reference to the discussion on the NWIO.[9] It was here that the USSR recognized most clearly the opportunity of profiting from the developing countries' demand to change the World Information Order and/or of interweaving its own aims with those of the developing countries.

THE CSCE AND THE SOVIET INTERPRETATION OF "BASKET 3"

After the Soviet Union had agreed to the participation of the United States and Canada in the Conference on Security and Cooperation in Europe (CSCE), talks concerning the issues to be covered in the Conference began in the early 1970s. The Western side insisted on discussing the issues of information across national borders, of humanitarian concerns, etc., and on incorporating them in the Final Act (Basket 3). The Soviet Union showed little interest in this subject, but eventually gave in to avoid jeopardizing the negotiations. In December 1973 the jamming of Voice of America, Deutsche Welle and BBC broadcasts was abandoned. The Soviet attempt to have the Western foreign broadcasts discontinued failed. The Soviet Union, however, was successful in achieving its demand that the preamble emphasize full respect for the sovereignty, the laws and customs of all countries. This made it clear how the Soviet Union would act both during the CSCE and after the signing of the Final Act. The Soviet Union signed the CSCE Final Act of 1975, which entailed agreement to the issues in "Basket 3"; however, in principle, the Soviet Union was not willing to change its policy of control over information flows. In that context the Secretary of the Soviet Commission for UNESCO affairs, Iu. Kashlev, wrote in 1976:

The socialist countries, the majority of the developing countries, the international public reject the imperialistic notion of a "free flow of information and ideas." Numerous discussions in the UN, UNESCO and other organizations concerning information problems have demonstrated this. At the Conference for Security and Cooperation in Europe, the Western countries failed in the attempt to smuggle that concept into the Final Act.[10]

THE SOVIET UNION AND THE 20TH UNESCO GENERAL
CONFERENCE

When the 20th UNESCO General Conference convened in Paris in October 1978, it discussed the draft of a declaration about which TASS stated that "the initiative for the draft had come from socialist countries and that experts from numerous countries had participated in the actual elaboration of the draft."[11] The text submitted was not accepted by the Western members of UNESCO. They wanted to prevent any restriction on, or governmental supervision of, the free flow of information. The Western position was primarily presented by West German Foreign Minister Genscher.

The document finally worked out was a compromise, only partially meeting the Soviet intentions, but also not fulfilling Western expectations. The developing countries did not simply side with the socialist countries; they cast different votes. By acclamation the "Declaration on the fundamental principles for the contributions of the mass media, the strengthening of peace and international understanding, for the promotion of human rights and for fighting racism, apartheid and warmongery" was passed. The reference to states' responsibility for the mass media had been abandoned, and the immediate threat to a free flow of information averted. Upon the request of the socialist countries, however, a reference to "special obligations and responsibilities of the mass media" was included.

That the declaration was not completely in line with Soviet intentions was explained by the Soviet side as resulting from insufficient incorporation of the socialist countries' experience in the document.[12] Nevertheless, the Soviet side praised the declaration as a success for its policy. Kashlev, for example, stated: "The Soviet Union can pride itself on the fact that this document was adopted on its initiative."[13]

SOVIET COUNTER-PROPAGANDA AFTER HELSINKI

The Soviet rulers were surprised by the unexpected consequences of the Final Act agreed to at the Helsinki Conference. Now the West demanded that the socialist countries reduce their barriers to information flows. At the same time dissidents in the USSR demanded that the government comply with and implement the Final Act. The first so-called "Helsinki Group" was founded in 1976 in Moscow in order to promote the implementation of the Helsinki decisions in the USSR.

Since the beginning of the 1970s, studies of Soviet public opinion research institutes had shown with increasing clarity that Soviet domestic propaganda did not have the desired results. On 27 November 1978, Brezhnev criticized the work of the propaganda and information apparatus of the CPSU in a speech before the Central Committee. On 6 May 1979, *Pravda* published the text of a Central Committee decision on further improvement of ideological and education efforts in the Soviet Union. In view of this situation, Soviet media functionaries thought it advisable to initiate "counterpropaganda activities" to weaken the threat respresented by the CSCE. This propaganda was based on the Soviet interpretation of the CSCE Final

Act. It began with the allegation that the West was obstructing the free flow of information from East to West; then gained further intensity with the assertion that there was no freedom of opinion and freedom of press, no free flow of information in the capitalist countries; and culminated in the accusation that the "capitalist countries" were engaged in upsetting the citizens of socialist countries with "ideological diversion" and in alienating the citizens of the developing countries from their traditional cultures. The number of articles, radio broadcasts, pamphlets and books published in the Soviet Union calling the free flow of information "a psychological war," "ideological diversion," "electronic imperialism," etc., has since increased dramatically.

The topic of "disinformation" targeted at the public in capitalist countries has become a standard subject in Soviet newspapers. Since 1978 articles and political cartoons have suggested that US citizens are exposed to a total surveillance, as described in George Orwell's *1984*. In short, and somewhat simplified, the conclusion that the Soviet citizen is supposed to draw is that the mass media are controlled and citizens watched all over the world.

At the Belgrade CSCE follow-up meeting in 1977/78, "Basket 3" was again a subject of discussion. The final resolution showed that the Soviet Union did not intend to change its position. In view of the incompatible positions, the final resolution eventually agreed upon contained only the statement that both sides intended to implement the CSCE Final Act. Since the late 1970s the "global political climate" has deteriorated with the deployment of Soviet intermediate-range missiles, the foundation of the "Solidarity" trade union followed by the imposition of martial law in Poland, the NATO dual-track decision to display intermediate-range missiles, and the Soviet invasion of Afghanistan. All of these have affected the NWIO discussion. In 1980 the Soviet Union, at the time of "Solidarity" in Poland, resumed the jamming of Western radio broadcasts.

THE MACBRIDE REPORT AND THE SOVIET COMMENT

The "Report of the International Commission for the Study of Communication Problems," the MacBride Report,[14] presented after a long delay to the 21st UNESCO General Conference of 1980 in Belgrade, had been compiled by a variety of agencies and individuals, among them the Director General of TASS. The report sought to give a global and encompassing picture of international communication, from folk songs to satellite communications, and was therefore inappropriate as a basis for a political decision. The formula "New World Information

Order" was now expanded to "New World Information and Communication Order."

The MacBride Report has been harshly criticized by some in the West. The report emphasized the problems of the developing countries resulting from their dependence on the Western industrial nations, while it was reserved about the censorship problem and other forms of obstruction of information flows. Reference to the state-controlled media systems of socialist countries was excluded, just as the imbalance in the information sector between East and West was virtually ignored. It is not possible to specify precisely where the Soviet side exerted influence on the wording of the report. Various votes allow the conclusion that the Soviets disagreed with some statements. A further indication that the report left some Soviet desires unfulfilled is given in Appendix I of the report, where four members of the commission added critical comments. Among those comments is one by TASS Director General S. Losev.

Losev asserts that the description of the situation of the developing countries was "blurred." He refers to the problem of sovereignty facing developing countries and states that the "role of the Western mass culture in the destruction of the national cultures of the developing countries" was "played down." But, above all, the "achievements and experience of the socialist countries and the developing countries in establishing national mass communication systems and in gaining autonomy in that sector" had been ignored. And further: "The practical experience of Bulgaria and Poland, Tanzania and India, Uzbekistan and Armenia, Azerbaidzhan and Georgia, Turkmenistan and Kirghizia, Yakutia and Tadzhikistan is missing in the report . . ." The listing which mixes socialist countries, non-aligned countries and Soviet republics as if they were all part of one interest group is misleading, for it clearly implies a degree of autonomy for political units of the USSR that does not exist.

Finally, the heart of the matter is addressed: "It is regrettable that we sometimes use obsolete terms and empty formulas, such as the concept of the 'free flow of information.'" The final version of the report is, says Losev, "somewhat too Western" in terminology and approach. Losev's critique concludes: "Finally, I would like to emphasize again that I consider this report and especially its contribution to peace and international understanding as extremely important; I would also like to express my satisfaction about the fact that it properly observes the Final Act of Helsinki."

THE 21ST UNESCO GENERAL CONFERENCE (1980)

At the 21st UNESCO General Conference the discussion of the MacBride Report was directly linked with the discussion of the participant countries' different proposals for a declaration. Once more, the three groups stood out clearly. The Soviet position was discernible prior to the start of the Conference. In their view any information must serve the interests of peace and progress (or rather what the Soviet Union understands as the only acceptable form of peace and progress). Any propaganda to instigate or promote war, hostility between peoples, racism, etc., must be prohibited. The use of information and propaganda to unmask enemies of "peace" and "progress" is permitted and necessary, as is the use of information and propaganda in support of those exploited by capitalism – for example, in support of "national liberation movements." Moreover, every state is supposedly responsible for information and propaganda originating from its territory, and each state has the right to ward off or to censor foreign information or propaganda. A free flow of information across national borders without permission violates a nation's sovereignty. To prevent this, binding provisions must be incorporated in international law. In addition, the flow of information between the industrial nations and the developing countries must be balanced both quantitatively and qualitatively, and the alienation generated by the capitalist mass media must be eliminated. Finally, the developing countries should, in cooperation with the socialist countries, fight "electronic imperialism," and the socialist countries are prepared to assist the developing countries in establishing a media system after the socialist model.

The final resolution again had to be a compromise. It demanded both freedom of the press and of information and warned of the negative effect of certain monopolies ("Be they public or private"); it called for eliminating the imbalance in control over information flows and points out the responsibility of journalists, and so on.

There is no way to postulate that the final resolution is a Soviet product, as Kashlev tried to: "This is a great success for the socialist countries and the developing countries."[15] What really happened in Belgrade, how other positions in the discussion were substantiated, was almost completely withheld from the Soviet public. Also withheld was the stand taken by the chief of the Afghan UNESCO Commission, Akhtar Mohammed Paktiawal, on 25 October 1980, at a meeting of Commission IV (Culture and Communication). Referring to the resolution on the Director General's report on the MacBride Report, passed by consensus, he stated that, given the possibility he would have voted no. He argued that the resolution represented nothing but a further empty formula unable to promote free communication between all men.[16] In that connection he pointed out the situation in his country which had been brought fully under Soviet control. He appealed to his colleagues to support his homeland in the struggle for freedom from Soviet domination. At the conference all one did was talk about a free flow of information, he noted. UNESCO could, however, ensure that the world would listen to Afghanistan. He continued: "But the resolution says nothing about the free flow of information . . . The news media in Afghanistan is under the control of the Soviet Union . . .'

The 21st General Conference also established an International Program for the Development of Communication (IPDC) designed to benefit primarily the developing countries. It also decided to create an Intergovernmental Council, with the majority of its thirty-five members from the developing countries. Soviet news reports on IPCD events in subsequent years were meager and totally distorted. On 24 June 1981, *Izvestiia* reported that the US delegation had been isolated because of its demand for a free flow of information and that the Third World representatives had condemned the Western information policy. Western reports, however, said that the developing countries were interested in cooperating with the Western states.[17] By that time apparently everybody had realized that aid from the Soviet Union could not realistically be expected. Similarly misleading were the Soviet news reports on the extraordinary UNESCO General Conference in November and December 1982 in Paris (the 4th extraordinary conference), at which 158 countries participated. A speech by the chief of the Soviet delegation, Deputy Foreign Minister V. Stukalin, consisted of praise for the efforts of UNESCO and of an enumeration of the Soviet Union's accomplishments.[18] The *Izvestiia* special correspondent reported that some Western delegations had attempted to undermine the efforts for peaceful coexistence among all peoples.[19] Applause in Paris had been supposedly reserved for the Soviet Union and the other socialist countries. In reality it took tenacious negotiations to combine numerous compromise into a package designed as the guiding program for the work of UNESCO in the period 1984–89. A direct confrontation had been averted; in the end a specially established commission once again succeeded in finding a mutually acceptable compromise.[20]

THE SOVIET RECOURSE TO THE 1936 "PEACE PACT WITH REGARD TO BROADCASTING"

A large number of countries had begun foreign radio broadcast services in the 1920s and 1930s. The "radio war" – that is, interference in the affairs of other countries through revolutionary broadcasts – had been started in 1929 by the Soviet Union, with Nazi Germany and fascist Italy initiating such broadcasts soon thereafter. Numerous countries protested against the Soviet radio propaganda war. Germany and Japan had already left the League of Nations when the so-called "Pact of Peace with regard to Broadcasting" was discussed and signed in 1936 in the League of Nations. The Soviet Union took part in the Conference and signed the pact, but did not ratify it. The pact envisaged, among other points, that governments should exert influence on the radio stations in their countries to prevent broadcasts which might disturb the internal order of other states.

This pact had no effect and, although it was mentioned in post-Second World War UN and UNESCO documents, nobody, including the Soviets, bothered to unearth it. After the discussion about a regulation of satellite television had begun (1972), the Soviets remembered the pact of 1936. After 1974, Soviet publications frequently referred to that pact, interpreting it as if it represented a basis or model for a kind of "Peace Pact with regard to Television," and claimed that the demand for a free flow of information had been devised by Goebbels and had been dusted off after the Second World War by Great Britain and the United States. In September 1982, the Supreme Soviet of the USSR ratified the convention dating from 1936, and Kashlev claimed in *Izvestiia* that this document on a broadcasting peace pact was in accordance with UN policy, with the CSCE Final Act and with the Soviet line.[21]

Shortly afterwards, in December 1982 at the 38th UN General Assembly, the resolution entitled "Principles Governing the use by States of Artificial Earth Satellites for Direct Television Broadcasting" was passed. This resolution was neither based on consensus nor was it binding under international law. It states, however, that satellite television broadcasts across national borders require the prior consent of the receiving countries. Also stated is a state's responsibility for broadcasts originating on its territory.

THE MADRID CSCE FOLLOW-UP MEETING

At the CSCE follow-up meeting in Madrid (1980–83) the USSR was at pains to keep the topics of human rights and "Basket 3," of Afghanistan and Poland, out of the discussion. The discussion on the flow of information and the freedom of information followed a pattern similar to that at the Belgrade CSCE follow-up meeting. The Soviet side proposed a CSCE decision to shut down Radio Liberty and Radio Free Europe because they were supposedly destroying mutual trust between peoples. The countries of the European Community demanded that

jamming be discontinued. The Soviet public was not told any details of
the discussion. The Madrid Conference did avoid a breakdown of the
Helsinki process, but it did not achieve any approximation of positions.
The final document was a laborious compromise. In the meantime, the
Helsinki groups in the Soviet Union were disintegrating after a series of
arrests and trials.

THE SOVIET UNION'S MAIN OBJECTIVE

The Soviet Union has succeeded in improving coordination with its
socialist allies in the joint struggle against a free flow of information; for
example, in its publications, the IOJ clearly supports the Soviet position.
Three books dealing with foreign propaganda were published in the
USSR in 1980 and 1981.[22] Symptomatically, they all discuss the subject
of a NWIO in more depth than earlier books and pamphlets. Kashlev's
book, *Mass Information and International Relations*, is devoted to the same
subject.[23] Somewhat simplified, one can find three main topics in each of
these books: Soviet foreign propaganda as a striving for peace;
"ideological diversion" by the capitalist countries; and the NWIO.
Since 1980 it has been evident that the Soviets have supported the idea of
a NWIO with only one main objective, which is to prevent the free flow
of information into socialist countries. Other Soviet publications in
recent years,[24] as well as publications of the IOJ,[25] prove that the Soviet
model for NWIO is designed to secure the existing monopoly on
information and opinion and to block any influence of the Western
democracies. In the Soviet Union this is called "counterpropaganda." It
is two-faced; one is the domestic face, the other the foreign. The Soviet
claim to act as the "true friend" of the developing countries can safely be
called a propaganda formula designed to subordinate North–South
problems to the East–West conflict. The Soviet Union has partially
achieved this goal in the United Nations and UNESCO to the detriment
of the overall interests of the developing countries and at the expense of
detente.

The Soviet Union's greatest fear is of a world-wide free flow of
information. The "Communist Manifesto" by Marx and Engels begins
with the famous sentence: "A specter is haunting Europe – the specter of
Communism. All powers of Old Europe have entered into a holy
alliance to exorcise this specter." Referring to the Soviet endeavors
toward a NWIO, one may use the following satirical paraphrase: "A
specter is haunting Europe – the specter of a world-wide free flow of
information. All powers of Socialism have entered into a holy alliance to
exorcise this specter."

NOTES

1 Vladimir Ilich Lenin, *Werke* (Berlin: Bietz Verlag, 1955ff.), vol. v, p. 10.
2 V. Kuibishev, in *Izvestiia*, 24 February 1931.
3 I. Zubkov, "Informatsiia – kategoria politicheskaia," *Zhurnalist*, no. 8 (1972), p. 8.
4 *Izvestiia*, 15 June 1983.
5 Sh. P. Sanakoev, *Voprosy sovetskoi vneshnepoliticheskoi propaganday* (Moscow: 'Mezhdunarodnye Otnosheniia, 1980), p. 63.
6 Iu. Kolosov, *Massovaia informatsiia i mezhdunarodnoe pravo* (Moscow: Mezhdunarodnye Otnosheniia, 1973); V. Korobeinikov, *Dukhovnoe obschchenie. Obmen informatsiei. Ideologicheskaia bor'ba* (Moscow: Politizdat, 1976); D. Nikolaev, *Informatsiia v sisteme mezhdunaronykh otnoshenii* (Moscow: Mezhdunarodnye Otnosheniia, 1978).
7 S. Beglov, *Vneshnepoliticheskaia propaganda* (Moscow: Vysshaia Shkola, 1980), p. 317.
8 K. Nordenstreng, T. Varis, "Za novyi informatsionnyi poriadok," *Demokraticheskii Zhurnalist*, no. 9 (1977), p. 6.
9 L. Sussman, *Mass News Media and the Third World Challenge* (London: Sage, 1977), p. 14.
10 Iu. Kashlev, "Obmen informatsiei – na sluzhbe mira," *Agitator*, no. 14 (1976), pp. 56.
11 TASS, 1 November 1978.
12 Iu. Poliakov, *Demokraticheskii Zhurnalist*, no. 5 (1979), p. 10.
13 Iu. Kashlev, *Novoe vremia*, 15 December 1978, p. 18.
14 "Bericht der Internationalen Kommission zum Studium der Kommunikationsprobleme unter dem Vorsitz von Sean MacBride an die UNESCO," *Viele Stimmen – eine Welt* (Konstanz: Universitätsverlag Konstanz, 1981).
15 Iu. Kashlev, "Die UNESCO und die Medien," *Neue Zeit*, no. 49 (1980), p. 22.
16 "Afghanistans Chefdelegierter klaft die Sowjetunion an," *Suddeutsche Zeitung*, 27 October 1980; "Afghanische Demonstration vor der UNESCO," *Neue Zürcher Zeitung*, 28 October 1980.
17 Associated Press, 23 June 1981.
18 *Izvestiia*, 27 November 1982.
19 A. Krivolapov, "IUNESKO na sluzhbe mira," *Izvestiia*, 7 December 1982.
20 "Verbschiedung des UNESCO-Programms. Im Zeichen von Kompromissen," *Neue Züricher Zeitung*, 7 December 1982.
21 Iu. Kashlev, *Izvestiia*, 2 September 1982.
22 Beglov, *Vneshnepoliticheskaia propaganda*; Sanakoev, *Voprosy sovetskoi vneshnepoliticheskoi propagandy*; Sh. Sanakoev and N. Kapchenko, *Vneshnepoliticheskaia politika i bor'ba idei* (Moscow: Mezhdunarodnye Otnosheniia, 1981).
23 Iu. Kashlev, *Massovaia informatsiia i mezhdunarodnye otnosheniia* (Moscow: Mezhdunarodnye Otnosheniia, 1981).
24 Iu. Kolosov and B. Tsepov, *Novyi informatsionnyi poriadok i problema podderzhaniia mira*. (Moscow: Nauka, 1983).
25 Iu. Kashlev, *The Mass Media and International Relations* (Prague: International Organization of Journalists, 1983).

5

Soviet propaganda and the process of national liberation*

ROGER E. KANET

In his monumental study of the Bolshevik Revolution, E. H. Carr claimed that "The initiative of introducing propaganda as a regular instrument of international relations must be credited to the Soviet Government."[1] More than ten years later Frederick C. Barghoorn began his classic study of *Soviet Foreign Propaganda* by stating: "Words and pictures have played a more continuous, and perhaps a more vital role than bullets or rubles in Moscow's struggle to undermine the social order of capitalism and to reconstruct society on 'Marxist–Leninist' foundations."[2] As these authors – and many others who have been concerned with detailing the record of Soviet propaganda activities – have demonstrated, propaganda of all sorts has been an important instrument in the efforts of Soviet leaders to accomplish their foreign objectives ever since the creation of the Soviet state.[3] During the two decades since Barghoorn published his study the foreign propaganda activities of the Soviet Union have expanded significantly and now extend across the entire world.

According to estimates of the US Central Intelligence Agency, the Soviet leadership spent more than $3 billion per year at the end of the 1970s on various forms of foreign propaganda; by 1982 the estimated cost of foreign propaganda had risen to more than $4 billion.[4] Soviet propaganda is conducted through a broad array of activities. In 1982, for example, the Soviets published books in 68 foreign languages, primarily for distribution abroad. In English alone almost 1,200 books and pamphlets were published in more than 24 million copies.[5] These publications have as one of their primary purposes getting across some aspect of the Soviet propaganda message. In addition to books and brochures, already by the early 1970s the Soviets were distributing

* The original version of this paper was prepared for presentation at the Conference on "Contemporary Soviet Propaganda and Disinformation," co-sponsored by the US Department of State and the US Central Intelligence Agency, Airlie House, Warrenton, VA, 25–27 June 1985.

abroad foreign-language editions of 91 Soviet periodicals.[6] The weekly *Moscow News*, for example, appears in more than 800,000 copies in English, French, Spanish and Arabic translations.[7] By 1980 a network of Soviet radio stations that included Radio Moscow, Radio Peace and Progress and a number of more specialized "unofficial" or clandestine stations were broadcasting more than 2,750 hours a week in over 80 languages to foreign audiences. Of the total hours of weekly foreign broadcasting, more than 60 per cent was targeted at Third World audiences: 270 hours were beamed toward Africa, 544 towards East Asia and the Pacific, 133 toward Latin America, 345 toward the Middle East and North Africa, and 370 toward South Asia.[8] Two Soviet press agencies, TASS and Novosti Press Agency, maintain a wide network of contacts with foreign newspapers, press agencies, and radio and television companies.[9]

Besides direct dissemination of its own propaganda materials, the USSR can rely on a wide network of foreign communist parties and front organizations to distribute Soviet-oriented propaganda. For example, *Problems of Peace and Socialism* (published in English as *World Marxist Review*), the international theoretical organ of communist parties allied to the CPSU, appears monthly in forty languages in a total edition of more than a half-million copies.[10]

The purpose of this network of propaganda facilities is to support the general and specific foreign policy objectives of the Soviet leadership – more specifically, "to weaken the United States and NATO; and to extoll the achievements of the Soviet Union, thereby creating a favorable environment for the advancement of Moscow's objectives."[11] The definition of "propaganda" to be used in this chapter is based on that developed by Baruch A. Hazan in his study of Soviet propaganda: propaganda is the preconceived, systematic and centrally coordinated process of manipulating symbols, aimed at promoting certain uniform attitudes, beliefs, values and behavior within mass audiencies – these expected attitudes, beliefs, values and behavior are congruent with the specific interests and ends of the propagandist.[12]

Related to, but distinct from, propaganda is disinformation, defined as any government-sponsored communication containing intentionally false and misleading material (often combined selectively with true information) which is passed to targeted individuals, groups, or governments with the purpose of influencing foreign elite or public opinion.[13] "Propaganda" differs from "disinformation" in two important ways. Propaganda is targeted at a mass audience and is not necessarily deceptive, while disinformation is aimed only at specific foreign targets and is always purposely deceptive.

Propaganda and disinformation belong to a category of activities which the Soviets refer to as "active measures" – including both overt and covert techniques employed for the purpose of influencing events and behavior in foreign countries.[14] "These measures are employed to influence the policies of other governments, undermine confidence in the leaders and institutions of these states, disrupt the relations between various nations, and discredit and weaken major opponents."[15] They are also used to generate abroad favorable views toward the Soviet Union and its policies and support of specific Soviet policy initiatives. Included among active measures are covert support for terrorist and insurgency activities, as well as propaganda and disinformation. Active measures, including both propaganda and disinformation, are an integral aspect of the "ideological struggle" between communism and capitalism that is, in the Soviet view, an essential component of "peaceful coexistence."[16]

To oversee and coordinate the broad array of propaganda and disinformation activities the Soviets have created a complex network of organizations and facilities,[17] (See Figure 5.1). At the top of the network is the Politburo of the Central Committee of the CPSU which approves the major themes of Soviet propaganda campaigns and the means used to implement them. Under the guidance of the Politburo, Party and governmental organizations carry out the propaganda and disinformation activities, as well as other active measures. The first of the three most important of these organizations, the International Department of the CPSU, headed from its creation in 1957 by Boris Ponomarev until he was replaced by Anatoli Dobronin in spring 1986, maintains ties with foreign organizations employed to disseminate Soviet propaganda – including more than seventy pro-Soviet communist parties, numerous international front organizations, and national liberation movements.

The second of the major coordinating organizations, the International Information Department of the CPSU, oversaw all aspects of Soviet foreign propaganda activities from 1978 until its abolition in March 1986. The head of the department throughout its entire history, Leonid Zamiatin, was director of TASS until he was appointed chief of the Information Department at the time of its creation in 1978. The functions formerly carried out by the International Information Department have apparently been assigned to the International Department and to the Propaganda Department, headed since March 1986 by Aleksander Yakovlev.

The third important organization involved in external propaganda and active measures is Service "A" (Disinformation and Active Measures) of the First Chief Directorate (Foreign Intelligence) of the Committee of State Security (KGB). Service "A" has responsibility for coordinating and planning the dissemination of "false and provocative

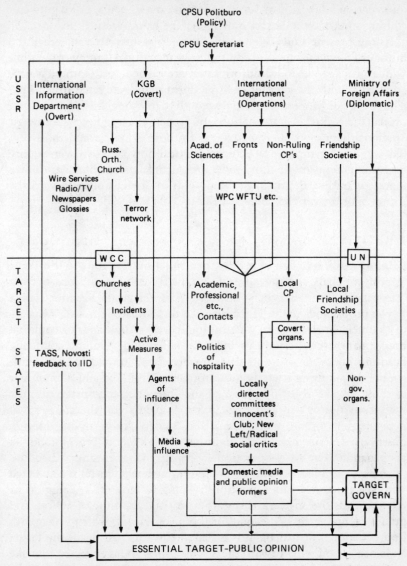

Note: a The International Information Department was disbanded in early 1986. Its functions have been taken over by the International Department and the Propaganda Department of the Central Committee.
Sources: Richard H. Shultz and Roy Godson, *Dezinformatsia: Active Measures in Soviet Policy.* (Washington: Pergamon-Brassey's, International Defense Publishers, 1984), p. 20; US Congress, House, Permanent Select Committee on Intelligence, Subcommittee on Oversight, *Soviet Active Measures,* Hearings July 13–14, 1982 (Washington: US Government Printing Office, 1982), pp. 228, 229.

Figure 5.1 Channels of Soviet propaganda and active measures

information" designed to deceive foreign governments or the public in countries outside the Soviet bloc under the name "active measures."[18]

In the present study we are not primarily interested in either the history of Soviet propaganda or in the organizational framework within which propaganda and disinformation are carried out. Rather, we are concerned with the content of Soviet propaganda directed toward the Third World. More specifically, we wish to examine the importance of propaganda and disinformation in Soviet policy directed toward "national liberation movements" (both those in power and those few that are still attempting to achieve political power). However, before beginning our assessment of Soviet propaganda and disinformation, we shall first outline the main developments in Soviet policy toward the Third World over the course of the past three decades.

THE NATURE OF SOVIET PROPAGANDA IN THE THIRD WORLD

In our discussion of Soviet propaganda and disinformation in the Third World we shall, for the sake of simplicity, employ the broad term "propaganda," unless otherwise noted. As we have already mentioned, Soviet propaganda in the Third World is disseminated through a variety of channels. In addition to distributing scores of thousands of copies of books, pamphlets, periodicals and newspapers in developing countries, beaming hundreds of hours of radio broadcasts to audiences in these countries, and using friendly local organizations to expand the number of those who receive Soviet propaganda messages; the Soviets also use such activities as cultural and sporting events for the purpose of generating favorable views about the Soviet Union among foreign observers. Barach Hazan distinguishes two different types of Soviet propaganda. The first, operational propaganda, is meant to produce "concrete specific results, i.e., a predetermined behavior. It is connected with specific issues, raises questions relating to those issues, suggests or recommends the answers, shows the way and the time of action, and guides the audience." A second form of propaganda, which Hazan calls impregnational propaganda, is oriented toward creating in the target audience "good will" toward the Soviet Union and is expected to make the target more amenable to accepting future operational propaganda. This form of propaganda employs means such as the arts, sports, etc., as well as other more traditional forms of propaganda.[19]

Since our major concern in the remainder of this chapter will focus on operational propaganda, we shall discuss only briefly those aspects of Soviet impregnational propaganda meant to "soften up" prospective targets. Already in the early years of Soviet involvement in the Third

World, a Soviet journalist pointed out that one of the purposes of a tour of Soviet musicians in Nigeria had been to overcome the "false views" of the Soviet Union and of Soviet society which had been implanted in Africa by the West.[20] In line with this view of artists and athletes as propagandists, one Soviet writer has asserted that: "Scientists, artists, writers, painters, musicians . . . as well as radio and television workers, are active fighters on the ideological front, passionate and insatiable propagandists of Communist ideas."[21] In his study of Soviet cultural diplomacy, Frederick C. Barghoorn noted that it is a special form of propaganda meant to generate attitudes generally favorable to the Soviet Union and to Soviet culture.[22] As Hazan has demonstrated, the Soviets have expended substantial efforts to establish in Third World states a broad network of facilities through which they are able to project the type of information meant to establish such an image. Cultural agreements have been signed with the majority of developing countries, thus creating the framework within which the Soviets are able to carry out their activities.[23]

Of special importance for the Soviets in their efforts to generate a positive image abroad has been the creation of local friendship societies, whose major function is to develop positive views toward and strengthen local "friendship" with the peoples of the USSR. Included within their activities are the promotion of the study of the Russian language; the development of libraries, reading rooms, and discussion groups; the showing of films; etc. Although the activities of friendship societies often extend into the area of supporting Soviet operational propaganda, their primary function is to influence the attitudes of as broad a range of the local population as possible toward the Soviet Union, the goals of socialism, and related topics.

Pro-Soviet international front organizations comprise a second important component of the network of organizations through which the Soviets attempt to influence general attitudes toward the Soviet state and to generate support for specific Soviet policy initiatives. This type of organization, designed to mobilize and unite individuals across national boundaries on the basis of sex, age, profession, etc., has been an integral part of Soviet policy since the 1920s, although officially these organizations have no connection with either the USSR or with the Soviet communist party. (See Figure 5.2)

The distribution abroad of films, books and periodicals – usually available at very low prices – represents another element of the Soviet attempt to generate a favorable image abroad and to create in target audiences attitudes conducive to the acceptance of specific aspects of Soviet operational propaganda and to support for Soviet policy

Figure 5.2 *Pro-Soviet International Front organizations*

Organization	Year founded		Claimed membership	Affiliates	Countries
Afro-Asian Peoples' Solidarity Organization	1957	Cairo	unknown	91	—
Christian Peace Conference	1958	Prague	unknown	86	c. 80
International Association of Democratic Lawyers	1946	Brussels	25,000	64	c. 80
International Organization of Journalists	1946	Prague	180,000	114	120 plus
International Union of Students	1946	Prague	10,000,000	118	109
Women's International Democratic Federation	1945	E. Berlin	200,000,000	129	116
World Federation of Democratic Youth	1945	Budapest	150,000,000	210	123
World Federation of Scientific Workers	1946	London	450,000	33	70 plus
World Federation of Trade Unions	1945	Prague	c. 206,000,000	90	81
World Peace Council	1950	Helsinki	unknown	135	142 plus

Sources: Richard F. Staar, ed., *Yearbook on International Communist Affairs, 1984: Parties and Revolutionary Movements*. Stanford, CA: Hoover Institution Press, 1984, p. xxiv; US Department of State, *Soviet International Fronts*. Publication 9360. August 1983.

objectives. Soviet involvement in international sporting activities also has clear political purposes. Foreign sports delegations competing in the USSR are usually exposed to a wide range of activities so that, in the words of *Moscow News* in referring to the Universiade–'73 Games: "Everything has been done so that our guests could become better acquainted with the Soviet way of life and spend their spare time usefully."[24]

In concluding his discussion of Soviet impregnational propaganda, Hazan notes:

While it may be pointed out that every country of the world is interested in improving its image and promoting goodwill and friendship, it can also be emphasized that no other country in the world attributes so much political importance to these issues. No other country strives so vehemently to promote the study of its language abroad, to demonstrate its achievements in culture, sports and arts, to prove its superiority, or to enhance its prestige.

What lurks behind this tremendous effort is an unusual attempt to facilitate the action of Soviet operational propaganda. In other words, to further Soviet foreign policy objectives and to project the best possible image of the USSR.[25]

After these introductory comments, we now turn to a discussion of the major elements of Soviet operational propaganda concerning the Third World and, more specifically, the process of national liberation.

SOVIET VIEWS OF THE NATIONAL LIBERATION PROCESS

For the Soviets "national liberation" is part of the broader world revolutionary process that will inevitably result in the destruction of the capitalist system and its replacement by a global socialist system. Already at the 2nd Congress of the Comintern in 1920 Lenin called on all communists to "give active support to the revolutionary movements of liberation."[26] More than thirty-five years later at the 20th Congress of the CPSU, Khrushchev introduced the idea of a world "peace zone" which united the communist countries, the "proletariat" in the advanced capitalist states, and the newly independent states and liberation movements in the developing world.[27] Soviet writers, even those who did not share Khrushchev's optimism about likely developments in the Third World, viewed national liberation as an objectively anti-imperialist process.[28] As S. Neil MacFarlane has noted in his excellent study of *Superpower Rivalry and Third World Radicalism*, since the beginning of the 1970s Soviet writers have argued most strongly "that the national liberation movement is an inseparable part of the world revolutionary process and a constructive factor of fundamental importance in world politics.[29] However, these analysts have continued to emphasize the primacy of the worldwide struggle between socialism and capitalism and of the role of the Soviet Union and the world socialist system in the world revolution.[30] The national liberation revolution is granted only secondary importance. As Karen Brutents, one of the chief Soviet specialists on the Third World, has argued: "The point is that left opportunist[s] and many nationalist ideologists of the Third World have clearly overrated the worldwide importance and revolutionary role of the national liberation struggle."[31]

In the Soviet view the national liberation movement can only be understood as an ongoing process that includes at least three important stages. The first of these stages, the winning of political independence and the gaining of national sovereignty by former colonies, was an "important prerequisite of their complete independence," in Khrushchev's view.[32] However, political independence alone is not the end in itself. It must lead to the second stage of national liberation, the elimination of economic dependence on the capitalist West. After political independence the goal of national liberation becomes the elimination of foreign economic domination, "which goes hand in hand with the plunder of the oppressed country, subjugation of its economic life to the purposes of this domination, and preservation of backward socio-economic forms."[33]

The final stage of national liberation involves the movement toward social revolution. Writing in the mid-1960s, V. Tiagunenko noted that national liberation would be completed only with the turn from capitalist forms of development towards socialism.[34] The Soviets have continued to emphasize the importance of radical social change as part of the liberation process – including even strong pressures on various Third World client states to establish vanguard political parties.[35]

It is within the context of this perception of the process of national liberation and of the global revolutionary process that pits socialism, represented by the Soviet Union and the other socialist states, against imperialist capitalism, that the specific aspects of Soviet propaganda to the Third World must be understood. In the following pages we shall examine the most important themes that characterize current Soviet propaganda toward the Third World and relate them to the broader aspects of Soviet policy.

GENERAL THEMES IN SOVIET PROPAGANDA TO THE THIRD WORLD

We shall divide our discussion of the major themes in Soviet propaganda into two broad categories – those of a general nature that have remained relatively permanent over the course of the past three decades and more specific propaganda campaigns meant to influence attitudes and behavior on specific issues of current concern. In reality, these types of propaganda are not always neatly divisible, and we shall attempt to show how issues of immediate concern to specific propaganda campaigns are also related to the long-term interests of general Soviet propaganda.

Themes concerning the world revolution, the future of Socialism, and Soviet unity with the Third World

One of the most important sets of themes characterizing Soviet propaganda in the Third World concerns the all-pervasive nature of Soviet efforts to associate the aspirations of the peoples and leaders of the developing countries with the historical experience of the Soviet Union and to demonstrate that the Soviet Union – alone among the industrialized states – can provide the assistance required for the further development of the struggle for national liberation.

The Bolshevik Revolution and the creation of a socialist state in the USSR are pictured as the most important developments of the modern era – events without which the colonial system created by the capitalist West would not have been overthrown. As was noted in an editorial in *Pravda* after the 23rd Congress of the CPSU, "the successes of the national-liberation movement are inseparably tied up with the successes of world socialism and the international working class."[36] The mere existence of the socialist states and the shift in the "international correlation of forces" in favor of the USSR no longer permits the imperialist powers to act with impunity in the developing world. For example, the victories of the national liberation movements in Mozambique and Angola and the successes of revolutionary forces in Ethiopia and in other African countries "are also a result of the enormous influence exerted on the course of world development by the policy of peaceful coexistence and detente . . ."[37]

Closely related to the Soviet emphasis on the importance of the Bolshevik Revolution and developments in Soviet policy for the success of the process of liberation are the specific claims that Soviet propaganda makes concerning the nature of direct Soviet support for national liberation. An analysis of Soviet propaganda to virtually any region of the Third World reveals that by far the most attention is given to continual expressions of Soviet solidarity with and support for all movements committed to liberation from Western imperialism. The Soviets are presented as committed to the just cause of exploited people chafing under the yoke of imperialist/Zionist/racist/reactionary oppression (depending upon the nature of the target of the propaganda).[38] While the imperialists continue to attempt to dominate the political and economic structures of the developing countries, the Soviets are committed to relations based on equality and mutual benefit.

One standard technique employed by Soviet propagandists has been to cite important foreign officials or publications concerning the significance of Soviet support for a particular liberation struggle. In 1957, for example, the Prime Minister of Syria was quoted as saying that Soviet policy toward the Arab states differed from that of the "Western imperialist powers." While the latter "have no aim but to preserve their positions in the Arab East, so that they may be free to exploit the national wealth of the Arab peoples," the Soviet Union "has no economic or other designs on the Arab East; all it desires is to strengthen peace in this area."[39] In the words of Anatolii Gromyko, Head of the African Institute of the Soviet Academy of Sciences and son of the long-time Soviet Foreign Minister: "The USSR and Africa's independent countries are closely cooperating to eliminate the vestiges of racism and colonialism and fight against neo-colonialism, and that brings notable results and promotes closer relations between this country and the young African states."[40] In North Africa, it is claimed:

The line pursued by the Soviet Union as regards the North African countries, as well as all the developing states, is highly principled and is based on the Leninist tenet that the forces fighting for socialism and national liberation are great international allies . . . the USSR has always furnished all manner of aid and support to the just struggle of the North African peoples for their legitimate national political and economic rights.[41]

Not only is the Soviet Union pictured as a firm and reliable supporter of national liberation whose interests coincide with those of the developing states, but the experience of the Soviet Union (in particular of Soviet Central Asia) is presented as a model for the developing countries. G. Kim, one of the most prolific of Soviet writers on the Third World, presents the experience of the peoples of Central Asia in state building as an example, especially for states of "socialist orientation." He notes that, at the beginning, representatives of the traditional propertied class had participated in the new state organs; as class-consciousness grew, however, they were gradually removed from positions of authority and replaced entirely by representatives of the workers and peasants. The Central Asian republics of the USSR, once "backward outlying regions of tsarist Russia," have become major industrial centers. "In opposition to the situation taking shape in the newly-free countries under capitalist development, the flexible purposeful policy of industrialization based on socialist relations ensures fundamental conditions for eliminating relative agrarian overpopulation."[42] Ever since the 1950s, when the Soviets first established relations with newly-independent states, they have emphasized the importance of Soviet experience in restructuring the economies of Third World states.[43]

The non-capitalist path of economic development has been extolled as the solution of the development problems of Third World states, as in a 1962 radio broadcast: "The Soviet Eastern republics have . . . shown the whole world that all the oppressed peoples . . . can throw off the imperialist yoke forever. . . . The Soviet Eastern Republics, like a bright torch, are an example to those countries where the labour of the peoples and the wealth of the country are still being plundered and looted by the Western monopolists."[44]

As Theodore H. Friedgut has noted, "The Soviet model of development presented in the newspapers and journals, is one of rapid transformation, the injection of newly activitated masses into the political system, destroying and removing old ruling classes and political structures."[45]

Another related theme in the general Soviet propaganda message concerns the status of the USSR as a global power with legitimate interests in all regions of the world. For example, in a speech to the 24th CPSU Congress in 1971 Foreign Minister Andrei Gromyko expressed the Soviet leadership's global aspirations when he stated: "Today, there is no question of any significance which can be decided without the Soviet Union or in opposition to it."[46] Several years later the Soviet Minister of Defense made explicit the global importance of Soviet military force when he stated: "the historic function of the Soviet armed forces is not restricted merely to their function in defending our Motherland and the other socialist countries." Aggression by the Western imperialist states should be resisted "in whatever distant region of our planet it occurs."[47]

Throughout the 1970s the Soviets devoted substantial effort to support the claim that the "international correlation of forces" had changed dramatically and that the forces of socialism and progress, headed by the Soviet Union, were far more influential in international political developments than those of imperialist capitalism. They pointed to the military strength of the Soviet Union, the successes of the socialist states and the growing number of developing countries that have chosen the non-capitalist path of development as evidence that supported this claim.[48]

Yet another of the general themes that runs throughout virtually all Soviet written and verbal propaganda disseminated in the Third World concerns the crucial role played by the Soviet Union in the struggle for peace and security in the world. As we shall see in more detail below, the United States and its imperialist allies (supported by reactionary elements in the Third World) are presented as the primary source of conflict and war. Yet, it is claimed, "The USSR's approach to the search for peace in the Middle East and to the task of easing the tensions there is appreciated not only by socialist countries but also by many Arab and West European political figures."[49] According to the Soviet writer, "The USSR has always opposed this course [the United States and Israeli attempt to force an unjust settlement] with the only correct alternative – to turn developments in the Middle East towards the search for an all-embracing and just Middle East settlement."[50]

The Soviets, primarily through their international front organizations, have been especially active within the United Nations network in disseminating their propaganda themes. The World Peace Council, which has consultative status with UNESCO, UNCTAD and UNIDO (United Nations International Development Organization), has persistently attempted to push Soviet initiatives (often with considerable success) within these bodies. The Council has been especially successful in influencing the deliberations of the Non-Governmental Organizations committees that are associated with various UN organizations. In all of these organizations the Soviets – usually through these front organizations – have managed to influence significantly the items on the agenda, the terms of discussion, and the orientation of resolutions. The extent to which the World Peace Council (WPC) operates within the UN network was the subject of a congratulatory article by WPC President, the Indian communist Ramesh Chandra, that appeared in the WPC's journal:

The World Peace Council has for the last 12 years and more been a member of the 20-member board of the Conference of Non-Governmental Organisations in Consultative Status with the UN (ECOSOC); it has been holding the position of vice-president of the Conference for nearly 10 years. Similarly the World Peace Council is a member of the 15-member bureau (and is rapporteur) of the Conference of Non-Governmental Organisations in Consultative Status with UNESCO. The World Peace Council's representative chairs the important NGO Sub-Committee on Racism, Racial Discrimination, Apartheid and Decolonisation, as well as the NGO Special Committee on Transnational Corporations. The World Peace Council also serves as vice-president of the NGO Special Committee on Disarmament.[51]

The Soviets and their allies have worked assiduously over the course of the past two decades or more to use the subsidiary bodies of the United Nations for their own purposes. To a very substantial degree they have succeeded, although there have been important recent setbacks. Yet, overall the Soviet Union has been extremely successful in setting the agenda and the terms of discussion concerning questions of peace and security within these international bodies.[52] The message here, as in all of Soviet propaganda targeted at the Third World, is well summarized in the following excerpt from a recent Soviet article on Asia:

It is an indisputable fact that the policy of the aggressive forces of imperialism, above all American imperialism, is the main obstacle to improving the international situation in Asia. These forces are stepping up their attempt to impede the onward march of the historical process on the continent, thwart social progress and the consolidation of the Asian states' independence, alienate them from each other, push them towards confrontation, and hamper the elimination of the smouldering seats of tension here . . .

It is the consistently peaceful policy of the USSR and other socialist countries, their close interaction on the international scene and growing cooperation between them and the progressive non-aligned states and all the forces of peace, democracy and social progress in Asia that were and remain a decisive factor of peace and stability on the continent.[53]

Themes concerning Western imperialism

Although the Soviets devote substantial efforts in their propaganda activities to extolling the virtues of socialism, the Soviet state, and Soviet support for the goals of national liberation, they give almost equal space and time to denigrating the United States and its allies and attributing virtually all the world's ills to the evils of imperialism. Conflict in the Third World results almost solely, according to Soviet propaganda, from the machinations of the West. According to one Soviet analyst, the one circumstance common to all conflicts in Africa is the fact "that the conflicts flare up exactly there where the forces of imperialism and its ilk try by means of force to suppress the national liberation movement, to reverse the march of history and erect obstacles to the independent development of young states."[54] In discussing the difficulty of reaching political settlements in local conflicts, Dmitry Volsky argues that "the reason is the same everywhere; the unwillingness of the imperialist quarters to recognize the principle of the equality of states and peoples, the striving of some countries to dominate others, to exploit their natural resources and to use their territory for their own strategic purposes."[55] Volsky even goes so far as to claim that US imperialist aggression in various regions of the world is interconnected:

It is hardly a coincidence that at the very time that the wide-scale incursion into Nicaragua was started, the threat of aggression against countries like Syria and Angola also increased. All these add up to a chain of interconnected operations prepared and carried out for the time being through the agency of others . . . Meanwhile the chain of conflict situations created by Washington's imperial policy encircles the whole globe at the Equator.[56]

Elsewhere Volsky has also asserted that "those who are bombing and shelling Third World countries are hatching militarist designs primarily targeted at the Soviet Union and other countries of the socialist community . . . This underscores the imperative need to strengthen the solidarity of the socialist and developing countries."[57] The message presented by Volsky – and by other Soviet propagandists who emphasize this theme – has two parts. First, it is the imperialist West, in particular the United States, that is the source of problems and conflicts in the Third World and that is currently threatening the security interests of "progressive" states; in addition, however, this threat makes it all the more imperative that developing countries ally themselves with the Soviet Union and the forces of world peace.

The picture presented by Soviet propaganda of the United States as the major source of conflict in the Third World and the ultimate source of opposition to revolutionary change is supplemented by the argument that the United States is invariably allied to the local or regional forces of reaction and aggression. In condemning the hypocrisy of US concerns for violations of human rights, for example, two Soviet writers ask: Where are the sources of the long-standing friendship those politicians clad as democrats and moralists maintain with all kinds of dictators, 'hereditary' and 'for life', like Duvalier of Haiti, with the racists who rule in South Africa, and with the South Korean, Salvadorean and Chilean generals who brutalize their own nations?"

The answer, they say, lies in the important assistance that such reactionary regimes provide Washington in its attempt to accomplish its imperial interests.[58] In their attempt to weaken relations between the United States and various Third World governments, the Soviets regularly attempt to tie the United States to those regional forces viewed as most hostile or oppressive by target populations. In Africa, for example, US policy aims reputedly include "coalescence with the racist upper crust" of South Africa; in the Middle East, Israel is pictured as carrying out US imperial aims in the region.[59]

Themes concerning Chinese hegemonism

During the past twenty years the People's Republic of China has been added to the list of states – along with the capitalist states – that represent a major threat to the security and developmental interests of the Third World. The post-Mao political leadership is accused of an "overt programme of military and political collusion with imperialism." China's main long-term goals in relations with developing states have remained unchanged during the past twenty years: "to subject them to its influence, isolate them from the socialist world and to harness the economic potential of the developing countries to its own 'four modernizations.'"[60] These accusations sound quite similar to those traditionally leveled against Western imperialism.

China has regularly been accused of attempting to undermine the security of liberation movements throughout the Third World – from Indochina and Afghanistan in Asia to Southern Africa.[61] In sum, China has shared with the United States and the West, though on a much more limited basis, in the diatribes and condemnations emanating from Moscow.

SPECIFIC THIRD WORLD THEMES AND PROPAGANDA CAMPAIGNS

While the major themes of Soviet propaganda toward the Third World discussed above have remained relatively constant over the course of the past three decades, other themes (often associated with a specific crisis or current developments in Soviet foreign policy) have changed. However, these more specific elements of the Soviet propaganda message are almost always associated with the more general themes of the global struggle between the forces of progress represented by the Soviet Union and those of reaction and imperialism led by the United States. In the following pages we shall discuss only a few of the specific themes that have characterized Soviet propaganda toward the Third World in recent years.

The state of Socialist orientation and vanguard parties

One of the major aspects of Soviet policy in the Third World in recent years has been the attempt to establish close ties with radical Marxist–Leninist regimes. In addition to granting military assistance, training internal security forces, and providing political support for the foreign policy objectives of these regimes, the Soviets have devoted substantial energy in the attempt to convince their leaders of the need for what they call "vanguard parties."

In recommendations made to leaders of these countries the Soviets have developed a model for political development that they now call the "state of socialist orientation."[62] What the Soviets recommend to radical Third World leaders on every possible occasion is the emulation of Soviet political experience. Given the fact that full-scale communist parties do not exist (or play only a secondary role) in most developing countries, the state of socialist orientation has been presented as an acceptable alternative approach to the eventual creation of full-scale communism. The state of socialist orientation should be ruled by what the Soviets refer to as a "vanguard party" – i.e., a party which, although not accepted by the Soviets as fully Marxist–Leninist, is modeled after the hierarchical structure of the CPSU. Such parties represent an alliance of the "progressive" forces in society, attempt to strengthen their organizational and ideological unity, and are committed to increasing their influence on the masses. In addition, such parties are in the process of "conversion to Marxist–Leninist teaching about the path of the revolutionary transformation of society" and are broadening and deeping all forms of cooperation with "the world Communist movement, and in the first instance with the ruling parties of the countries of the socialist commonwealth."[63]

Virtually all Soviet writing on the developing world in recent years has presented the state of socialist orientation with a vanguard party as the model to be followed eventually by all developing countries. To supplement their advice the Soviets have devoted substantial resources to the establishment of relations between the CPSU and the existing "vanguard parties" and, especially, to training and educating their leadership cadres. The purpose is to institutionalize the revolutionary process as a prelude to the establishment of full-scale communist regimes oriented toward and dependent upon the USSR. Propaganda is one aspect of the Soviet attempt to convince Third World leaders of the necessity of following a socialist path of development.

A new international information order

The Soviets have been in the forefront of those who have been arguing for the need to eliminate the dominant position of Western news media and news agencies in the dissemination of information. In fact, the Soviets have two major concerns in this area: first, they are interested in increasing their own control over the flow of information about the USSR and its policies that is disseminated throughout the world. Their second concern is to be able to control the flow of information into the USSR itself. Ever since the establishment in 1979 of a UN Committee on Information the Soviets have presented themselves as the active supporters of those countries in the Third World which are most committed to the development of guidelines on the international flow of information which would, in effect, create a form of international censorship.

At the meeting of the UN Committee on Information held in New York in mid-1984, the Soviet delegation, headed by Iurii Kashlev, called for an "end to the use of information channels for interference in the internal affairs of sovereign states, subversion and psychological warfare."[64] Examples of the type of activity referred to were limited to Radio Liberty, Radio Free Europe and Radio Marti. No agreement could be reached at the meeting because of "the intransigence of the United States and its allies" and their refusal to accept any of the proposals advanced by developing countries. However, as Kashlev put it: "This obstructionist line is countered by the growing resolve of most countries – the socialist and many developing countries – to secure the elimination of 'information imperialism,' and the use of information media to strengthen peace, to promote mutual understanding among nations and social and national progress."[65]

According to the Soviets, the slogan "free exchange of ideas" which is so widely propagated by the West is merely a "screen to cover imperialism in the field of culture." The only purpose of this type of exchange is "to spread the influence of the bourgeoisie, to subject the majority of people in countries with market economies to its domination." After noting the spiritual bankruptcy of the capitalist states and the vibrant nature of cultural development in the Soviet Union, one Soviet author concludes:

Today culture is an arena of acute ideological struggle. Cultural exchanges have many enemies, in the first place because the art of socialist realism proclaims as its main task the promotion of the Soviet way of life, the norms of lofty communist morality.

The contrast between the destructive consequences of cultural imperialism and the burgeoning of culture in socialist countries can be clearly observed today by all honest people the world over. This is a contrast between a forward-looking society and a moribund system which is desperately struggling for survival.[66]

The objective of a "new international information order" becomes quite clear when one reads statements such as this that permeate Soviet writing about and propaganda toward the Third World.

Although not directly related to information and the media, Soviet condemnation of Western student exchange programs does fit into the general argument that the West is committed to cultural imperialism in its relations with the Third World. According to two Soviet writers "the imperialist states have made personnel training for the developing countries a major instrument of neocolonialism."[67] In addition to siphoning off the brightest of those trained to remain in the host country, the imperialists are involved in brainwashing those personnel who will return home to inculcate anti-socialist views into particularly important targeted areas (especially within the state administration and production management).[68]

Western economic exploitation and a New International Economic Order

Another theme that has been widespread in Soviet propaganda targeted at Third World countries has been the inherent exploitative nature of economic relations between the capitalist West and the developing countries. The primary goal of the capitalist countries in their economic relations with the developing states is to maintain and strengthen control over developing economies. The capitalists are interested solely in extracting resources at cheap prices and selling the products of their industries. Western capital exports, one of the most important elements of capitalist economic policy, are meant "to strengthen the sway of foreign capital in the developing countries in order to 'accelerate' the pace of their technico-economic modernization."[69] The capitalists have discovered that, unless the developing economies make progress in the technical fields, their own ability to benefit from the latter's long-term economic dependence on the capitalist states will be reduced. Thus, capital exports and so-called economic assistance from the West have the sole purpose of maintaining and strengthening the economic, financial and technological dependence of developing countries on international capitalism.

Western "aid" is also used as a means to interfere in the internal affairs of Third World states. Among the more heinous recent examples of such interferences, according to a Soviet writer, has been the attempt by the United States to benefit politically from the famine in Ethiopia. The United States and other Western countries and organizations have been using Ethiopia's need for food as a means to put pressure on the progressive government of Mengistu Haile Mariam to change its policies. All of the efforts by charitable organizations to gain unlimited access to areas of the country controlled by anti-government rebels "clearly bear the stamp of the CIA, whose agents are active in the border regions of Ethiopia and Sudan."[70]

As we have already seen, the solution that the Soviets continually present to Third World leaders to reduce the opportunities for capitalist exploitation is the socialist path of development combined with closer relations with the Soviet Union and the other socialist states.

In the past two years, or so, the Soviets have given special attention to the issue of Third World debt. Articles with such vivid titles as "In the Clutches of Present-Day Shylocks" speak of the "predatory policies being pursued by the developed capitalist states" that result in "financial bondage" for developing states.[71] The current debt faced by Third World states is the direct result of "their inequitable economic and commercial ties with the United States" and of the policies of the US-controlled International Monetary Fund.[72]

Closely associated with Soviet propaganda concerning Western economic exploitation are calls for the establishment of a New International Economic Order. In fact, for a number of years, ever since the Group of 77 raised the issue of major structural reform of the international economic system, the Soviets have provided substantial verbal and propaganda support for the concept.[73] They have attempted to demonstrate that the restructuring of the international economy that developing countries envisage is integrally involved with "problems of limiting the arms race, disarmament and consolidating security – further progress in political and military detente, which is of paramount significance for strengthening general peace, will at the same time contribute to the normalization of the world economic situation."[74]

In their discussions of a New International Economic Order, Soviet spokesmen have been careful to emphasize the fact that the economic problems facing the developing countries stem exclusively from the past and present policies of monopoly capitalism. An official Soviet government statement put the issue in the following terms:

The stance of monopoly circles in capitalist states has been and still is the chief obstacle to the radical restructuring of international economic relations on a democratic basis . . . The course of continuing and deepening the exploitation of developing countries for their part remains essentially unchanged. It is impossible to count on forcing them to abandon it with the help of all kinds of narrow group negotiations. . . .[75]

The Soviets continue to emphasize in all of their propaganda concerning "pressing economic problems" the close connection between economic and political/security problems. In discussing the debate at the 38th UN General Assembly on economic measures, two Soviet authors note the "West's obstructionist policy aimed at preventing the discussion of pressing world economic problems, the delegations of the socialist countries submitted a good number of initiatives on the most urgent issues." These proposed "economic" measures included proposals for the limitation of the arms build-up, reduction of military spending and the channeling of resources squandered on war preparations to peaceful purposes.[76]

In all of its propaganda concerning the international economy the Soviet message is the same – the West is the cause of the world's economic problems (in particular those of the developing countries); the West is opposed to all change in the international economic system, for that would reduce the opportunities for economic exploitation; and the USSR and its allies are alone among the developed states committed to a fair and equitable international economic system in which the interests of developing countries would be protected.

Arms races in the Third World

As we have already seen, according to Soviet propagandists, the West (in particular the United States) is the primary cause of military conflict in the Third World. One of the factors given great emphasis in Soviet propaganda is the role of Western arms merchants in flooding the Third World with all sorts of military equipment. Needless to say, no reference is made to the role of the Soviets in the international arms trade, except to note that the Soviets provide security assistance to Third World governments threatened by Western-supported reactionary governments. "Monopoly capital uses the arms trade to solve various tasks of its economic neocolonialist expansion in the developing countries,'' according to one Soviet author.[77] The first goal is supposedly to increase its influence on the social and economic development of arms recipients. The provision of arms has also been a means "for establishing direct or indirect control over big masses of liquid assets, especially the capital accumulated by the oil-producing countries."[78] However, there is also the purpose of creating military forces in the Third World which can be used as proxies by the West against progressive forces.[79]

The massive increase in Western arms sales to developing countries has had, according to Soviet propagandists, a very deleterious effect on prospects for future economic development. It has only been the USSR, according to the message projected from Moscow, that has been committed to limiting the sale and transfer of conventional weapons. The "Western death merchants," however, have prevented any form of agreement.[80]

One of the more interesting aspects of Soviet propaganda concerning the place of arms sales in the policies of the West is the degree of what in psychological terms would be called projection that appears in Soviet arguments. Virtually every one of the points made about the importance of arms sales for the United States and Western Europe is a direct counterpart to Western assessments of the place of arms transfers in Soviet policy in the Third World.[81]

Related to Soviet accusations that Western sales of arms to the Third World are among the major sources of instability is the Soviet charge that the United States is carrying out "state-sponsored terrorism." This aspect of the Soviet propaganda campaign is obviously a response to Western accusations of the USSR's involvement in various forms of international terrorism. The Soviet delegation, for example, introduced onto the agenda of the 39th Session of the UN. General Assembly a proposal "On the Inadmissibility of the Policy of State Terrorism and Any Actions by States Aimed at Undermining the Socio-Political Systems in Other Sovereign States." Prime examples of state terrorism, according to the Soviets, have been the "undisguised aggression of the USA against Grenada," the support for terrorists operating against the progressive government of Nicaragua, and "the shelling of defenceless villages in mountain regions of Lebanon," as well as earlier "US aggression against Vietnam."[82]

REGIONAL THEMES IN SOVIET PROPAGANDA

Before concluding this examination of Soviet propaganda activities in the Third World, I wish to provide some additional specific themes of

Soviet propaganda targeted at individual Third World countries or regions. These themes, in general, fit directly into the pattern that has already been outlined above.

East and Southeast Asia

The United States and Japan remain the principal targets of Soviet propaganda about and targeted at Asia. Although condemnation of China has been muted since Sino-Soviet relations began to improve in 1982, China is still accused of conducting a hostile campaign against the Soviet Union and of collusion with the West in formenting subversion and providing support for opponents of the Soviet-supported governments in Afghanistan, Kampuchea, Vietnam and elsewhere.[83]

The Soviets continue to support the Vietnamese occupation of Kampuchea, but have failed to obtain international acceptance of the Vietnamese-backed regime of Hen Samrin as the country's legitimate government. The United States and its allies are accused of attempting to intimidate the countries of ASEAN with talk of a Soviet threat for their own political purposes in the region. Japan, in particular, has been accused of attempting to extend its influence in the area, in part by pitting the countries of Southeast Asia against one another.[84]

US–Japanese relations and increased Japanese defense spending are singled out as specific threats to peace in Asia, as are Japan's closer ties with China, South Korea and the ASEAN states. In the words of one Soviet commentator, "The US ruling circles are increasingly drawing Japan into war preparations in South Korea . . . Washington's militaristic policy, Seoul's war preparations and the resultant buildup of tension on the Korean peninsula and all over the Far East are serious obstacles to the national reunification of the country [Korea] and interfere with the peace forces' efforts to strengthen security in the region."[85]

South Asia and the Middle East

Since the Soviet invasion of Afghanistan in late 1979, major propaganda resources have been devoted to the attempt to justify the invasion and the continuing presence of more than 100,000 Soviet combat troops and to gain international recognition for the regime headed by Babrak Karmal. The United States and China, in particular, are charged with conducting an undeclared war of aggression against Afghanistan by arming and training "reactionary bandits" in the neighboring countries, with Iran and Pakistan acting as accomplices in these activities. The regime in Afghanistan is presented as one committed to peace and progress that is increasingly obtaining the support of the broad working masses of the population.[86]

Propaganda directed at India stresses the mutual benefits of Indo-Soviet friendship and praises the independence of Indian foreign policy, while warning Indians against the allegedly hostile policies of the United States, China and Pakistan.[87]

As noted above, Soviet propaganda attempts to discredit the United States in the Middle East by accusing the latter of supporting – and even instigating – the "predatory," "aggressive," and "expansionist" policies of Israel. The Deputy General Secretary of the Communist Party of Israel, writing in a major Soviet journal, summarizes the main Soviet view of US–Israeli policy as follows:

US imperialist policy in the Middle East makes the outbreak of a new war ever more probable. The Washington leaders and their Zionist henchmen now in power in Israel use the threat to exert pressure on the peoples of Lebanon and Syria. Simultaneously, imperialism, Zionism and the Arab reactionary forces continue their intrigues against the Palestine Arabs and the PLO, striving to perpetuate Israeli occupation of the Arab territories and do away with the Palestine problem.[88]

The United States is pictured as a "hegemonistic" power interested in gaining strategic advantages in the Middle East that have as their ultimate target the Soviet Union. It attempts to "entangle the independent states in the Middle East in a web of military bases, encircle the region with its naval fleets . . . and bring into play the whole arsenal of the means of blackmail, pressure and provocations which should be viewed in the context of this policy."[89]

Africa

Soviet propaganda about and to Africa has focused on issues concerning "imperialist" and "neocolonialist" intervention, particularly in southern Africa, and "capitalist exploitation" of developing countries. South Africa's Western "patrons," especially the United States, are accused of helping South Africa with its nuclear ambitions and with the creation of a war machine with which to attack and destabilize neighboring states. Western interests in supporting South Africa are based on the wealth of minerals in that country and throughout the entire region, according to the Soviets, as well as on the "apartheid regime's" opposition to the development of progressive socialist governments in neighboring countries.[90]

The United States is accused of attempting to split the Organization of African Unity, in order to facilitate its efforts to extend its military presence and domination on the continent,[91] while Israel is presented as penetrating Africa "with Washington's help" in order to engage in "large-scale subversive activities against most countries of Black Africa."[92]

Concerning Namibia, the Soviets denigrate the mediation efforts of the five Western members of the UN Security Council as merely supporting South Africa's delaying tactics for their own interests, and Soviet solidarity is voiced for those fighting for the liberation of southern Africa from colonialism and racism.[93] The Soviets continue to condemn Somalia as an agent of US imperialism, while the Marxist government in Ethiopia is presented as a progressive regime struggling against local reaction and Western imperialism.

As should be clear, all Soviet propaganda concerning Africa – as that targeted toward other geographic regions of the Third World – fits within the broad general themes that were discussed earlier in this essay. The West, in particular the United States, is presented as the major security threat to Africa,[94] while the Soviets and their allies are the sole friends of the African peoples seeking independence and economic development.

South and Central America

As can be expected, US policy in Central America has been a major target of Soviet propaganda and disinformation activities in recent years.[95] Soviet sources seek to blame the United States for political instability and economic problems throughout Latin America. In particular, they attack US involvement in Central America and the Caribbean, while making much of the Soviet Union's friendly ties with the progressive governments of Cuba and Nicaragua.[96] Emphasis is given to the CIA's alleged war against national liberation throughout Central America[97] and the supposed role of reactionary elements in Central America in supporting US reaction.[98]

Latin America, in the Soviet view, is an area of major conflict between "patriotic progressive forces" represented by Cuba, Nicaragua and those fighting for national liberation elsewhere on the continent and "local imperialism-backed oligarchies intent on retaining their privileges at any cost."[99] The United States has allied itself throughout the continent with the forces of reaction, in order to retain and strengthen its domination over the peoples of the continent. Soviet commentary on Grenada has emphasized the "aggressive" nature of US policy and has argued that the US intervention in the island nation is a prime example of "state-sponsored terrorism."[100]

In sum the Soviet propaganda message concerning and to Latin America is virtually the same as that aimed at other regions of the Third World; only the specific illustrations of US perfidy and Soviet friendship differ.

PROPAGANDA IN SOVIET POLICY TOWARD THE THIRD WORLD

By this point the significance of the Soviet propaganda offensive in the Third World as a complement to other forms of policy should be most evident. The Soviets have expended substantial effort and resources in an attempt to influence attitudes, values and behavior of both elites and masses in developing countries. The message, repeated over and over, is virtually always the same: the inevitability of world revolution; the unity of the Soviet Union with progressive, peace-loving forces; the opposition of the forces of imperialism to independent development and progress; and the role of Western imperialists causing, or attempting to exacerbate, all of the problems and tensions that exist in the developing countries.

It is outside the scope of the present article (which has had as its primary purpose the documenting of the major themes of Soviet propaganda) to discuss the success of this massive Soviet propaganda effort. However, it is important to recognize that there is substantial evidence of success. For example, various UN affiliates – such as UNESCO and some of the committees of Non-Governmental Organizations – are strongly influenced by Soviet front organizations. The issues discussed and the positions taken by these groups are often virtually identical with Soviet positions. Moreover, until quite recently at least, the so-called non-aligned movement increasingly supported major policy positions advocated by the USSR and its allies and clients.[101] These are indications that the Soviet propaganda effort has had an effect.

NOTES

1 E. H. Carr, *The Bolshevik Revolution, 1917–1923* (London: Macmillan, 1950), p. 137.
2 Frederick C. Barghoorn, *Soviet Foreign Propaganda* (Princeton: Princeton University Press, 1964), p. 3.
3 A number of major studies have provided substantial detail about the history and organization of Soviet propaganda and disinformation activities. See, for example, Barghoorn, *Soviet Foreign Propaganda*; John Barron, *KGB Today: The Hidden Hand* (New York: Reader's Digest Press, 1983); John Clews, *Communist Propaganda*

Techniques. (New York: Praeger, 1964); Barach A. Hazan, *Soviet Propaganda: A Case Study of the Middle East Conflict* (Jerusalem: Israel Universities Press; New Brunswick, NJ: Transaction Books, 1976); Donald Jameson, "Trends in Soviet Covert Action," in *Intelligence Requirements for the 1980s: Covert Action*, Roy Godson, ed. (New York: National Strategy Information Center, distributed by Transaction Books, New Brunswick, NJ, 1981); US Congress, House, Permanent Select Committee on Intelligence, Subcommittee on Oversight, *Soviet Active Measures*, Hearings, 13, 14 July 1982 (Washington: US Government Printing Office); and a host of other publications.

4 US Congress, *Soviet Active Measures*, p. 30.

5 *Pechat'v USSR* (Moscow: Finansy i Statistiki, 1983).

6 USIA, *External Information and Cultural Relations Programs of the Union of Soviet Socialist Republics* (Washington: USIA Office of Research Assessment, 1973), pp. 36–37.

7 Sh. P. Sanakoev, ed., *Voprosy sovetskoi vneshnepoliticheskoi propagandy* (Moscow: Mezhdunarodnye Otnosheniia, 1980), p. 191.

8 USIA, *Communist International Radio Broadcasting in 1980* (Washington: USIA Office of Research, 1980).

9 By the late 1970s more than 300 foreign news agencies, services and companies in 93 countries used TASS materials. See USIA, *External Cultural and Information Activities and Themes of Communist Countries in 1977* (Washington: USIA Office of Research, 1978), pp. 1–6. At the beginning of the 1970s Novosti had dealings with more than 100 news agencies, 120 publishing firms, more than 100 radio and television firms, and 7,000 newspapers and magazines. See USIA, *Information and Cultural Relations*, pp. 36–37. For more recent estimates, see Foreign and Commonwealth Office, London, "Soviet External Propaganda," *Background Brief*, October 1984. For a valuable discussion of the role of radio broadcasts in Soviet policy toward the Third World, see Patrick Lemoine and Jacques Rupnik, "Les Émissions radiophoniques," in *L'URSS et le Tiers-Monde: Une Stratégie Oblique*, edited by Groupe d'études et de recherches sur la stratégie Soviétique (Paris: La Fondation pour les Etudes de Defense Nationale, 1984), pp. 133–46.

10 Richard F. Staar, *USSR Foreign Policies After Detente* (Stanford, CA: Hoover Institution Press, 1985), p. 77.

11 Richard H. Shultz and Roy Godson, *Dezinformatsia: Active Measures in Soviet Strategy* (Washington: Pergamon-Brassey's, International Defense Publishers, 1984), p. 39.

12 Hazan does not include the reference to attitudes, beliefs and values in his definition, although they are implied in his definition and explicitly discussed later in his book. See Hazan, *Soviet Propaganda*, pp. 12, 16.

13 Shultz and Godson, *Dezinformatsia*, pp. 37–38.

14 The "Interagency Intelligence Study: Soviet Active Measures" includes within "active measures" the following activities: manipulation or control of the media, written or oral disinformation, use of foreign communist parties and front organizations, manipulation of mass organizations, clandestine radio broadcasting, economic activities, military operations, and other political influence operations. See US Congress, *Soviet Active Measures*, p. 32.

15 Shultz and Godson, *Dezinformatsia*, p. 16.

16 For an excellent discussion of the importance of the continuation of the ideological struggle during the period of peaceful coexistence, see Alvin Z. Rubinstein, *Soviet Foreign Policy Since World War II: Imperial and Global* (Cambridge, MA: Winthrop Publishers, 1981), pp. 269–71.

17 The following discussion draws heavily on the 1980 CIA study of Soviet propaganda and covert operations. See "CIA Study: Soviet Covert Action and Propaganda," in US Congress, House, Permanent Select Committee on Intelligence, Subcommittee on Oversight, *Soviet Covert Action (The Forgery Offensive)*, Hearings, 6, 19 February 1980 (Washington: US Government Printing Office, 1980), pp. 59–87. For a good survey of the organization aspects of Soviet propaganda and active measures, see Schultz and Godson, *Dezinformatsia*, pp. 17–39. See also, Foreign and Commonwealth Office, London, "Soviet Party's Role in External Propaganda and Policy," *Background Brief*, March 1985; and Lawrence B. Sulc, *Active Measures, Quiet War and Two Socialist Revolutions* (Washington: The Nathan Hale Institute, 1985).

18 US Congress, *Soviet Active Measures*, p. 235.

19 Hazan, *Soviet Propaganda*, p. 29.

20 A. Tarelin, "Travel Notes from Nigeria," *New Times*, no. 38 (1961), p. 27.

21 F. Krotov, *Leninskaia Teoriia Propagandy i Sovremennost'* (Moscow: Politizdat, 1972), p. 123.

22 Frederick C. Barghoorn, *The Soviet Cultural Offensive: The Role of Cultural Diplomacy in Soviet Foreign Policy* (Princeton: Princeton University Press, 1960), p. 12.

23 Hazan devotes an entire chapter of his study of Soviet propaganda to impregnational propaganda. In the following section I have drawn on that discussion. *Soviet Propaganda*, pp. 96–143.

24 *Moscow News*, no. 34, 1973, p. 15.

25 Hazan, *Soviet Propaganda*, p. 137.

26 Bela Kun, ed., *Kommunisticheskii Internatsional v Dokumentakh . . . 1919–1932* (Moscow: Partiinoe izdatel'stvo, 1933), p. 128.

27 Leo Gruliow, ed., *Current Soviet Policies II: the Documentary Record of the 20th Communist Party Congress and its Aftermath* (New York: Columbia University Press, 1957), p. 37.

28 N. Simoniia, "O kharaktere natsional'no-osvoboditel'nykh revoliutsii," *Narody Azii i Afriki*, no. 6 (1966), p. 8.

29 S. Neil MacFarlane, *Superpower Rivalry and Third World Radicalism* (Baltimore: The Johns Hopkins University Press, 1985), p. 146. Relevent Soviet publications that have taken this line include: V. Tiagunenko, "Mirovoi sotsializm i natsional'no-osvoboditel'naia revoliutsiia v svete Leninizma," *Mirovaia Ekonomika i Mezhdunarodnye Otnosheniia*, no. 5 (1977), p. 27; K. N. Brutents, *National Liberation Revolutions Today* (Moscow: Progress Publishers, vol. 1, 1977), vol. 1, p. 51.

30 See, for example, R. Ul'ianovskii, "National'no-osvoboditel'noe dvizhenie v bor'be za ekonomisheshuiu nezavisimost'," *Kommunist*, no. 14 (1980), p. 20; and Tiagunenko, "Mirovoi sotsializm," p. 54.

31 Brutents, *National Liberation*, vol. 1, p. 15.

32 N. S. Khrushchev, "Otchotnyi Doklad TsK KPSS XX S"ezda Partii," *Pravda*, 15 February 1956, p. 3.

33 Brutents, *National Liberation*, vol. 1, p. 29.

34 V. Tiagunenko, "Zakluichitel'noe Slovo," to "Diskussiia: sotsializm, kapitalizm, slavorazvitye strany," *Mirovaia Ekonomika i Mezhdunarodnye Otnosheniia*, no. 6 (1964), p. 78.

35 For more recent references to Soviet views on the importance of social change, see Anatoly Gromyko, "Soviet Foreign Policy and Africa," *International Affairs*, no. 2 (1982), p. 31; Brutents, *National Liberation*, vol. 1, p. 29. For a Soviet discussion of

the importance of vanguard parties, see Iu. Irkhin, "Avangardnye revoliutsionnye partii trudiashchikhsia v osvobodivshikhsia stranakh," *Voprosy istorii*, no. 4 (1982), pp. 55–67.

36 "Velikaia sila internatsional'noi solidarnosti," *Pravda*, 11 April 1966, p. 1.

37 E. A. Tarabrin, ed., *USSR and Countries of Africa: Friendship, Cooperation, Support for the Anti-Imperialist Struggle*, (Moscow: Progress Publishers, 1977), p. 14.

38 Two studies of the content of Soviet propaganda toward the Middle East can be found in Hazan, *Soviet Propaganda*, pp. 144–229, and Karen Dawisha, *Soviet Foreign Policy Towards Egypt* (New York: St Martin's Press, 1979), pp. 186–88.

39 BBC, *Summary of World Broadcasts, Part I: The Soviet Union/877* (30 October 1957), in Arabic; cited in Hazan, *Soviet Propaganda*, p. 194.

40 Gromyko, "Soviet Foreign Policy," p. 33.

41 A. Shvedov, and A. Podtserov, "The Soviet Union and North African Countries," *International Affairs*, no. 6 (1983), p. 55.

42 G. Kim, "The USSR and National-State Construction in Developing Countries," *International Affairs*, no. 1 (1983), pp. 41, 38.

43 See Roger E. Kanet, "The Soviet Union and Sub-Saharan Africa: Communist Policy Toward Africa, 1917–1965." Unpublished Ph.D. dissertation, Princeton University, 1966, pp. 275–97.

44 BBC, *Summary of World Broadcasts, Part I: The Soviet Union/1074/A4/4* (16 October 1962); cited in Dawisha, *Soviet Foreign Policy*, p. 187.

45 Theodore H. Friedgut, "The Domestic Image of Soviet Involvement in the Arab–Israeli Conflict," in *The Limits to Power: Soviet Policy in the Middle East*, Yaacov Ro'i, ed. (New York: St Martin's Press, 1979), p. 171.

46 Andrei Gromyko, Speech to the 24th CPSU Congress, 1971, *Pravda*, 4 April 1971, pp. 8–9.

47 Andrei A. Grechko, "The Leading Role of the CPSU in Building the Army of a Developed Socialist Society," *Voprosy istorii KPSS* (May 1974), translated in *Strategic Review*, vol. III, no. 1 (1975), pp. 88–93.

48 For discussions of the Soviet concept of the correlation of forces, see Michael J. Deane, "The Soviet Assessment of the 'Correlation of World Forces': Implications for American Foreign Policy," *Orbis*, vol. xx, no. 3 (1976), pp. 625–31; Haus Rissen, ed., *Das sowjetische Konzept der Korrelation der Kräfte und seine Anwendung auf die Aussenpolitik* (Hamburg: Haus Rissen, Internationales Institut für Politik und Wirtschaft, [1980?]); and Roger E, Kanet and Daniel R. Kempton, "Western Europe in Soviet Global Strategy: Soviet Power and the Global Correlation of Forces," unpublished paper, 1985.

49 A. Osipov, "NATO's Militaristic Strategy in the Middle East," *International Affcirs*, no. 4 (1985), p. 65.

50 O. Kasyanov, "Crimes of Imperialism and Zionism in Lebanon," *International Affairs*, no. 9 (1984), p. 59.

51 Romesh Chandra, Supplement to *Peace Courier* (Journal of the World Peace Council), March 1984, cited in Foreign and Commonwealth Office, "Soviet External Propaganda," p. 2.

52 See Foreign and Commonwealth Office, London, "The Soviet 'Peace Campaign' and the United Nations," *Background Brief*, February 1985.

53 N. Isayev, "Peace and Security for Asia," *International Affairs*, no. 5 (1985), pp. 18, 23.

54 Y. Tarabrin, "Africa in Confrontation with US Imperialism," *International Affairs*, no. 10 (1984), p. 33.

55 Dmitry Volsky, "Local Conflicts and International Security," *New Times*, no. 5 (1983), p. 5.

56 Dmitry Volsky, "The Face of Imperial Policy," *New Times*, no. 16 (1983), p. 9.

57 Dmitry Volsky, "Washington Plot Against the Third World," *New Times*, no. 10 (1983), pp. 5–7.

58 Victor Samarin and V. Tolstov, "Washington's Reliance on Repressive Regimes," *International Affairs*, no. 9 (1984), p. 104.

59 Y. Tarabrin, "US Expansionist Policy in Africa," *International Affairs*, no. 10 (1983), p. 42; V. Victorov, "US Policy of Expansion in the Middle East," *International Affairs*, no. 6 (1983), pp. 81–89; Osipov, "NATO's Militaristic Strategy."

60 I. Alexeyev, and F. Nikolayev, "Some Trends in PRC Policy," *International Affairs*, no. 12 (1984), pp. 34, 39.

61 See M. Isayev, "Indochina: Fighting for Peace and Progress," *International Affairs*, no. 1 (1985), pp. 21–30.

62 For excellent discussions of the "state of socialist orientation" and the "vanguard party," see Sylvia Woodby Edgington, "The State of Socialist Orientation: A Soviet Model for Political Development," *Soviet Union*, vol. VIII, part 2 (1981), pp. 223–51; David E. Albright, "Vanguard Parties in the Third World," in *The Pattern of Soviet Conduct in the Third World*, Walter Laqueur, ed. New York: Praeger, 1983, pp. 208–25.

63 See C. P. Nemanov, "Parties of the Vanguard Type in the African Countries of Socialist Orientation," *Narody Azii i Afriki*, no. 2 (1979), cited from Albright, "Vanguard Parties," p. 217; and E. Primakov, "Strany sotsialisticheskoi orientatsii: trudnyi no real'nyi put' perekhoda k sotsializmu," *Mirovaia Ekonomika i Mezhdunarodnye Otnosheniia*, no. 7 (1981). The list of vanguard parties in the Third World includes the ruling parties of Afghanistan, Angola, Benin, Congo, Ethiopia, Mozambique, and South Yemen.

64 Yuri Kashlev, "Information Imperialism: Session of the UN Committee on Information," *New Times*, no. 33 (1984), p. 15.

65 *Ibid.*

66 A. Romanov, "Imperialism and West's Spiritual Crisis," *International Affairs*, no. 2 (1984), p. 100.

67 O. Pobokova and A. Smirnov, "The Trojan Horse of Neocolonialism (On the Training of Developing Countries' Personnel in the West)," *International Affairs*, no. 12 (1984), p. 126.

68 According to Pobokova and Smirnov, "In the USA, for instance, the strategic aspects of these matters are dealt with by the foreign relations committees of both chambers of Congress, the President and the Secretary of State . . . In France, the general supervision of organizing the training of foreign citizens is exercised by the Ministry for External Relations." Similar high-level officials in other Western countries supposedly coordinate the "brainwashing" of foreign students. *Ibid.*, pp. 126–27.

69 A. Kodachenko, "Newly-Free Countries: A Strategy of Independent Development," *International Affairs*, no. 2 (1984), p. 46.

70 Y. Bochkaryov, "Grain and Slander," *New Times*, no. 21 (1985), p. 21.

71 A. Baryshev, "In the Clutches of Present-Day Shylocks," *New Times*, no. 20 (1985), p. 24.

72 Pyotr Nikolayev, "Latin America in the Debt Noose," *New Times*, no. 26 (1984), p. 16; *Ekonomicheskaia gazeta*, no. 4 (1984), p. 22; no. 9 (1985), p. 21.

73 See Robert H. Donaldson, "The Second World War, the Third World, and the New International Economic Order," in *The Soviet Union in the Third World: Successes and Failures*, Robert H. Donaldson, ed. (Boulder, CO: Westview Press, 1981), pp. 358–83; Peter Knirsch, "The CMEA Attitude to a New Economic Order," *Intereconomics*, no. 13 (1978), pp. 106–7.

74 "In the Interests of Cooperation," statement of the Soviet Government, *Pravda*, 5 October 1976, p. 1.

75 *Ibid.*

76 N. Evgenyev and G. Alexandrov, "Needed: Co-operation, Not Confrontation. Economic Debate at the UN General Assembly," *New Times*, no. 3 (1984), p. 5.

77 E. Nukhovich, "The Arms Race and the Developing Countries," *International Affairs*, no. 8 (1983), p. 109.

78 *Ibid.*

79 Nikolai Gnevushev, "Saddling the Third World with an Arm Race," *New Times*, no. 20 (1984), p. 18.

80 Nukhovich, "The Arms Race," p. 113.

81 See Roger E. Kanet, "Soviet Military Assistance to the Third World," in *Communist Nations' Military Assistance*, John F. Copper and Daniel S. Papp, eds. (Boulder CO: Westview Press, 1983), pp. 39–71.

82 V. Lomeiko, "State-Sponsored Terrorism Should be Outlawed," *International Affairs*, no. 2 (1985), pp. 96, 99.

83 Isayev, "Indochina," p. 23; I. Alexeyev and F. Nikolayev, "PRC State Council Premier Visits the USA," *International Affairs*, no. 4 (1984), pp. 45–51.

84 F. Anin, "ASEAN in the Focus of Japanese Diplomacy," *International Affairs*, no. 3 (1982), pp. 41–45.

85 Vladimir Tikhomirov, "Reunification: Two Approaches," *New Times*, no. 23 (1985), pp. 21, 22.

86 One of the forgeries planted by the Soviets in their disinformation campaign against the United States – supposedly an official document recovered from the burned US embassy in Pakistan – referred to a CIA courier who was in contact with President of Amin of Afghanistan prior to his overthrow in 1979. This was meant to substantiate the Soviet claim that both Taraki and Amin were, in fact, US agents. See US Congress, *Soviet Active Measures*, pp. 46, 89.

87 A recent example of Soviet disinformation aimed at exacerbating US relations with India was a planted story about alleged CIA involvement in the assassination of President Indira Gandhi of India. See Elizabeth Pond, "Disinformation," *The Christian Science Monitor*, 27 February 1985, p. 16.

88 Tewfik Tubby, "The Struggle Against Aggression and Expansionism," *International Affairs*, no. 6 (1984), p. 26.

89 The Soviet disinformation campaign has been especially active against the United States in the latter's relations with countries in the Middle East. In a falsified interview, the then Vice-President Mondale allegedly made derogatory statements about President Sadat of Egypt. In another forgery, former Secretary of State Vance supposedly made very negative statements about President Sadat and King Hussein of Jordan. All of these forgeries were planted in Middle Eastern newspapers or sent to the Egyptians anonymously with the purpose of undermining US relations with friendly countries in the region. See US Congress, Permanent Select Committee on Intelligence, Subcommittee on Oversight, *Soviet Covert Action*, pp. 68, 145–46, 161–65.

90 L. Goncharov, "The Driving Forces of Aggression," *New Times*, no. 41 (1983), p. 21.

91 Y. Tarabrin, "US Expansionist Policy in Africa," *International Affairs*, no. 10 (1983), pp. 44–48.

92 V. Golubev, "Israeli Penetration of Africa," *International Affairs*, no. 12 (1983), pp. 59, 63.

93 Another example of Soviet disinformation aimed at the United States was the distribution of forged letters on Ku Klux Klan stationary threatening Third World athletes who might come to the Los Angeles Olympics. Pond, "Disinformation," 27 February 1985, p. 16.

94 Other examples of Soviet disinformation that surfaced in early 1983 were a forged West German document that accused the United States of plotting to overthrow the Rawlings government of Ghana and a forged US embassy memo recommending the assassination of two prominent Nigerian political figures. US Department of State, *Soviet International Fronts*, Publication 9360, August 1983, pp. 4–5.

95 The series on disinformation that appeared in *The Washington Times* in April 1985 provides clear evidence of the ways in which Soviet-oriented groups have been able to influence broader organizations opposed to US policy in Central America. See John Holmes, "Network. Target: Reagan's Central American Policy," a five-part series written by Roger Fontaine, John Holmes, Bill Outlaw, and Ed Rogers, *The Washington Post*, 8 April 1985, pp. 1A, 5A; 9 April, pp. 1A, 5A; 10 April, pp. 1A, 4A; 11 April, pp. 1A, 6A; and 12 April, pp. 1A, 4A.

96 S. Losev, "The People of Nicaragua Defend Their Revolution," *International Affairs*, no. 8 (1984), pp. 32–40.

97 V. Petrusenko, "CIA in Action Against the Peoples of Central America," *International Affairs*, no. 3 (1985), pp. 84–93; G. Petrov, "CIA's Testing Ground in Guatemala," *International Affairs*, no. 10 (1983), pp. 109–16.

98 V. Krestyaninov and G. Petrov, "Honduras – The Jumping-off Ground for Aggression," *International Affairs*, no. 4 (1984), pp. 75–80.

99 L. Klochkovsky, "Imperialist Expansion in Latin America," *International Affairs*, no. 1 (1985), p. 1.

100 Lomeiko, "State-Sponsored Terrorism," p. 97.

101 William M. LeoGrande, "Evolution of the Nonaligned Movement," *Problems of Communism*, vol. XXIX, no. 1 (1980), pp. 35–52.

PART 2

CMEA economic involvement in the Third World

6

Soviet economic policy in the Third World

HEINRICH MACHOWSKI AND SIEGFRIED SCHULTZ

Since the mid-1950s the Soviet Union has intensified its efforts to develop ties with the non-communist countries of the Third World and has endeavored to assert its political influence in these parts of the world. Whereas Khrushchev's efforts were classed by the West under the rubric "commitment and adventurism," Brezhnev's later policy has been praised as "highly rationalistic, realistic, pragmatic, and, until Angola, cautious."[1] The reference to Soviet–Cuban intervention in Angola (1975–76) is an expression of growing Western fear that the spectacular spread of Soviet power in the Third World could inflict damage on the economic interests of Western industrialized countries. The Soviet invasion of Afghanistan in 1979 not only heightened these fears, it triggered (primarily in the United States) an outright "perception revolution"[2] with regard to the future goals of Soviet policy towards the Third World and the very nature of Soviet foreign policy in general.

Analysis of political and economic relations between the Soviet Union and the developing countries encounters fairly serious difficulties. There is no public Soviet discussion of goals and resource commitment; the same applies to gains and costs incurred by the Soviet Union through its relations with "the South." Soviet public policy statements and press accounts are laden with ideology and propaganda; often they are hollow slogans that do not lend themselves well to analysis. Moreover, published Soviet economic statistics have only limited information value and are incomplete.

Only with reservation is the term "The Third World" used by Soviet authors, as it is a reminder of the concept of the "third way" (between the two major political groupings) against which the Soviet Union has consistently fought. Similarly, the Chinese concept of "three worlds" does not fit into the Soviet view of the global antagonism between communism and imperialism. China developed into the Soviet Union's major rival for influence in the developing countries. Since the 1960s

China has succeeded, to varying degrees, in neutralizing Soviet influence in many countries and regions. A policy of self-reliance was propagated by the Chinese as better suited to the needs of the Third World. The present Chinese program of modernization, should it succeed, constitutes a major challenge to the USSR. Consequently, an important goal of Soviet policy in the Third World is the struggle against the "Chinese threat."[3] Since the late 1950s China has become Moscow's rival, for it has attracted as a model a number of developing countries viewed by Moscow as candidates for "socialist development" and, therefore, potential allies.

Soviet policy toward the Third World has an ideological, a politico-strategic, and an economic dimension. The main objective of Moscow's foreign policy over the past twenty-five years and also the chief determinant of its policy in developing regions has been "its claim to act, and to be treated, as a superpower equal to the United States."[4] This claim – somewhat exalted in view of the clearly weaker Soviet economic power – explains the nuclear armaments effort and the development of a global naval fleet. Genuine superpower equality with the United States requires not just corresponding military strength, but an equal worldwide presence, at least in key regions. A large portion of Soviet commitments in the Third World may be explained by this necessity.

GENERAL TRENDS IN TRADE

According to Soviet sources, the USSR maintains trade relations with a total of eighty-nine non-European, non-communist developing countries (LDCs) in the Third World; with seventy-three of these countries it concluded long-term (presumably five-year) trade treaties.[5] Soviet exports to the LDCs during the period 1970–84 increased by over six and a half times in nominal terms and in 1984 amounted to more than $13 billion (see Table 6.1). Soviet imports from this group of countries went up in the same period by more than seven times to over $9 billion. The share of Soviet trade directed to the non-socialist developing countries has held rather steady: at about 15 per cent on the export side and at 11 per cent on the import side, respectively.

From Soviet sources one can conclude that real overall growth in Soviet exports to and imports from the LDCs was impressive, too; exports increased in real terms from 1970 to 1975 by more than 20 per cent, whereas real growth of imports was in the range of 60 per cent. This growth relationship changed dramatically in the following five-year period 1976–80: Soviet exports in real terms went up by a further 45

Table 6.1 Soviet foreign trade with the Third World,[a] 1970–84 in billion US dollars

Years	Exports, f.o.b.			Imports, f.o.b.			Export surplus			Share in total trade in %	
	Total	Specified	Unspecified	Total	Specified	Unspecified	Total	Specified	Unspecified	Export	Imports
1970	2.04	1.24	0.80	1.27	1.26	0.01	0.77	−0.02	0.79	16.0	10.8
1971	2.03	1.33	0.70	1.41	1.38	0.03	0.62	−0.45	0.67	14.7	11.3
1972	2.45	1.36	1.09	1.63	1.62	0.01	0.82	−0.26	1.08	15.9	10.1
1973	3.97	1.82	2.15	2.36	2.28	0.08	1.61	−0.46	2.07	18.6	11.3
1974	4.49	2.44	2.05	3.16	3.11	0.05	1.33	−0.67	2.00	16.4	12.7
1975	4.60	2.69	1.91	4.17	4.13	0.04	0.43	−1.44	1.87	13.8	11.3
1971/75	17.54	9.64	7.90	12.73	12.52	0.21	4.81	−2.88	7.69	15.8	11.4
1976	4.96	2.59	2.37	3.78	3.69	0.09	1.18	−1.10	2.28	13.3	9.8
1977	7.27	3.35	3.92	4.09	4.04	0.05	3.18	−0.69	3.87	16.0	9.8
1978	8.41	4.24	4.17	4.17	4.14	0.03	4.24	0.10	4.14	16.0	8.2
1979	9.65	5.35	4.32	4.87	4.82	0.05	4.78	0.51	4.27	14.8	8.4
1980	10.55	5.81	4.74	7.82	7.62	0.20	2.73	−1.81	4.54	13.8	11.5
1976/80	40.84	31.32	19.52	24.73	24.31	0.42	16.11	−2.99	19.10	14.8	9.6
1981	12.03	6.98	5.05	10.79	10.58	0.21	1.24	−3.60	4.84	15.1	14.8
1982	14.04	7.46	6.58	9.25	9.03	0.22	4.79	−1.57	6.36	16.1	11.9
1983	14.23	7.18	7.05	9.69	9.41	0.28	4.54	−2.33	6.77	15.5	12.1
1984	13.43	6.44	6.99	9.30	9.12	0.18	4.13	−2.68	6.81	14.7	11.6
1981/84	53.73	28.06	25.67	39.03	38.14	0.89	14.70	−10.08	24.78	15.3	12.6
1971/84	112.11	59.02	53.09	76.49	74.94	1.52	35.62	−15.95	51.57	15.2	11.3

[a] Asia (without China, Japan, North Korea, Mongolia, Vietnam); Africa (without South Africa), Middle East (without Israel), America (without Canada, Cuba, USA).

Source: USSR Foreign Trade Yearbook, Vneshniaia Torgovlia SSSR. Statisticheskii Obzor, various editions.

per cent, whereas real growth of imports declined to only 15 per cent. From this follows implicitly that the Soviet terms of trade have declined over the period examined by 15 to 20 per cent.

Table 6.1 also documents the long-recognized significance of the "unspecified" exports in Soviet–LDC trade. Forty-seven per cent of total Soviet exports over the years 1970 to 1984 can be identified neither by country of destination nor by commodity type. This share of "unspecified" exports increased from 39 per cent in 1970 to over 51 per cent in 1984; i.e., these deliveries were by far the most dynamic part of the Soviet trade with the LDCs.

While gaps in official Soviet statistics on trade with the LDCs have always existed, the quality of these data has deteriorated sharply since the mid-1970s. For instance, since 1977 it is impossible to calculate unit values for virtually all Soviet exports and imports of fuels, metals and minerals. Beginning with 1977, it is consequently almost impossible to separate price and real trade trends for Soviet trade with the Third World.

Global and regional analysis of USSR–LDC trade is largely affected by these data problems. The significance of the Third World as trade partner to the USSR is relatively small. Among the 25 most important partner countries, to whom 86 per cent of total Soviet foreign trade fell in 1983, there are only 4 non-communist developing countries: India, Argentina, Libya and Iran. The main feature is the extreme concentration of Soviet trade. In 1983, three-quarters of Soviet exports were taken by 10 countries, with the corresponding figure for imports being almost 85 per cent. The concentration of Soviet trade with LDCs is higher on the import side than on the export side.

From an LDC perspective, the USSR has never been an important market for exports or an important supplier of goods (see Table 6.2). Moreover, its share both of LDC exports and of LDC imports fell during the period 1970–80. A reversal of this trend seems to have occurred in the early 1980s with the respective shares going up to 2.4 and 4.3 per cent in 1983. In comparison with the USSR, slightly more than one-fifth of LDC trade was conducted with the European Economic Community, 18 per cent with the United States and 14 per cent with Japan.

Of the countries for which one can make rough trade share estimates, only Afghanistan, Argentina, Ethiopia, India, Libya, Sudan, Syria and North Yemen have conducted 10 per cent or more of their reported export and/or import trade with the USSR. Available data do not suggest widespread high Soviet trade shares in the Third World. The alleged deepening of Soviet–LDC economic interdependence may have

Table 6.2 *Share of the USSR in Third World trade by major commodity groups (per cent)*

SITC Position	Year	Soviet share of Third World	
		Exports	Imports
All commodities	1970	3.1	4.7
(SITC 0 to 9)	1975	2.7	3.1
	1980	1.7	3.1
	1982	2.4	3.9
	1983	2.4	4.3
Food items	1970	5.9	2.8
(SITC 0+1+22+4)	1975	10.7	2.3
	1980	10.3	1.1
	1982	14.7	1.5
	1983	13.2	1.4
Agricultural raw materials	1970	7.4	3.4
(SITC 2 less 22, 27, 28)	1975	6.2	4.2
	1980	3.5	2.7
	1982	4.3	4.3
	1983	3.9	2.4
Ores and metals	1970	2.1	3.5
(SITC 27+28+67+68)	1975	1.8	1.5
	1980	1.9	1.2
	1982	2.6	1.7
	1983	2.2	1.4
Fuels (SITC 3)	1970	0.2	3.3
	1975	0.6	2.8
	1980	0.3	3.0
	1982	0.2	4.0
	1983	0.3	4.7
Manufactured goods	1970	2.9	3.0
(SITC 5 to 8 less 67, 68)	1975	2.2	1.7
	1980	0.7	1.5
	1982	1.0	1.6
	1983	0.8	1.9

Sources: UN Statistical Yearbook 1975 and 1983; Monthly Bulletin of Statistics, May 1977, 1981 and 1985.

been less than is often perceived in the West and claimed by the Soviets. However, the USSR seems to be an important customer for LDC foodstuffs since 1975.

In examining Soviet trade trends with developing countries one can distinguish three groups using standard economic criteria (i.e., OPEC, the least developing countries, or LLDCs, and the newly-industrializing countries, or NICs), and a fourth group according to presumed political orientation. One-third of the specified Soviet exports to the LDCs over the period examined went to OPEC countries, and the share of the LLDCs increased significantly (up 7 per cent). The role of "developing countries of socialist orientation" as an outlet for Soviet exports increased sharply over the thirteen years (from 4 to 20 per cent). The bulk of specified Soviet imports from the Third World stem from OPEC countries and NICs, respectively. The increase of the NICs' share is especially spectacular. This, of course, results from grain imports from Argentina and Brazil. This points to the conclusion tending to confirm one's first impression that the pattern of Soviet exports to the Third World is more heavily influenced by political factors and less by economic factors than is the pattern of Soviet imports from the developing countries.

The Soviet Union has achieved an export surplus in trade with the Third World every year since 1970 (see Table 6.1). For the total period the cumulative surplus amounts to more than $35 billion. This results entirely from the "unspecified" trade where the cumulative surplus was about $51 billion. Since most Western observers believe the "unreported" exports consist of arms deliveries, the Soviet surplus would consist of these shipments. To put it another way, in "civilian" trade with the LDCs, the USSR has achieved a cumulative deficit of more than $16 billion.

Soviet literature is equally deficient in information that permits one to determine whether the USSR has provided credit toward financing its export surpluses under conditions that would qualify them as development aid. Further, it is not known exactly with which developing countries the Soviet Union carries on trade on the basis of payment in convertible currency. Presumably this would apply to its dealings with OPEC countries; the USSR has achieved an export surplus of more than $4 billion with these partners over the past thirteen years, making the exchange of goods with OPEC countries an important source of convertible currency income for the USSR.[6]

Along with rising prices for some primary products, there has been a growing tendency in Soviet–Third World trade to include more and more convertible currency payments in the settlements. This new method of payment, which was introduced mainly by LDCs, has not been strongly opposed by the USSR which saw in it new possibilities of selling its manufactures for cash. The number of clearing agreements between LDCs and the USSR rapidly diminished: from twenty in 1970, sixteen in 1975 down to nine at the end of 1983, as reported by the International Monetary Fund. In fact, by early 1982, the USSR declared officially that it had bilateral clearing accounts with only seven countries: India, Afghanistan, Iran, Bangladesh, Pakistan, Syria and Egypt.[7] In 1983 these countries accounted for more than one-third of identified imports and more than one-half of identified Soviet exports.

In 1982, 49 per cent of identified Soviet exports to the LDCs consisted of machinery, vehicles and equipment; in 1970, however, the figure has been 61 per cent. The second most important export items were fuels and industrial raw materials, whose share more than doubled to 37.5 per cent in the past thirteen years – a development that may be primarily attributed to energy price increase. This commodity group has increased its share on the import side by almost 20 points to 27.5 per cent, since Third World energy imports have also increased in importance to the Soviet economy, even though the USSR has remained an important net energy exporter. Identified Soviet imports from the Third World remain, however, dominated by agricultural products of all kinds (55 to 60 per cent). Among them foodstuffs increased their share by 10 points to more than 42 per cent. Here Soviet grain imports from Argentina are primarily noticeable: because of the American partial embargo on grain exports enacted by President Carter in January 1980, and lifted by President Reagan in April 1981, the USSR bought approximately 15 billion tons of grain from Argentina. The USSR became an important trade partner of Argentina; in 1981 its share of the country's exports amounted to 83 per cent for grain, 88 per cent for corn, 63 per cent for barley, 100 per cent for rye, 22 per cent for soybeans, and 24 per cent for meat.[8] The growing role of food in Soviet imports from the LDCs could partly be seen as an aberration, reflecting the series of bad Soviet grain harvests in the late 1970s and early 1980s, combined with a need for grain imports from the developing countries as a result of restricting US policies.

The picture of the commodity structure of Soviet exports to the developing countries differs significantly if one uses UN foreign trade data. The exports were dominated by arms, while machinery and transport equipment, which made up one-third of all Soviet exports in 1970, lost constantly in subsequent years. To quote Tom Wolf:

Taking the export and import development together, one is struck by a commodity composition of Soviet–LDC trade which appears to be increasingly dominated in real terms by arms and petroleum exports and the import of food. For the 1970s as a whole, there is little evidence of a significant "deepening" of the international division of labor between the Soviet Union and the Third World. Soviet exports of "civilian" manufactured goods to the LDCs have been growing at relatively moderate rates, while imports by the USSR of Third World manufactures have largely stagnated.[9]

Given this picture, which still shows the predominantly traditional pattern of exchange between North and South, no dramatic change in this structure is likely to take place. Even if the value of imports of manufactures from LDCs should rise substantially in the future, their share will likely remain constant, because of the considerable amounts of food and raw materials that the USSR will need to import. There may be a growth in trade, but its pattern will remain rather traditional.

ECONOMIC ASSISTANCE

With the exception of a few sporadic and very general reports, there is no systematic public reporting in the Soviet Union on the subject of foreign aid. This applies to both the "internal" aid flows to communist LDCs and to Third World countries outside the CMEA groupings. For a detailed analysis of the volume and structure of Soviet aid it is necessary to rely on Western estimates. These are exposed to quite some degree of uncertainty because of the risk of double counting of repeated aid offers, not to speak of non-transparent information on what is concessional development aid and what is commercial credit or military aid.

As to the volume of Soviet assistance, there are quite a number of figures employed in different sources. This is partly the result of conceptual differences, because in Eastern sources there is a preference for counting promises of future aid (commitments), while in Western sources disbursements of aid are emphasized. Of the two Western organizations continuously compiling information on assistance from the USSR (and Eastern Europe), i.e., OECD and the CIA, the former is preferred here because this source is not only more elaborate on the methodology applied but also more suitable for comparison with aid provided by Western and OPEC states, because of the definitions and criteria employed.

Soviet assistance was initially limited to centrally planned developing countries; thus to make a fair assessment of total Soviet aid performance, the aid flow to the CMEA members must also be considered. After having concluded the first cooperation agreements with Afghanistan and India some thirty years ago, the Soviet Union has extended economic aid to a growing number of developing countries. But there were always definite differences with regard to volume (and conditions) between political affiliates and other developing countries. While commitments used to be considerably higher,[10] according to OECD estimates,[11] disbursements (net of repayments) are thought to have been on average around $850 million annually in the early 1970s. In the second half of that decade the annual average was up by close to half a million dollars before, in 1979, the period of noticeable annual increases began, which came to an end with the record level of more than $2.4 billion in 1981.[12] These stepped-up aid flows are said to be due to increased contributions to the Cuban and Vietnamese five-year plans and to a growing involvement in Afghanistan, Kampuchea and Laos. According to preliminary information, the peak value is believed to have been almost reached again in 1984.[13] The record amounts are chiefly explained by an unchanged high level of aid going to Cuba and an allegedly unplanned rise of economic aid to Vietnam.

It should be mentioned that the considerable annual fluctuation of aid contributions to non-CMEA members, one of the main characteristics of Soviet development assistance, is not necessarily a reflection of the donor's change in policy. Rather, it results from a few large framework agreements, differing in size, and concluded at irregular intervals. Projections of the dispersion of a particular loan over time are cumbersome and misleading because the delay in implementation varies project by project.

It should be pointed out that the economically less developed members of CMEA accounted for about three-quarters of total Soviet net aid on average in the 1980s, with only the remainder available for the majority of the developing countries. This percentage seems to have declined since 1982. Moreover, this volume of net aid receipts of the Third World is heavily affected by an increasing volume of repayments on previous loans. For these countries as a group, disbursements from the USSR are supposed to be negative for two consecutive years.

Customarily net aid disbursements are related to GNP in order to have some kind of yardstick to measure the burden of an international "development tax" for the respective donor economy. However, this approach poses some problems with CMEA countries. Besides the fact that they have never accepted the 0.7 per cent target of the UN Development Strategy – allegedly "conscience money" of the West – there are conceptual difficulties which can only insufficiently be tackled. The GNP concept does not apply to most of the centrally planned economies. Various attempts (World Bank, UN, US-Congress/Joint Economic Committee, *et al.*) have been made to derive GNP figures from the Soviet type Net Material Product applying different methodologies, but the results obtained diverge considerably.

For years, the ratio of Soviet development assistance to GNP (the ODA/GNP ratio) was estimated to have moved in the neighborhood of

0.10 and 0.15 per cent. Even with the stepped-up volume of aid since 1979 and with the lowest adjustment for the value added by the service sector, the resulting ratio has not reached 0.3 per cent in recent years.[14] These figures refer to the entire foreign assistance program. When one excludes the "bloc"-internal assistance, (in particular, the substantial support for Cuba and Vietnam), the USSR's ratio – with all the methodological reservations and statistical qualifications which have to be made – slips to a magnitude of less than 0.01 per cent[15] which, by world standards, is extremely low.

Soviet authorities have attempted to counter Western statements about the low level of their economic aid by asserting, for the first time in 1982 at the UN Economic and Social Council (ECOSOC) meetings, that the USSR had contributed 30 billion rubles (about $44 billion at the official exchange rate) in net aid to developing countries during the period 1976–80, pushing up the ODA/GNP ratio from an average of 1.0 per cent to 1.3 per cent.[16] For years the Soviet Union had rejected demands to publish data on its development assistance and had argued for the differing quality of its aid which, in contrast to Western aid, cannot be expressed in quantitative terms. Basically the same figures were repeated in Belgrade at UNCTAD VI,[17] and in May 1984 at UN ECOSOC, with the additional information economic assistance to the developing world of 8.5 billion rubles in 1982 which is supposed to be 1.27 per cent of the Soviet GNP.[18] According to the USSR permanent representative's statement in May 1985 at the UN, the volume of aid for 1983 stood at 9 billion rubles or 1.2 per cent of GNP; a *note verbale* of June 1985 claimed a GNP ratio of "more than 1 per cent" on average during the period 1976–82.[19]

The OECD Secretariat has attempted to reconcile its own evaluations with the above information; however, the differences could not be fully explained because of the absence of more detailed and verifiable data. Although it admits that the OECD figures may well underestimate the real Soviet aid effort (e.g., possible budget and balance-of-payments support could not be taken into account), it maintains that even if price subsidies (to CMEA members) were added this would not raise the aid/GNP ratio into a different range of magnitude.

One of the few Soviet indicators available to check the magnitude of Soviet aid flows (gross disbursements) is the item in the foreign trade statistics entitled, "Equipment and materials for projects built abroad with technical assistance of the USSR." According to this source the USSR provided assistance valued at more than 8 billion valuta rubles to developing countries between 1970 and 1983. That is about the equivalent of $11 billion, very roughly $2 billion more than the US estimates of Soviet disbursements to Third World countries in these thirteen years.

Because of the definite Soviet preference for bilateral assistance, multilateral contributions of the USSR are negligible; about 1 per cent of overall commitments. They are limited to small payments to the UN Development Fund[20] and to UNICEF and special contributions to UNIDO. The contributions are in non-convertible currency, which further diminishes their usefulness because it is a *de facto* tying of procurement to Soviet goods. Since the Soviet Union has no intention of supporting pro-Western developing countries, but rather of deliberately promoting the "non-capitalist road to development," it has no interest in supporting international development institutions, which would curb its liberty to decide independently which countries should receive development aid.

In 1973 CMEA member countries decided to establish a special fund for financial assistance endowed with 1 billion transferable rubles ($1.3 billion), five per cent of which are to be paid in convertible currencies for the purchase of some equipment and know-how in third markets. The fund is administered by the Moscow-based International Investment Bank of the CMEA and is supposed to extend loans with maturities of up to fifteen years at low interest rates to Third World countries. The fund suffers from a lack of adequate finance and from restrictive operating rules; as yet it does not seem to have been put to any significant use. In contrast, the scholarship fund for the multilateral financing of students and trainees from developing countries, also set up in 1973 and predominantly furnished by the USSR, is fully operational.

With regard to regional distribution, the bulk of Soviet aid is concentrated on a small number of countries, primarily the underdeveloped CMEA members which account for about 75–80 per cent of total disbursements. The geographic distribution of aid to other developing countries in the long run reflects to a large extent the desire to strengthen relations: (a) with sympathetic governments (Angola, Ethiopia, Kampuchea, North Korea, Mozambique and the Yemen PDR); (b) with politically and strategically important countries (Afghanistan, India, Nicaragua, Pakistan, Syria and Turkey);[21] and (c) with countries that provide markets for Soviet exports and/or are a source of essential raw materials (Algeria, Egypt, Guinea, Iraq, Morocco, Peru). The lion's share goes to the Middle East and South Asia, i.e., predominantly to neighboring countries or to countries close to the southern Soviet border. Also a few key positions on the African coastline are involved.[22]

The demands made of the CMEA countries by the least developed group have received only a limited response. While Western countries were prepared, after negotiations at UNCTAD, to write off debts and to provide assistance in the form of grants, the CMEA countries have scarcely reacted to similar demands made of them. However, at UNCTAD VI the Soviet Union expressed its "special understanding for the problems of the least developed countries," and claimed to have set aside funds for this target group amounting to 0.18 per cent of its GNP.[23]

FINANCIAL TERMS

The overall concessional component of Soviet commitments is heavily influenced by the substantial assistance in grant form to less developed member countries of the CMEA (Cuba, Mongolia and Vietnam) which is not typical at all of overall Soviet commitments.[24] Soft aid is also extended to newly acquired spheres of influence like Afghanistan, Ethiopia, Kampuchea and Laos. The USSR assistance to other developing countries extended in the form of development loans carries, as repeatedly reported by different sources, 2.5–3 per cent interest with a repayment period of twelve years. However, the interest rate, as well as the repayment period, may vary according to the recipient or the project – a trend towards diversification which could be observed recently. Interest rates of concessional loans ranged from 0 to 5 per cent and repayment periods of ten, but sometimes also twenty, years have become more frequent. (In the case of Vietnam and Laos the maturities are supposed to have reached twenty-five and fifty years, respectively.) The precise grant element of these loans is difficult to calculate, since the loan agreements do not stipulate the beginning of the grace period. The latter depends not on the commitment date, but on the actual disbursment of the funds. Repayments, made in annual installments, usually start one year after or upon completion of the project or delivery of the goods, but in certain instances are deferred for five or ten years. Taking into account all these qualifications, the overall grant element is believed to be in the neighborhood of 60 per cent on average for all recipients, but considerably higher for CMEA developing countries (about 80 per cent). The trend seems to point to a hardening of Soviet loan terms. As a general rule, the USSR finances only the foreign currency portion of aid projects. Occasionally local cost financing has been provided (through the delivery of goods for sale on the local market). These exceptions to the rule were made mostly in favor of the least developed countries.

Outright grants are provided mainly for relief aid, scholarships, hospitals, schools, agricultural machinery and scientific equipment. Whereas grants represent only a small fraction of Soviet aid for Third World countries, they account for a substantially larger part of assistance to communist developing countries. The major part of the USSR's technical assistance is provided not on a grant but on a credit basis. The cost of the provision of experts, teachers and training places is included in the project agreement, and in many instances outlays for technical assistance are believed to have totalled one-third of the credit received. Only scholarships for university, technical and secondary school students are usually in grant form.

Since 1970 the USSR has provided debt relief on several occasions. These operations, which frequently cover both economic and military assistance, carry much more favorable conditions than standard lending terms. This may be partly because of criticism by several recipient countries of hard financial terms. As a rule, these relief operations are on a strictly bilateral basis. Again there is a bias in favor of CMEA members whose repayment load has been rescheduled more readily or written off altogether. As exceptions to this rule, Afghanistan, Peru, Uganda and Zambia are also said to have obtained rescheduling or partial cancellation in 1983.

In general, all Soviet aid, including contributions to UN programs, is characterized by tying the procurement to Soviet goods and expert services. This situation is partly explained by the shortage of foreign currency and the close link between aid and trade. Needless to say, there is no price competition among potential USSR suppliers.

Repayments on loans are usually made either in goods or in local currencies but have sometimes, depending on the conditions laid down in the aid agreement, also been effected in freely convertible currencies. When repayments occur in the form of local goods, the USSR – in principle – accepts them at world market prices. However, several recipient countries have complained about the arbitrary determination of prices, claiming that Soviet goods were overpriced by international standards and deliveries from the recipient countries undervalued. Repayments in goods rather than convertible currency can, however, be attractive to developing countries since certain goods delivered to the USSR may not always be easy to sell elsewhere. When repayments are in local currencies, allegedly most aid agreements include a gold clause as a guarantee against devaluation. In this case too, recipient countries have occasionally complained about artificial exchange rates for the settlement of outstanding debts. Many agreements contain a clause providing that the USSR can collect money due, partially or fully, in convertible currency, if the assisted country is unable to supply sufficient goods within a specified period. It appears, however, that this clause is rarely used. In the past repayments in kind took the form of raw materials traditional to the developing country, but following pressure by the developing countries (India in particular), manufactured and semi-manufactured goods, predominantly those produced by plants built with Soviet assistance, are more frequently used. In some instances the USSR has also accepted raw materials as well as (non-project related) semi-finished and finished goods in excess of its own need as repayment. Though the payment agreements usually prohibit the reexport of delivered goods, the fear has been expressed that Soviet exports of certain products (mainly commodities like oil, sugar and cotton) at discounted prices endanger Third World exports.

SPECIAL FEATURES

Soviet relations with LDCs, whether they are CMEA members or not, can be characterized by a few features that go beyond traditional economic ties and cannot be found to the same extent in West–South relations.[25] The most important of these features include long-term cooperation agreements, which are considered to be one of the cornerstones of East–South cooperation. Concluded bilaterally, they are supposed to serve economic and scientific–technical cooperation. Intergovernmental commissions, convening at regular intervals, are the institutional body with steering capacity. In the context of medium and long-term planning of a number of LDCs, the cooperation agreements allegedly produce an important element of stability and predictability. With this kind of cooperation the USSR is, *inter alia*, aiming at the strengthening of key sectors, notably heavy industry and the public sector, in the partner country.

The Soviet cooperation program has a relatively high training component. With regard to Soviet experts, previously predominantly attached to specific projects, there has been a growing tendency to provide non-project personnel, mainly in the field of education, planning, health and agriculture. Medical teams have been sent mostly to African countries. As to students, there has been a partial shift to overseas training to ease the pressure on Soviet academic institutions. This applies in particular to less advanced education and preparatory language courses. In addition, large groups of skilled workers and specialists have obtained practical training from Soviet experts in the recipient countries, either in connection with aid projects or through vocational and other educational institutes set up and staffed with Soviet assistance. Nonetheless, substantial numbers of students and trainees continue to travel to the USSR for advanced training and higher education. Courses taken include technology and management, mainly related to the steel and aluminium and petroleum industries, to land reclamation.

Besides straightforward sales and purchases, commercial and industrial cooperation may embrace other forms such as production-sharing arrangements, joint ventures, mixed companies and cooperation in third markets. In this context repayment agreements may be mentioned, which allow the debtor country to pay back part of its debts in the form of output of the factory whose establishment had been credited. When representatives of the "Group of 77" inquired about the breakdown of Soviet aid statistics, the reply is supposed to have amounted to an unquantified list of forms of aid which are said to carry favorable terms.[26]

Assistance through pricing is another form of Soviet economic cooperation worth mentioning. In particular, the Cuban economy has for a number of years been supported by the USSR through favorable pricing arrangements. These have taken the form of higher than world market prices for purchases of nickel (until 1979) and sugar. Conversely, there were lower than world market prices of crude oil deliveries to that country. Vietnam is supposed to have also benefited from lower than world market oil prices, although on a much lower scale. To the extent that procurement took place, as reported,[27] in OPEC countries (Iraq and Venezuela) at official rates, in principle these transactions would qualify as concessional flows even under OECD-DAC criteria. Since, however, the quantities involved are unknown, the matter is dealt with in Western statistics as a memo item. It is also said that there may be offsetting movements through refusal of world market prices for LDCs' deliveries (as allegedly happened with bauxite from Guinea as well as Iranian and Afghan natural gas).

THE SOVIET POSITION IN THE NORTH–SOUTH DIALOGUE

Since the decolonization process is more or less completed, Third World interest has moved away from the struggle for the demand for political independence to concern for economic development. The developing countries formulated their aims within the framework of the Non-Aligned Movement, the traditional political forum of the Third World. The 1973 Summit Conference of the non-aligned countries in Algiers marked the starting point for the demands which were later brought together under the title "The New International Economic Order" (NIEO). After the first oil crisis of 1973–74, the OECD countries showed themselves to be increasingly willing to take more account of the needs and demands of the developing countries. In addition, the UN special session in September 1975 marked an important development: within the "Group of 77" – which had by this time well over 100 members – there was growing optimism that the South could achieve more concessions from the West by negotiation than by mere confrontation.

Moscow was thus faced with a new situation. Until then the Kremlin had derived considerable benefit from the antagonism and conflict between Western industrial countries and the Third World. Its military aid and diplomatic backing for liberation movements and anti-Western regimes, together with strong declarations of solidarity, had previously been enough to make the USSR appear the "natural ally" in many parts of the Third World. The North–South dialogue which had been intensifying since the mid-1970s was uncomfortable for Moscow insofar as it felt obliged to adopt a much more well-defined stance regarding the demands of the developing countries. The self-consciousness of the Third World could no longer be met with mere platitudes, especially since these countries began to address their demands for economic development directly to the CMEA countries.

The major demands of the developing countries in the Manila Declaration made toward the CMEA countries included:[28]

The volume of trade should be increased;

All customs and other barriers to imports from developing countries should be eliminated unilaterally and without discrimination;

Going beyond bilateral arrangements, general preferential treatment should be granted;

The CMEA economies should take account of the export requirements of developing countries in their central planning, particularly as regards finished and semi-finished products;

The CMEA countries should abandon the requirement for an even trade balance;

If desired, trade surpluses of developing countries should be reimbursed in convertible currency;

Existing payment arrangements within the CMEA (in transferrubles) should be to the benefit of developing countries to allow the transfer of a positive balance in one country to any other member country; and

The CMEA countries were called upon to increase their financial and technical aid, in order to reach the aim of the international development strategy of one per cent of gross national product.

This list indicates that the developing countries were prepared to address the CMEA group separately, which at first sight might be to its political advantage. It also shows, however, that the Third World was no longer prepared to spare this group of countries from their demands. To summarize the ideas with reference to trade policy, it could be said that trade between developing and CMEA countries should be more multilaterally organized. This was seen as the only way to improve conditions for increased cooperation between different countries, regardless of their economic system. This touches on some of the basic problems of centrally planned economies which have acted, and continue to act, as a barrier to East–West economic relations.

Moscow's most pressing problem has been to find an optimal position in a dialogue which it neither brought about, nor on which it can exert much influence. The notion of a world divided between the "rich North" and the "poor South" concealed dangerous consequences, too. In this dichotomy the USSR belonged to the "rich North" and would in principle be subject to the same demands from the Third World as the West. Finally, Moscow and its allies would have had to accept unpleasant limitations on its scope for decision making if the South succeeded in achieving real influence in international organizations and official bodies – for example, the Integrated Program for Commodities and in particular the Common Fund idea, as demanded by the developing countries.

The Soviet announcements and contributions to the World Trade Conferences at Nairobi (1976) and the subsequent meetings in Manila (1979) and Belgrade (1983) were noteworthy for their willingness vociferously to support the aims of the "Group of 77" so long as this did not involve obligations for the USSR. However, when concrete demands from developing countries were debated, whose acceptance would have affected the CMEA countries financially, the Soviet negotiators did not shy from rejecting them flatly. There was an overall attempt to stress wherever possible the common or related interests of the communist industrial countries and the "Group of 77" against the OECD countries and to play down the increasingly obvious differences.

With regard to concrete demands, the USSR and the other CMEA countries are only prepared to consider a "further increase" of their technical and economic aid.[29] Where trade is to take place without reciprocity under preferential treatment, then they will carry it out only "on normal and equitable terms." Commodity agreements would be considered, but bilateral trade agreements are clearly preferred as a "central element" of any such commodity agreement. Also obligations to supply or accept certain quantities would be dealt with within trade agreements. The question of indexation – touching upon the interdependence of commodity and manufactures' prices – is viewed as a "complex question" requiring detailed study. Efforts to improve compensatory financing facilities are rejected. A stabilization of revenue is not considered as one of the most important steps.

As far as the transfer of technology is concerned, the USSR refers mainly to existing socialist development assistance to increase capacity in the developing countries' technology sector. The Third World's demand for a revision of the international patent system and for the development of a comprehensive code of conduct for the transfer of technology meets with approval, but must proceed, in the socialist view, on the basis of equal rights, mutual advantage, and the maintenance of sovereignty. There is no mention of the demand made by the "Group of 77" for the institutional establishment of any preferential treatment of developing countries in the context of the transfer of technology.

With regard to the NIEO, the USSR displayed for a number of years a rather passive, wait-and-see attitude.[30] The East expressed at best a great deal of criticism concerning the imperfections of current foreign trade mechanisms, but at the same time there was a lack of constructive proposals for real improvements. The statements of the East were essentially a rejection of the demands of the Third World for a NIEO, sometimes with categoric bluntness, sometimes with elastic formulations with a constructive appearance. An equal amount of energy was devoted to the promotion of their alternative concept (i.e., long-term agreements, support for the expansion of productive capacity, the opening up of natural resources, development of the public sector, help with planning). However, the limitations of such a policy were clearly hinted at: first, potential partners must act reasonably and be willing to cooperate on the basis of equal rights. Secondly, it was recognized that the Soviet Union's first concern was the well-being of its people and the preservation of peace and world security in the face of "attacks from aggressive, imperialist circles." This is a euphemism for the fact that the USSR considers the strengthening of its defensive capabilities as first priority.

The current position as regards the NIEO is probably best summed up as follows: the identity of interests of the USSR and the developing countries in the economic sphere, which had previously been so strongly emphasized, no longer seems valid. The western industrialized countries have without doubt prevented the realization of major elements of the NIEO with their opposition to changes in the world economy. The decisive change in attitude has been the attenuation of verbal support, on the part of the USSR and its allies, for the developing countries. This has occurred despite political disadvantages which were outweighed by economic advantages: supporting the views of the Third World would ultimately have entailed the demands of the developing countries for unilateral concessions from CMEA countries. As C. W. Lawson has noted: "While the economic costs of implementing the LDC demands would have been considerable and identifiable, the political losses from opposing them were slight."[31] Economic reality led to a sober and pragmatic reappraisal of Soviet policy towards the South which led to the conclusion that the "accepted" international division of labor was such that the Third World could, on the basis of comparative advantage, concentrate on its role as supplier of raw materials and fuel for the industrial countries of the North,[32] while in turn buying from them machinery, equipment and sophisticated manufactures.

ELEMENTS OF CHANGE IN SOVIET—THIRD WORLD RELATIONS

Thirty years of Soviet efforts to achieve influence in the Third World have had mixed results: indisputable successes together with set-backs and some sensitive losses. Such evaluations are made with the reservation that these areas of the world are subject to rapid change and switches of alliances (as shown by the changing regimes of Egypt and Somalia as well as Angola and Ethiopia) which make final judgments and forecasting extremely difficult.[33]

Since the death of Stalin, the USSR has constantly played the role of a friend and supporter of the newly independent states in their struggle against Western domination. The ways and means may have changed considerably; the aim – to gain influence in the Third World – has remained the same. After 1964–65 the Soviet trade and aid policy, which until then had been purely politically motivated and somewhat arbitrary, underwent a change and developed into a pragmatic program ("new realism")[34] geared to the economic advantage of the USSR. It is also carefully turned to the strategic needs of the world's second largest economy. The USSR has turned its back on spectacular declarations of intent and instead is working patiently at a system which brings considerable advantages, which is flexible and therefore better suited to serve the interests of a superpower under the most diverse conditions of political development. Also, the interest of Soviet development experts has shifted from questions of non-capitalist development to the problems of economic development aid and its efficiency.[35] They gradually came to the realization that the poor economic performance in some of the "progressive" developing countries led to political instability and thus reduced the attractiveness of a non-capitalist development strategy for other countries.

There are different causes for the switch to a more rational policy, some of which are to be found in the Third World, some in the Soviet Union itself. The most important are the following:

Opportunities to aid classical liberation movements have declined;

The Soviet Union's role as a superpower brings with it responsibilities and limitations. As in the West, more and more attention has to be devoted to the problems arising from the consolidation and management of a complex system of duties and alliances;

It was wrong to expect that the newly independent countries would automatically develop into natural allies of the Soviet Union;[36] thus, considerable political and economic capital was invested in some countries with no return in the form of a reliable partnership;

The increase in material demands from successful revolutionary governments for economic support on a permanent basis puts stress on the Soviet economy;

The Soviet Union's economic performance on the "home front" has a definite bearing on the extent of engagement abroad.[37] In this respect the consistently weak performance of Soviet agriculture has brought about severe constraints abroad.

While some developing countries have an economic order based on Marxist–Leninist principles or are in their bilateral relations politically inclined to the socialist camp, the "Group of 77" (the organized representation of the developing countries) does not approve of the main principles of the socialist development concept. The developing countries want financial support and economic concessions, and socialist analysis is not considered as relevant to their present needs. The socialist states are regarded as relatively successful industrial countries of which, in principle, the same economic demands can be made as of the former colonial rulers. The special structure of the Eastern trade and economic system is considered as only a partial excuse for the low level of development assistance. The developing countries do not accept the dichotomy between capitalist and socialist countries as a useful distinction in global economic relations.

CONCLUSIONS

On the basis of the above analysis we can reach the following conclusions:[38]

Soviet–Third World economic relations have become less laden with ideology, but ideology is still an important factor. A somewhat more pragmatic approach to economic issues is covering up orthodox recipes. There is a discernible shift in emphasis away from ideology towards a growing understanding of the importance of underpinning aspirations with economic deeds.

Exhibiting worldwide presence has its economic price. The Soviet Union's claim for extensive cooperation cannot be properly backed up by economic potential. Consumer demands, capital expenditure, the military budget and an inefficient economy curtail economic capacity to match political aspirations on a worldwide scale.

The USSR strongly emphasizes the significance of its cooperation with the Third World along the lines of bilateral country-to-country relations assuring equal treatment and mutual benefits. This view contrasts with that of the developing countries which demand a privileged position in world trade.

Claiming to stand up for the improvement of the international trading conditions of LDCs, while securing advantages from the exchange of goods with the Third World in the conventional pattern, causes a dilemma for the Soviet Union.

There are special features but no special relations in Soviet–Third World cooperation. They are neither extremely cordial nor shock-resistant – as a number of sudden "divorces" has proven.

Growing export surpluses *vis-à-vis* developing countries will aggravate the problem of indebtedness and dependency of the Third World.

Recent negative net disbursements of aid to some recipient countries must lead to the provision of new funds, debt relief, or a deterioration of relations.

International image seems to be a (new) governing force in the USSR: although it has never accepted any international aid target, the Soviet claim of a significant ODA/GNP ratio looks like a signal of change in attitude.

The concentration of aid on CMEA members and the reluctance to enlarge the group of beneficiaries are reflections of a growing resistance against increasing the economic burden.

In the NIEO discussion, the problem arises from the fact that the Soviet Union's demand structure and its supply profile resembles that of the North.

The vast majority of LDCs are no longer looking for those responsible for their present economic state; rather they prefer to be helped out of it quickly.

What conclusions can be drawn from the behavior of the Soviet Union in the past about its future relations with the developing countries? Future Soviet attitudes towards the Third World are likely to have the following elements:

There is little evidence that a "socialist division of labor" would differ greatly from the capitalist one which currently assigns to the Third World the role of primary commodity producer and customer for manufactures.

The autonomy of the Soviet planning authorities will not be unnecessarily encroached by entering into long-term global obligations of a recurrent nature. The government will emphasize the liberty to provide (and withdraw) aid and to set stipulations as it deems fit. The possibility of concentrating resources on selected recipients or sectors will be maintained.

In general, the USSR faces in the developing countries basically the same obstacles and constraints as providers of Western assistance, e.g., lack of local skills and poor management. There is no magic key to overcome these problems more efficiently than the West.

As in the West, Soviet economic policy has different dimensions including humanitarian, ideological, political, and economic interests. Despite a trend indicating the growing importance of economic considerations in shaping trade and aid policy towards the Third World, foreign policy will never lose its prime role.

NOTES

1 Joseph G. Whelan, *Soviet Policy and United States Response in the Third World* (Washington: US Government Printing Office, 1981), pp. 37–38.
2 A. v. Borcke, "Wie expansionistisch ist das Sowjetregime? Innenpolitische Determinanten des aussenpolitischen Entscheidungsverhaltens der sowjetischen Führung," in *Sowjetunion 1980/1981*, ed., Bundesinstitut für Ostwissenschaftliche und Internationale Studien, ed. (Munich/Vienna: Hanser, 1981), p. 102.
3 Helmut Hubel and Siegfried Kupper, *Sowjetunion und Dritte Welt*. Arbeitspapiere sur Internationalen Politik, no. 14 (Bonn: Forschungsinstitut der Deutschen Gesellschaft für Auswärtige Politik), 1981, pp. 88–91.
4 John C. Campbell, "Introduction: The Role of the Soviet Union in World Politics in the 1980s," in *Soviet–American Relations in the 1980s: Superpower Politics and East–West Trade*, Lawrence T. Caldwell and William Diebold, Jr, eds. (New York: McGraw-Hill, 1981), pp. 12–13.
5 A. Kodatchenko, "Wirtschaftliche Zusammenarbeit zwischen RGW und Entwicklungsländern," *Deutsche Aussenpolitik*, no. 1 (1981), p. 55.
6 Heinrich Machowski and Siegfried Schultz, *RGW-Staaten und Dritte Welt*. Arbeitspapiere zur Internationalen Politik, no. 18. Bonn: Forschungsinstitut der Deutschen Gesellschaft für Auswärtige Politik, 1981), pp. 18–20.
7 Giovanni Graziani, *Commercial Relations between Developing Countries and the USSR: Recent Trends and Problems*. Universita' Degli Studi Della Calabria, Working Paper no. 5 (1984), pp. 9ff.

8 Olga Shurawljowa, "Der Nahrungsgüteraspekt der witschaftlichen Zusammenarbeit zwischen den sozialistichen Ländern und den Staaten Lateinamerikas," *Aussenhandel der UdSSR*, no. 1 (1983), p. 46.

9 Thomas A. Wolf, "Soviet Trade with the Third World: A Quantitative Assessment," unpublished manuscript (May 1984), pp. 10–11.

10 A precise compilation of commitment figures is difficult for various reasons, the main problem being that a reported commitment may only confirm or reactivate an earlier one or may be part of a previous frame agreement. In practice, first agreements of a general nature are often confirmed in whole or in part at a later stage of negotiations.

11 OECD, *The Aid Program of CMEA Countries, 1970–1980* (Paris: OECD, 1981).

12 Recently the figures compiled by OECD were twice revised upwards: in early 1984, connected with the inclusion of aid to Mongolia, and during the preparation of the 1985 Chairman's Report.

13 This order of magnitude happens to match the CIA amount for 1983 of "Soviet Economic Aid Extended to Less Developed Countries." To this figure another $15 billion (1982) of Soviet economic aid to communist countries (less developed CMEA members plus North Korea) would have to be added to approximate the foreign assistance total. Applying a 45 per cent utilization ratio, the USSR total disbursement may have been somewhere near $8 billion, thus indicating the wide margin between the two main Western sources. Cf., CIA, *Handbook of Economic Statistics, 1984*, Tables 80 and 86.

14 The DAC Secretariat's estimate of the ratios originally corresponded to the results of a British study. See Foreign and Commonwealth Office, "Soviet, East European and Western Development Aid, 1976–82," *Foreign Policy Document No. 85* (London: 1983).

15 Or even below zero if repayments outpace gross disbursements as reported by the OECD for 1981 and 1982.

16 UN/ECOSOC, E/1982/86 (12.7.1982).

17 UNCTAD, TD/302 (10.6.1983), p. 3.

18 UN/ECOSOC, A/39/273; E/1984/103 (25.5.1984), p. 4.

19 UN/ECOSOC, A/40/303; E/1985/76(13.5.1985), p. 2 and A/40/407; E/1985/131 (25.6.1985), p. 7.

20 None of the CMEA countries contribute to IFAD, WFP, UNHCR, UNWRA or the regional development banks. The USSR's cumulative share in the provisions to UNDP since its inception is slightly above 1 per cent. For comparison: The USSR's contribution is outnumbered by that of India alone or about equivalent to the amount provided jointly by Argentina, Brazil, Colombia and Indonesia. UNDP, *"Generation" – Portrait of the United Nations Development Programme, 1950–1985* (New York: United Nations, Division of Information, 1985), pp. 74ff.

21 Michael Libal, "Interessen und Ideologie in der Dritte-Welt-Politik der Sowjetunion," *Europa-Archiv*, no. 7 (1985), p. 198.

22 Daniel Pineye, "The Bases of Soviet Power in the Third World," *World Development*, vol. XI, no. 12 (1983), p. 1087.

23 UNCTAD TD/302, p. 3.

24 This section draws extensively on OECD material produced over the years by the Secretariat of the Development Assistance Committee, i.e., the annual Chairman's Report and various special reports on the subject of CMEA assistance.

25 Mette Skak, "CMEA Relations with Africa: A Case of Disparity in Foreign Policy Instruments," *Cooperation and Conflict*, vol. XXI (1986), pp. 3–23.

26 Quintin V. S. Bach, "A Note on Soviet Statistics on Their Economic Aid," *Soviet Studies*, vol. xxxvii, no. 2 (April 1985), pp. 269ff.

27 OECD/DAC, DD/83/5, passim.

28 Manila Declaration and Programme of Action of 7 February 1976. Cf., Immo Stabreit, "Der Nord–Süd-Dialog und der Osten," *Europa-Archiv*, no. 14 (1976), p. 483.

29 Henning Wegener, "Sozialistische Länder und neue Weltwirtschaftsordnung," *Europa-Archiv*, no. 10 (1977), pp. 295ff.

30 Leon Zurawicki, "The New International Economic Order: A View from the Socialist Corner," *Intereconomics* (March/April 1982), pp. 91–92.

31 C. W. Lawson, "Socialist Relations with the Third World: A Case Study of the New International Economic Order," *Economics of Planning*, vol. xvi, no. 3 (1980), p. 159.

32 Elizabeth K. Valkenier, "Die Wirtschaftsbeziehungen der Sowjetunion zur Dritten Welt: Vom Optimismus zur Ernüchterung," manuscript circulated by Stiftung Wissenschaft und Politik/AZ 2424 (Ebenhausen: 1985), p. 48. Updated summary of *The Soviet Union and the Third World: An Economic Bind* (New York: Praeger, 1983).

33 Hubel and Kupper, *Sowjetunion und Dritte Welt*, p. 68.

34 Coined by Valkenier; see also in this context her article "Die Sowjetunion und die Dritte Welt," *Europa-Archiv*, no. 5 (1973), p. 162.

35 Edward Böhm, "Der Wandel in den Beziehungen der Sowjetunion zur Dritten Welt," Haus Rissen, loose-leaf communication 11/84.

36 Valkenier, *"Die Sowjetunion und die Dritte Welt,"* p. 163.

37 Thomas J. Zamostny, "Moscow and the Third World: Recent Trends in Soviet Thinking," *Soviet Studies*, vol. xxxvi, no. 2 (April 1984), p. 224.

38 Cf., Ruben Berrios, "The Political Economy of East–South Relations," *Journal of Peace Research*, vol. xx, no. 3 (1983), *passim*; Skak, "CMEA Relations," pp. 4, 7–11; Pineye, "Bases of Soviet Power, p. 1083; Zamostny, "Moscow and the Third World," p. 233.

7

Eastern Europe and the Third World: economic interactions and policies*

LAURE DESPRÉS

The interests of the East European countries in the Third World are usually much less discussed than those of the Soviet Union. It is assumed that East European relations with the developing countries are more or less aligned with Soviet policy, only with less important stakes. Very few specific studies have been devoted in the West to this topic.[1] This is paralleled by a disproportion in the amount of literature published in the Soviet Union and in the East European countries. There is nothing comparable in the latter to the number of general and specialized Soviet institutes dealing with the Third World.[2] To our knowledge only Hungary has a Center for Development Studies attached to the Institute for World Economics of the Academy of Sciences. In the other East European countries the institutions dealing with the developing countries are mostly interested in civilization, geography and language studies, and only marginally in economic problems.

This paper aims to present the main conclusions of a group research project on East–South relations.[3] An earlier article from this project by Marie Lavigne has stressed the major differences between Soviet and Eastern European patterns of trade and cooperation in the Third World.[4] Here we would like to elaborate on a particular aspect of this pattern – the gains in hard currency derived from those relations.

The expansion of trade between Eastern Europe and the Third World has, in general, been greater than the growth of the total trade of the six smaller CMEA members. It has also been erratic, as Figures 7.1 to 7.7 in the Appendix show. The most obvious trend, beginning already in 1975

* The research for this article is part of a group project conducted under the direction of Marie Lavigne at the Center for International Economics of Socialist Countries, University of Paris 1, Panthéon–Sorbonne. The research is sponsored by the Commissariat Général du Plan, Paris, whose financial support is gratefully acknowledged. Portions of the project are scheduled for publication as *East–South Relations in the World Economy*, Marie Lavigne, ed. (Boulder. CO: Westview Press, 1987).

141

Table 7.1 Trade balances[a] of the East European countries with the West and with the Third World ("South") (billion dollars)

	1970	1971	1972	1973	1974	1975	1976	1977	1978	1979	1980	1981	1982	1983	1984[a]
Bulgaria															
West	−65	−55	−41	−79	−526	−843	−475	−388	−416	−43	−22	−718	−619	−445	−570
South	44	27	31	74	154	282	246	373	399	702	1010	1331	1269	822	1160
Czechoslovakia															
West	−133	−145	−123	−234	−393	−581	−773	−732	−804	−803	−452	−332	−146	−29	196
South	116	172	138	54	57	215	174	109	635	318	458	635	633	805	600
GDR															
West	−292	−294	−522	−842	−901	−1018	−1428	−1308	−1092	−1855	−1644	−507	788	884	735
South	3	37	62	53	−175	−8	−134	−153	−79	77	62	599	838	423	320
Hungary															
West	−60	−231	−51	25	−593	−642	−487	−720	−1216	−745	−707	−1066	−580	−75	181
South	−11	−20	−19	−44	−100	−134	−131	−146	−102	100	2	263	234	21	−18
Poland															
West	77	53	−317	−1313	−2310	−2943	−3258	−2498	−2051	−1605	−843	−568	495	704	910
South	65	59	45	21	163	270	325	342	219	−79	−141	591	950	698	650
Romania															
West	−171	−115	−180	−121	−456	−425	−80	−476	−776	−387	−146	241	369	2196	2516
South	56	52	64	77	84	337	69	380	62	−603	−1771	67	159	−221	460
The Six															
West	−655	−787	−1234	−2564	−5176	−7452	−6500	−6122	−6355	−5438	−3814	−2936	1306	3235	3900
South	248	328	321	236	184	962	551	904	1022	517	−379	3536	4066	2608	3200

[a] Estimates.

Sources: National foreign trade statistics (compiled in the Data Bank CRIES – Calculs sur les Relations Internationales des Economies Socialistes); ECE/GEAD (UN) Trade Data (WEST).

but intensifying since 1981, has been the emergence of high surpluses in this trade. A comparison of balances with the industrialized West and with the Third World (see Table 7.1) shows that in 1981 the deficit of the Six as a whole with the West was more than offset by a surplus with the developing countries; in the following years, the positive balance with the West was complemented by continuing surpluses with the South.

In this chapter we shall explore four questions: (1) where do these surpluses originate? (2) what goods are generating them? (3) what percentage of the surplus is in hard currencies? (4) how can we evaluate the aid granted by the Six to the Third World in view of their gains in the field of trade?

THE PARTNERS: DEFICITS AND SURPLUSES

The trade of the Six with the Third World is heavily concentrated on a limited number of countries.[5] The top five partners usually account for more than a half of total trade, and the top ten for over three quarters. If we look at the main partners of the Six over the 1970–83 period (for three sample years, 1970, 1975, and 1983), shifts have occurred – mainly the loss of the two first positions held by Egypt and India in 1970. However, the most constant partners fall into three groups: oil-exporting Islamic countries of the Middle East (Iran, Iraq, Libya, Algeria); non-oil-exporting countries in the Middle East (Egypt, Turkey, Syria) and in Latin America (Brazil, Argentina); and India (see Table 7.2).

The group of oil-exporting states was a source of surpluses over the period (except in 1979–80 because of heavy purchases of oil), the second group is a source of constant deficits; and for India the picture is mixed, with deficits (in 1972–73, 1976–79, 1981) alternating with periods of surpluses, the balance being slightly positive in the whole period.

Turning from individual partners to broader groupings, Table 7.3 gives the most significant balances in trade with the oil-exporting countries and Latin America. One may observe that, contrary to the situation that exists in OECD countries' trade with developing countries, Eastern Europe is deriving surpluses in its trade with oil exporters and suffering deficits in its trade with Latin America as a whole. We have, therefore, to look in more detail at the commodities traded with these partners, in order to understand the origin of the gains or losses.

Table 7.2 Ranking of the top ten partners of the Six in the South (1970, 1975, 1983)

| | Bulgaria 1970 | | Bulgaria 1975 | | Bulgaria 1983 | | Czechoslovakia 1970 | | Czechoslovakia 1975 | | Czechoslovakia 1983 | | GDR 1970 | | GDR 1975 | | GDR 1983 |
	X	M	X	M	X	M	X	M	X	M	X	M	X	M	X	M	X+M
Egypt	1	1	7	1			1	1	3	1	1	1	1	1	2	2	6
India	2	2	6	2		6	2	2	4	3	2	2	2	2	3	4	5
Iran	9		3	7	3	2	6	7	6	4	6	7		7	8	10	2
Iraq	3		2	8	2				1	8	3				1	1	1
Libya	7		1		1	1	3		2		1		5				
Algeria	6	3		4	5	3	9	4	8	2	9	4	7	3	6	3	7
Brazil		3		3	7		10		6		10		3	3	5		3
Morocco	8	8		5			10						10	8	8	6	
Syria	8	4	10	6	4	7	4	6	5		4	6	4	8	4	6	4
Turkey	8	5	5				8	6	10				6	6	7	7	
Afghanistan																	
Angola					8			8				8					8
Argentina		9		10		4		8		9		8		5		9	
Columbia													8				
Ecuador			8														
Indonesia			8												3		
Kuwait																	
Lebanon	5	10	9		10		7		7		7			9			
Malaysia						9		5		5		5					
Nigeria	10	6	4		6		10				10						
Pakistan	4				9	5	5				5						
Peru						10	3		7		3		4		5		
Saudi Arabia																	
Singapore																	

	Hungary 1970		Hungary 1975		Hungary 1983		Poland 1970		Poland 1975		Poland 1983		Romania 1970		Romania 1975		Romania 1983	
	X	M	X	M	X	M	X	M	X	M	X	M	X	M	X	M	X	M
Egypt	1	3	5	6	8	8	2	3	10	4	7	8	2	2	4	2	3	4
India	2	1	3	3	5	9	1	1	1	2	8	4	4	3	5	6	7	8
Iran	4	5	2	4	2	3		10	4		5	2	1	1	1	1	2	1
Iraq	10		1	1	1	6	3		5		2				6		1	10
Libya			7		4	1	9		2		1	1	5		2	3	6	3
Algeria	6	2	5	5	3	3	4	4	7	5	10		7	8	10	5	9	
Brazil				2	6	2		7	3	3	4	3		7	8			6
Morocco							7	7	9	1		6	8		7			
Syria	8	9	8				5	8	8		3	5	6	9		9	8	1
Turkey	3	4			9												5	7
Afghanistan																		
Angola																		
Argentina	7						8	5		6			10	6	9			
Columbia	10						10											
Ecuador			10	10			6		6		6	9						
Indonesia															9			
Kuwait	5	8	8															
Lebanon	6		6	9	7	7	3	3					3		3		4	
Malaysia		9		9		7			10	10								
Nigeria	9	8				10	6	2	8		9		10	5				
Pakistan	7						10	2	8	8			10	5				
Peru		6						6	7	7								
Saudi Arabia					10													
Singapore													4		10		5	
Tunisia									9						9			9

Table 7.2 (contd.)

	The Six					
	1970		1975		1983	
	X	M	X	M	X	M
Egypt	1	2	5	1	5	5
India	2	1	4	2	9	7
Iran	4	4	3	4	3	2
Iraq	3		2	6	1	
Libya	10		1	8	2	1
Algeria			10	7	7	
Brazil	9	3	9	3	10	4
Morocco		9		5		
Syria	8		7		6	3
Turkey	6	7	8		4	8
Afghanistan						
Angola						
Argentina		5				9
Columbia						
Ecuador						
Indonesia						
Kuwait	7		6		8	
Lebanon				10		
Malaysia		10				
Nigeria						10
Pakistan	5	8		9		
Peru	6					
Saudi Arabia						
Singapore						
Tunisia						6

Source: Databank CRIES
Note: X = export; M = import

Table 7.3 *Trade balances of the East European countries in trade with oil exporting countries and with Latin America (million dollars)*

	1970	1971	1972	1973	1974	1975	1976	1977	1978	1979	1980	1981	1982	1983
Bulgaria														
Oil exporting countries	27	34	47	66	82	282	247	297	422	448	762	749	957	702
Latin America			−11	−13	−42	−39	−52	−50	−19	−21	−39	−8	−30	−63
Czechoslovakia														
Oil exporting countries	56	39	37	64	108	224	203	143	256	312	376	498	367	449
Latin America	−29	−18	−16	−67	−42	−44	−118	−147	−147	−147	−188	−176	−183	−118
Hungary														
Oil exporting countries	5	5	26	−1	11	75	121	103	102	155	442	325	91	
Latin American	−44	−29	−39	−39	−68	−92	−170	−287	−220	−226	−260	−257	−204	−218
Poland														
Oil exporting countries	45	35	49	58	162	257	339	336	175	−59	−145	439	605	198
Latin America	−8	−4	12	−56	−58	9	31	−49	−157	−308	−509	−372	−61	69
Romania														
Oil exporting countries	35	14	16	16	−9	81	−261	−181	−49	−1283	−2096	−516	39	−110
Latin America	−9	−8	4	−20	−21	33	2	−67	−70	−6	−129	−116	−88	−56
The Five														
Oil exporting countries	168	127	149	233	342	855	602	716	383	−549	−1044	1838	2280	1330
Latin America	−90	−60	−51	−194	−230	−133	−306	−599	−611	−749	−1113	−936	−500	−379

Source: Same as Table 7.1. GDR is excluded since it does not give export/import trade data by individual countries.

THE COMMODITY COMPOSITION OF TRADE

Trade with Latin America deserves closer examination for two reasons. First, over 70 per cent of the deficit is realized in trade with countries with which most of the Eastern European countries have clearing agreements, especially Brazil (see below on the settlement of balances). Second, the structure of import trade needs to be mentioned. At first glance, it is a typical North–South pattern with primary commodities comprising about 85 per cent of total trade (and food commodities alone making up 60 to 70 per cent). But, contrary to the case of the USSR, the food exports are not primarily composed of grain, but mainly and increasingly of animal food (e.g., fish-meal and soy concentrates). This is significant if we remember that meat exports are important hard currency earners for most of the East European Six.

In the remainder of this chapter we shall concentrate on the gains in East European trade with OPEC countries. Both exports and imports will be considered, for a significant portion of imports is earmarked for export against hard currency.

East European exports to OPEC countries are concentrated on manufactured goods (over two-thirds of total trade), although food products also account for a significant part of total exports (over 20 per cent). The distribution is not even among the East European countries. The share of machinery is higher for the northern countries (Czechoslovakia, GDR and Poland); while Hungary, Bulgaria and Romania are the main exporters of food, especially to Islamic Middle Eastern countries. Bulgaria in particular has stepped up its sales of lamb and mutton to these countries (mainly to Libya) since the end of the 1970s in return for animal hides for processing.

An important question concerning East European sales of machinery and equipment concerns the share of arms exports in these sales. Arms sales do not appear in East European trade statistics, as is the case for the USSR, in the form of an undeclared "residual." If total exports to the Third World are compared with exports to individual countries, this "external residual," which is very high for the USSR (over 50 per cent of the total exports), is low for the East European countries and decreasing over time. It has occasionally been significant for some countries (Romania in 1977–79, Poland in 1977–81), but has always remained in the range of 10–20 per cent of total exports. As for OPEC trade with the Six, the residual has always been negligible. However, data on machinery sales are far from complete, and arms sales may appear in the "internal residual" thus resulting.

However, given the absence of specific data on arms exports in East European statistics, we must rely mostly on Western sources (CIA, Arms Control and Disarmament Agency [ACDA]; and the Stockholm Institute for Peace Research – International [SIPRI]) to obtain an esimate of the amount of these sales.[6] According to ACDA data,[7] most of the sales are made to oil exporters of the Middle East and Libya, especially in the post-1978 period when over 90 per cent of total arms sales had that destination. For the years 1978–82, arms sales to the developing countries amounted to 16 per cent of Czeckoslovakia's total sales to the Third World, 15 per cent for Poland, and 11 per cent for Romania (see Table 7.4). These three countries appear as the major East European suppliers of arms; the share of sales of the three others is marginal (with Bulgaria and the GDR more involved in military cooperation).

The main East European import from OPEC countries is oil. The major oil importer is Romania, which is also the only country to maintain a structural trade deficit with the OPEC countries since 1976. This results from the fact that, for all the East European countries except Romania, OPEC countries are only supplemental oil suppliers; the main bulk of oil imports (over 80 per cent) comes from the USSR. Romania began to import oil from the Soviet Union only in 1979, and the OPEC countries remain its primary suppliers. From slightly less than 50 per cent of the oil imports of the CMEA six from OPEC suppliers in 1975, Romania claimed 66 per cent in 1979, the year of the highest amount of total oil imports by the Six (almost 20 million tons). Since then, Romania's share has decreased to only 46 per cent of the total in 1983.

The top three OPEC oil suppliers of Eastern Europe have always been Iran, Iraq and Libya, but in varying positions. Iran was the primary exporter in the beginning of the 1970s; Iraq took the lead in 1972–73, but its share decreased sharply after the beginning of the Iraq–Iran war in 1980. Libya became the main supplier in 1982.

Several additional factors make this trade with OPEC countries particularly profitable. First, these countries provide good markets for the exports that the CMEA countries have to offer: machinery, arms, and food. Their ability to finance imports opens to Eastern Europe opportunities for large-scale investment contracts. Technical assistance, in the form of experts and training on the spot, is also a source of gain for the East.

Second, the oil which OPEC provides is used by the East European countries largely for reexport, either in the form of crude oil (by Hungary, Poland, and on a minor scale by Bulgaria and Czechoslo-

Table 7.4 *Arms sales of the East European countries to the Third World (million US dollars)*

	Sales of East European countries			Sales of Selected countries (4) (1978–82)		
	CIA (1)	Department of State (2)	Congressional Res. Serv. (3)	Czech.	Poland	Romania
1970	75					
1971	125					
1972	75	75				
1973	130	130				
1974	210	210	390			
1975	285	280	630			
1976	330	335	825			
1977	345	355	730			
1978	470	550	1,195			
1979	525	635	1,045			
1980		525	1,300			
1981		775	2,470			
1982			3,750			
1983			2,105			

	Czech.	Poland	Romania
Middle East	520	650	915
Libya	430	330	240
Subtotal	950	980	1,160
All recipients	1,000	1,040	1,270
Share of Middle East and Libya of total sales	16%	15%	11%

Source: For sales to the non-Communist developing countries (1), CIA, National Foreign Assessment Center, *Communist Aid Activities in Non-Communist Less Developed Countries, 1979 and 1954–79*, October 1980; (2), US Department of State, *Soviet and East European Aid to the Third World, 1981*, February 1983; (3) For sales of all other Communist Countries (USSR excluded) to the Third World as a whole (including Communist developing countries), Congressional Research Service, report by R. F. Grimmett, *Trends in Conventional Arms Transfers to the Third World by Major Supplier, 1974–1981*, 12 August 1982; and *Trends in Conventional Arms Transfers to the Third World by Major Supplier, 1976–1983*, 7 May 1984. For the trade of selected countries, see Arms Control and Disarmament Agency, *World Military Expenditures and Arms Transfers, 1984*, pp. 95–98.

vakia), or refined products (by the GDR, and especially Romania, whose refining capacities are more than double its declining domestic production of oil).

But it may be argued that the reexport of oil (crude or refined) is not by essence a profitable operation when it implies purchases in hard currencies. Here one must take into account the conditions of these deals. By the early 1970s the East European countries had special barter agreements with Iran (beginning in 1967), Iraq (1969), and Libya (1971), that provided for oil exports in return for machinery or technical services. A similar agreement was signed in 1972 between Romania and the United Arab Emirates. These deals, agreed to before the oil price explosion, were profitable to the OPEC countries especially since some countries happened to be blacklisted by Western markets (Iraq and Libya, for instance). After 1974–75 all the barter or clearing agreements were suspended. But the sluggish demand for oil on the world market brought about the resumption of barter deals by the early 1980s. Algeria and Libya first offered such agreements in order to conceal a reduction of the OPEC oil price through a swap – oil for arms or machinery. Iran resumed barter deals in 1983. In addition, Hungary and Poland have succeeded in obtaining (in 1982 and 1983) Libyan crude on credit. These agreements may be expected to last as long as the oil market remains soft.[8]

THE SETTLEMENT OF THE BALANCES

The case of oil transactions demonstrates the complexity of the settlements. This question is generally approached in the following way. On the basis of the clearing agreements still in force (their number began to decrease at the end of the 1960s), one may determine which part of total trade is covered by clearing agreements; from this, one may derive estimates of the settlements in hard currencies. Table 7.5 summarizes the clearing agreements in force in 1983, while Table 7.6 is a computation of exports to and imports from countries that have concluded a clearing agreement for the same year. For each East European country (except the GDR, which does not publish export–import data by partner country), the share of clearing in imports and exports has been computed. Finally, the "apparent balance in hard currencies" has been estimated as the total balance minus the algebraic value of the clearing balance. The clearing balance reduces the currency balance when it is positive (the debtors do not have to pay); it increases, for the opposite reason, the hard currency balance when it is negative (the CMEA country does not have to pay).

Table 7.5 *Clearing agreements in force between the East European countries and the developing countries (end-1983)*

	Bulgaria	Czecho-slovakia	GDR	Hungary	Poland	Romania
Afghanistan		x	x	x		
Algeria[b]		x		x	x	
Bangladesh	x	x	x	x	x	x
Benin				x		
Brazil	x	x	x		x	x
Columbia	x	x[b]		x	x	x
Congo	x					
Costa-Rica					x	
Ecuador[a]		x	x		x	x
Ghana						x
India		x	x		x	x
Iran	x	x	x	x	x	x
Lebanon[b]		x[d]			x	x[d]
Mali[c]				x		x
Malta	x				x	
Nepal					x	
Pakistan[b]	x	x		x	x	
Peru					x	
Sao Tome			x			
Sri Lanka[b]	x	x	x	x	x	x

Sources: IMF, *Annual Report on Exchange Restrictions, 1984;* Euromoney Trade Finance Report.
Notes: [a] For most of the settlements.
[b] For some settlements only.
[c] Non-working agreement.
[d] In process of liquidation.

The share of trade conducted under clearing agreements is still important and comprises about one-quarter of total exports and one-third of total imports (for the year 1983). Romania, Hungary, and to a lesser extent Bulgaria are in deficit on their clearing accounts; Poland and Czechoslovakia maintain a surplus. In total, this affects the overall trade balance with the Third World quite marginally (it increases it by a mere 4 per cent).

Czechoslovakia usually has a surplus in its clearing accounts because it has no clearing account with the Latin American countries with which it is in deficit. Poland, on the other hand, generally maintains a deficit in clearing; the peculiar situation of 1983 results from a substantial decrease

Table 7.6 Trade balances of the East European countries with the Third World in 1983 according to the types of settlements (million dollars)

	Exports under clearing regime	Ratio of clearing to total exports (%)	Imports under clearing regime	Ratio of clearing to total imports (%)	Positive clearing balance	Negative clearing balance	Total balance with Third World	Apparent hard currency balance
Bulgaria	266.7	16.7	274.2	36.0	17.4	−24.7	821.6	828.9
Czechoslovakia	288.9	19.5	221.9	33.0	78.3	−11.3	805.3	738.3
GDR	(913.8)	(34.7)					482.8	
Hungary	399.0	35.0	491.9	44.3	139.7	−232.6	21.1	114.0
Poland	416.8	27.9	265.8	37.0	179.0	−27.8	698.2	547.0
Romania	500.3	22.5	701.1	28.5	46.0	−246.7	−221.2	−20.5
The Five	1,871.7	23.9	1,954.8	34.2	460.4	−543.1	2,125.1	2,207.8

Source: Same as in Table 7.1.
Note: The GDR does not identify its export/import trade with individual countries. The figures are given for the aggregate exports + imports.

in imports from its main clearing creditor, Brazil. The deficits of the three other countries are attributable to a few partners: first of all Brazil and Colombia, then Iran (for Hungary and Romania), and to a lesser extent Pakistan (for Bulgaria), and Sri Lanka (for all three East European states).

The first question is, of course, what happens with the deficits in clearing accounts? How are they settled? Why are they tolerated by the developing countries themselves? The clearing account deficits occur mostly with Latin American countries: for example, all of Eastern Europe except Czechoslovakia run deficits in their trade with Brazil and Columbia and all but Bulgaria and Czechoslovakia in trade with Ecuador. The clearing agreements were originally concluded to provide markets for food commodities such as coffee, cocoa, soya, sugar, bananas exported by the Latin American countries. Colombia, for instance, could never have expanded its sales of coffee without the clearing arrangements, because the East European countries would not have bought its coffee. The lobby of the coffee exporters in Colombia has pressed for the renewal of the clearing agreement. Recently, additional reasons have emerged to influence Latin American governments to sign such agreements. For Brazil, which is heavily indebted to the industrialized countries and under IMF control, such agreements also make it easier to import East European products, such as coal from Poland or potash fertilizers from the GDR.[9]

In principle the clearing balances have to be settled, after delays specified in the agreements, in hard currencies. More and more frequently they are settled through triangular compensation deals. For instance, in 1983 Hungary supplied a Brazilian engineering firm with tar and foodstuffs for construction projects in Iraq; the GDR supplied Brazil with Pakistani rice, Canadian sulphur and US ammonium sulfide. But some East European countries seem to be unable to repay their clearing debts. Poland has accumulated a debt of over $2 billion towards Brazil, which has been included in the rescheduling of the total Polish debt towards other governments. Brazil signed new clearing agreements with Hungary, Poland and Romania at the end of 1983.[10]

We now turn to a discussion of trade conducted under the system of hard currency settlements. May we assume that all the surpluses are effectively hard currency gains? The answer is obviously negative. First, one has to deduct from the hard currency exports the supplies of equipment and machinery exported within the framework of cooperation agreements. Usually available data (for instance, that of the CIA, which is based on estimates of aid commitments of the East European countries) gives the amount of the loans granted to developing countries. Unlike the Soviet Union, the East European countries do not publish the annual amount of the aid actually provided in relation to those commitments. One must estimate their share in total machinery sales from assumptions about the effective time-schedule of the deliveries specified in the cooperation agreements.

In addition, some developing countries are unable to pay for their imports or to repay their loans, so that positive trade balances with those countries must be considered as only apparent surpluses. This is probably the case with the African countries with a "socialist orientation," and the other least developed countries with which the East European states conduct trade.

Conversely, the East Europeans do not always pay for their imports in cases when these imports are a reimbursement for previous loans. Again, it is not easy to estimate the amounts involved because the goods used for repayment are often the traditional exports of the developing countries. Especially in the field of minerals, the East European countries have signed a number of agreements that aim at securing supplies of commodities (rock phosphate, iron ore, nonferrous metals) in return for cooperation in the development of such resources. The resulting Third World exports include both the repayment of the loans and regular commercial sales.

Finally, apart from the above-mentioned agreements, which fall into the category of cooperation, there is a whole complex of purely commercial deals conducted under the system of compensation, barter, and triangular settlements.[11] Bulgaria has concluded such agreements with Nicaragua, Guyana and Mexico. The GDR has barter agreements with Mexico and Tanzania (bicycles, medical equipment and drugs in return for coffee, tea, tobacco and cotton) and has concluded since 1982 compensation deals with Indonesia and the Philippines. Romania has signed bilateral barter agreements with Malaysia, Indonesia, and Pakistan. It appears that agreements of this type have tended to occur recently with a number of heavily indebted countries such as Brazil or Nigeria, or with countries generally used to compensation agreements, such as India. If it is assumed that barter or compensation agreements aim to achieve a balanced trade, then it has no influence on the total balance. But in all cases barter reduces the overall flow of hard currency transactions in both directions, by a greater amount than is implied in the clearing agreements themselves. Overall, we estimate that the net hard-currency increase from trade for Eastern Europe is about $700 million (around 30 per cent of the apparent hard currency balance for the year 1983).

ARE THERE HARD CURRENCY DISBURSEMENTS TO THE THIRD WORLD?

The "Group of 77" has asked the socialist countries to increase their economic assistance program so as to reach the level required from the developed market economies (0.78 per cent of GNP), to increase the share of aid extended in hard currency, and to activate the "Special Fund" of one billion transferable rubles supposedly created within CMEA in 1973, with a share of 5 per cent extended in hard currencies.[12]

The traditional answer of the socialist countries[13] was that such requirements could not be put before them, because their cooperation was of a different nature than the so-called aid of the capitalist countries and they could not be held responsible for the past colonial exploitation exerted by these countries, for which assistance was a sort of reparation. But in July 1982 the Soviet representative at the Economic and Social Council of the United Nations stated that USSR economic assistance to the developing countries, when computed according to the Western methodology, was indeed 1 per cent of GNP over the 1976–80 period.[14] Three East European Countries, Bulgaria, Czechoslovakia and the GDR, followed this line and publicized the amount of their net aid at UNCTAD VI in 1983 in Belgrade.[15] Figures were given for the amount of aid in 1976–80 (Bulgaria) or in 1982 (GDR and Czechoslovakia), in national currencies and in dollars (expressed in "devisa currencies," at the official exchange rates used in foreign trade statistics), and as a percentage of national income: 0.79 for Bulgaria and the GDR; 0.74 for Czechoslovakia.

These figures are very difficult to understand, especially as they refer to a "GNP" which is supposed to be calculated according to the Western methodology, and is not to be equated to the NMP (net material product) published in the statistical yearbooks. For instance, when deriving the GNP from the percentages given, one gets about $84 billion for Czechoslovakia and $61 billion for GDR in 1982, which leads to a GNP figure of $5,500 per capita in Czechoslovakia and $3,640 in GDR. These figures are to be compared with the last figures published in the World Bank Atlas for the year 1980, giving $5,820 for Czechoslovakia and $7,180 for GDR! The discrepancy is obvious and also contradicts data published in Eastern Europe, which always lists the GDR as ahead of Czechoslovakia for the level of national income per capita. In addition, the 1982 figure for the absolute amount of aid does not fit with the usual estimates of Western agencies (CIA, Department of State, OECD, etc.) according to which the GDR is the main donor within Eastern Europe. The figures published in the DAC Chairman's report estimate GDR aid as $195 million in 1982 (40 per cent of the official figure of the GDR) and the aid by Czechoslovakia as $138 million (22 per cent).[16]

However, the amount of aid extended in hard currency must be very low by any account. First, the greatest part of total aid (over 80 per cent) is extended to communist developing countries (Cuba, Vietnam, Mongolia, Korea, Laos), which are included in these figures. As we are concerned here with the "other" developing countries, the total volume of net assistance is small (in the range of $100 million),[17] mainly extended in the form of deliveries of equipment on credit and of training of specialists or scholarships for Third World students in Eastern Europe. As for multilateral contributions, according to the OECD they are steadily declining ($14 million in 1980, $9 million in 1983). Moreover, these data include Soviet aid. Most of these funds are disbursed in non-convertible currencies. The multilateral "Special Fund" of the CMEA has never been put in operation.

The figures quoted above do not include military assistance, which is extended in the form of military equipment and training. The share of Eastern Europe in recent years is about 10 per cent of the overall number of military experts from the Soviet Union and Eastern Europe active in the Third World. The ratio of military to civilian experts is relatively low, about one-sixth in total, but is higher in the countries with a socialist orientation (Angola, Mozambique, Ethiopia, South Yemen – but not in Afghanistan where training is overwhelmingly provided by the USSR). The ratio of military staff trained in the East European countries to the number of civilian students is still lower, by about 4 per cent. In both cases, the GDR is the leader; this country has signed military cooperation agreements with Angola (1973), Ethiopia (1979), and Nicaragua, where military assistance is supplemented with medical help.

CONCLUSION

Based on our analysis of East European economic relations with non-communist developing countries, we reach the following conclusions:

1   The East European countries derive substantial hard currency gains from their trade with the Third World; these gains were particularly high in 1981–84; that is, during the period when these countries were striving to restore their balances of payments with the developed market economies.

2   These gains were achieved by a vigorous export drive during the year 1981 and by a strong decline in imports (as with developed

countries) in 1981–82; the following years seem to show a stabilization of both exports and imports.

3   Arms sales play a significant but, unlike the Soviet case, not a major role in achieving these surpluses.

4   A peculiar feature of this trade is that not only exports, but also imports, help to achieve hard currency gains, for imported oil is reexported either in crude or in refined form. This, in turn, is made possible by the fact that the Soviet oil supplies, paid in non-convertible currency except in the case of Romania, cover the main domestic needs.

5   The outlook for the future is mainly related to the prospects of trade with the Middle East countries, and hence to the state of the world oil market.

6   Both the clearing and the hard currency forms of settlements benefit Eastern Europe overall, as these combine deficits on clearing accounts and surpluses in hard currencies.

7   Economic assistance does not cause a drain on hard currency earnings; first, because the amount of economic assistance to non-communist developing countries is small; secondly, because assistance is mainly granted in forms other than hard currency disbursements. The GDR is the major supplier of both civilian and military assistance.

Appendix

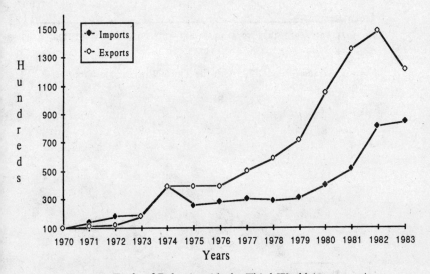

Figure 7.1 Trade of Bulgaria with the Third World (1970 = 100)

Figure 7.2 Trade of Czechoslovakia with the Third World (1970 = 100)

160

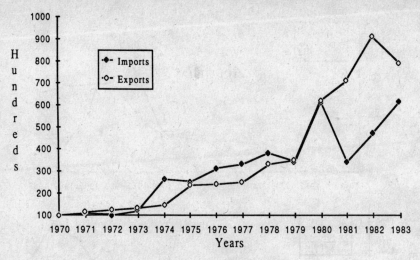

Figure 7.3 Trade of the GDR with the Third World (1970 = 100)

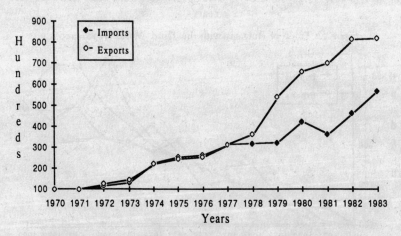

Figure 7.4 Trade of Hungary with the Third World (1970 = 100)

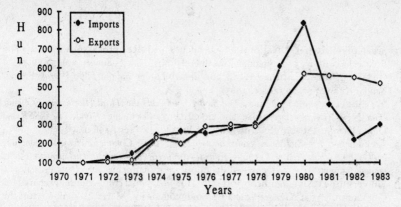

Figure 7.5 Trade of Poland with the Third World (1970 = 100)

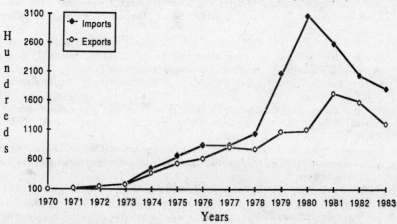

Figure 7.6 Trade of Romania with the Third World (1970 = 100)

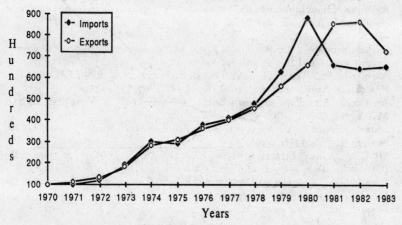

Figure 7.7 Trade of The Six with the Third World (1970 = 100)

NOTES

1 See Colin Lawson, "National Independence and Reciprocal Advantages: The Political Economy of Romanian–South Relations," *Soviet Studies*, vol. XXXV, no. 3 (1983), pp. 362–75; Michael Radu, ed., *Eastern Europe and the Third World: East vs. South?* (New York: Praeger, 1981).

2 See Elizabeth Kridl Valkenier, *The Soviet Union and the Third World: An Economic Bind* (New York: Praeger, 1983) and Cole Blasier, *The Giant's Rival: The USSR and Latin America* (Pittsburgh: University of Pittsburgh Press, 1983).

3 *Les Relations Est–Sud dans l'économie mondiale*, vol. I: *Commerce et coopération: une analyse d'ensemble:* vol. II: *Les pays socialistes européens et les pays en dévelopement. Etudes monographiques* (Paris: Centre d'Economie Internationale des Pays Socialistes, Université de Paris I, Panthéon Sorbonne, 1985). This is a compendium prepared for the Commissariat Général du Plan and edited by Marie Lavigne, with the participation of Giselda Akaishi, Sonia Bahri, Iris Balvany, Frederic Brommer, Barbara Despiney, Laure Després, Alexandre Dimitri, Dominique Don, Anne Elkoubi, Françoise Renaudie, Elisabeth Tison, Bernadette Veyrat, and Jorge Zumaran.

4 See Marie Lavigne, "Eastern European–LDC Economic Relations in the Eighties," in *East European Economies: Slow Growth in the 1980s*, Vol. II: *Foreign Trade and International Finance* (Selected Papers Submitted to the Joint Economic Committee, Congress of the United States) (Washington: US Government Printing Office, 1986), pp. 29–59.

5 The East European definition of the Third World excludes communist countries, whether they are CMEA members (Cuba, Mongolia, Vietnam) or not (North Korea, Laos and probably Kampuchea).

6 This problem has been analyzed in more detail in Laure Després, *Les Ventes d'armes et la coopération militaire Est–Sud* (Paris: Centre d'Economie Internationale des Pays Socialistes, 1985).

7 *World Military Expenditures and Arms Transfers, 1967–1976* (Washington: ACDA, 1977), pp. 157–60, and *1978–1982* (Washington: ACDA, 1983), pp. 95–98.

8 See the study by Sonia Bahri, "Les Relations économiques entre les pays socialistes européens et les pays de l'OPEP," in Lavigne, ed., *Les Relations Est–Sud*, vol. II.

9 See the study by Giselda Akaishi, Elisabeth Tison and Jorge Zumaran, "Les Relations économiques entre les pays socialistes européens et les pays de l'Amérique latine," in Lavigne, ed., *Les Relations Est–Sud*, vol. II'

10 *Ibid.*

11 Frederic Brommer, "Les Accords de paiement entre les pays socialistes et les pays en development," in Lavigne, ed., *Les Relations Est–Sud*, vol. I.

12 "Group of 77," Program of Manila, January 1976, doc. UNCTAD TD/195; Program of Arusha, February 1979, doc. UNCTAD TD/236.

13 Joint declaration of the socialist countries, UNCTAD IV, Nairobi, doc. TD/211, May 1976.

14 Letter addressed to the President of the Economic and Social Council, United Nations, 12 July 1982, E/1982/86'

15 UNCTAD, doc. TD/291, 7 June 1983 (Bulgaria); TD/301, 10 June 1983 (Czechoslovakia); TD/304, 14 June 1983 (GDR).

16 See OECD, *Cooperation for Development*, Annual Report of the Chairman of the Developmental Assistance Corporation, for 1982, p. 92.

17 Després, *Les Ventes d'armes*, ch. 2.

8

The non-European members of the CMEA: a model for developing countries?

GIOVANNI GRAZIANI

The Council for Mutual Economic Assistance (CMEA) is a mixed organization. Apart from the USSR and Eastern Europe it includes three developing countries: Mongolia, Cuba and Vietnam. Mongolia was admitted in 1962 with few problems, probably because of its low population. Cuba entered in 1972 after a long delay, and Vietnam joined in 1978 in spite of opposition by at least one industrialized member, Czechoslovakia. Among those developing countries with the status of observers, Laos failed to gain admission once and Mozambique has been rejected twice.[1]

This chapter will concentrate on only one very important aspect of foreign economic relations of the three developing members of CMEA, namely the foreign trade sector. The foreign trade of developing countries is generally characterized by an extreme dependence on one or a few partners and/or commodities; by a predominance of raw materials and intermediate goods in their exports, and of machinery and equipment, together with fuels and foodstuffs, in their imports; by a high degree of vulnerability to price fluctuations in the world market; and, lastly, by huge trade deficits. With these facts in mind, it is useful to try to determine whether joining the CMEA has meant the end of dependency relations for the three countries in question or rather the transformation of their old bonds into new, more sophisticated ones.

Western scholars usually present these countries (particularly Cuba) as political assets and economic liabilities for the Soviet Union for several reasons: (a) all of these countries turned to the USSR after a social revolution (Mongolia in 1924 and Cuba in 1959) or a national liberation war (North Vietnam in 1954, unified Vietnam in 1975); (b) all hold strategic geographic positions (Mongolia as a buffer state between China and the USSR; Cuba as a far outpost near the United States; Vietnam at the heart of Southeast Asia, bordering China); and (c) entry into the CMEA by the two last members (Cuba and Vietnam) was probably pushed by the USSR for political reasons, as a seal to an already established exclusive relationship when other economic partners were excluded (the West in the case of Cuba after the US embargo; China and in part the West, in the case of Vietnam after the start of the Cambodian war). Political factors were certainly decisive in the establishment of Soviet relations with these countries and are still significant. However, we must not forget that these political relations were accompanied by economic ties from the beginning in the case of Cuba (the "sugar for oil" barter), and more gradually in the other cases. These new relations, which were clearly costly for the Soviet Union at first, have yielded increasing returns over time, especially after the European members began to restructure intra-CMEA policy. Non-quantifiable political returns and current economic advantages should also be taken into consideration in creating a general balance sheet.

THE INCREASING POLARIZATION OF TRADE TOWARDS THE USSR

The establishment of political and economic relations between the USSR and the three countries meant a dramatic reorientation of trade away from previous partners towards the Soviet Union, which soon became their primary trade partner. In what way has the entry into the CMEA modified this situation? To answer this question our analysis will focus on the last fifteen years, which are the most important period for the history of the organization, since it began with the so-called Complex Program (1971), which set the way for further integration among member countries.[2]

The main features of the impact of CMEA membership for the three countries have included an increase in trade with the USSR and a decrease in the relative importance of trade with Eastern Europe, the industrialized West and other developing countries. First, there was a dramatic increase in the USSR's share of the three countries' total trade. In the case of Mongolia it was already higher than 80 per cent at the end of the 1960s and reached nearly 90 per cent in 1983. If the share of Eastern Europe is added to this, then more than 98 per cent of Mongolian goods are traded inside the CMEA (see Table 8.1).

The Soviet share in Cuban exports seems to followed a similar path, although at a lower level of trade concentration; from roughly half the total in 1970 to 72 per cent in 1984. The most dramatic jump occurred in the early 1970s, when Cuba joined the CMEA, and again in the 1980s, probably as a result of increasing difficulties on the world sugar market and of new economic agreements with the USSR. The Soviet share of

Table 8.1 *Geographic distribution of foreign trade of Mongolia, Cuba and Vietnam* (in % of total turnover)

Years	USSR		Eastern Europe		Other socialist economies		Industrial countries		Developing countries	
	Exports	Imports	Exports	Imports	Exports	Imports	Exports	Imports	Exports	Imports
Cuba:										
1970	50.4	52.7	14.2	9.5	9.5	6.0	15.4	29.3	10.5	1.7
1975	56.3	40.2	7.8	8.1	3.7	2.3	23.5	38.9	8.6	10.5
1980	56.8	62.2	10.2	12.9	2.9	2.6	17.9	17.8	12.0	4.5
1984	72.1	66.3	13.4	13.8	4.1	4.0	5.2	11.2	5.2	4.7
Mongolia:										
1970	81.8		17.3					1.0		—
1975	84.6		13.0					0.8		1.7
1980	86.8		10.8					1.5		0.8
1983	89.2		9.2					1.1		0.5
Vietnam:										
1975	20.2		14.3				39.8		25.7	
1980	42.4		20.9				23.5		13.2	
1983	63.2		11.8				12.3		12.7	

Note: A breakdown of exports and imports is not available for Mongolia and Vietnam.

Sources: Date for Cuba were calculated from *Anuario Estadistico de Cuba*, various years, and IMF, *Direction of Trade Statistics, Yearbook*, 1985.
Data for Mongolia were calculated from mirror data published in UN, *Monthly Bulletin of Statistics*, various years; IMF, *Direction of Trade Statistics, Yearbook*, various years; *Statistiches Jahrbuch der DDR*, 1984.
Data for Vietnam were calculated from mirror data published in: UN, *Monthly Bulletin of Statistics*, July 1985; IMF, *Direction of Trade Statistics, Yearbook*, 1982 and 1985; *Statistiches Jahrbuch der DDR*, 1984.

Table 8.2 *Share of individual European CMEA countries in non-European members' trade with CMEA, 1983*
(in % of total turnover)

	Mongolia	Cuba	Vietnam
USSR	90.7	81.8	84.3
Bulgaria	1.1	4.2	1.2
Czechoslovakia	2.9	3.2	4.1
GDR	2.9	7.1	6.7
Hungary	0.5	0.8	1.2
Poland	0.8	0.8	2.0
Romania	1.2	2.2	0.6

Sources: Calculated from UN, *Monthly Bulletin of Statistics*, July 1985; *Anuario Estadistico de Cuba*, 1984; *Statistiches Jahrbuch der DDR*, 1984.

Cuban imports showed a slight decrease around the middle of the 1970s, but a swift pick up in the 1980s (66 per cent in 1984). If one adds the share of Eastern Europe, in 1984 almost 83 per cent of Cuban trade is directed towards the European members of the CMEA.

The progression was even faster in the case of Vietnam. In 1975 the United States was still its main trading partner, with the Soviet Union coming second with a mere 20 per cent of Vietnamese trade. After joining the CMEA in 1978 and signing a fundamental Treaty of Friendship and Cooperation with the USSR that same year, the Soviet share of total Vietnamese turnover jumped to 42 per cent in 1980 and to 63 per cent in 1983. Adding the share of Eastern Europe, three quarters of Vietnamese commodities are traded inside the CMEA.

The same polarization of trade towards the USSR shown above on a world level occurs also within the CMEA. The CMEA countries which trade most with the USSR are Mongolia (91 per cent), Vietnam (84 per cent) and Cuba (82 per cent) (see table 8.2).

Briefly, the Soviet Union takes an enormous percentage of the trade of the CMEA developing countries. For each of them, the USSR is its main trade partner. Conversely, in 1984, their shares in Soviet trade turnover were the following: Cuba, just above 5.2 per cent (ranked seventh among Soviet trade partners); Mongolia, 1 per cent; and Vietnam, 0.9 per cent.[3]

On the other hand, the relative importance of Eastern Europe in the trade of the three communist less developed countries (LDCs) diminished over the period. This trend is very clear for Mongolia, where trade with Eastern Europe was only 9 per cent of total trade turnover in 1983, but more erratic in the case of Vietnam. In the case of Cuba, after an initial loss, the share of Eastern Europe became important again in the 1980s, when it reached almost 14 per cent. Cuba and Vietnam seem to be more interested than Mongolia in trading with Eastern Europe. All three of these countries tend to trade more with the most advanced members of the CMEA; for example, the GDR is one of the major trading partners of both Cuba and Vietnam (see table 8.3).

A third development in the trade of the three communist LDCs has been a sharp reduction in the share of the industrial countries. Apart from Mongolia, for which trade with the West has always been negligible (1 to 2 per cent), the industrial countries have traditionally been important trade partners both for Cuba and Vietnam. However, after an increase in trade in the early 1970s, their share in Cuban trade plummeted to roughly 8 per cent in 1984 (from 30–35 per cent in the 1970s). In the case of Vietnam trade fell steadily to 12 per cent in 1983. Some industrial countries stand out. Japan is among the ten top partners of Cuba and of Vietnam, for which it ranks second. Hundreds of Japanese businessmen visit Hanoi every year in an attempt to expand Japanese economic involvement in the region.

In addition, trade of the three communist developing countries with the Third World has decreased. While trade with the Third World was negligible for Mongolia, the LDCs' share in Cuban trade increased up to 1975, but fell in the 1980s (to 4 per cent in 1984). The Cuban choice of trade partners seems to be based on political grounds (China and Algeria), but also on economic motives (the importation of grain from Argentina in 1983). The downward trend in trade with LDCs was even more pronounced in the case of Vietnam, where the share still remains important (13 per cent). Vietnam is relatively more open to the Third World countries (three of them figure in its top ten partners). Apart from India, substantial trade is carried out with Hong Kong and Singapore. In fact, the registered trade might very well be only the tip of an iceberg composed of counter-trade and, as is well-known, of clandestine trade. Moreover, the major part of Vietnamese trade in Southeast Asia is carried out through these free ports, where the destination and origin of the goods traded is often "adjusted." Ties with Singapore are even closer, since many Singapore businessmen act as intermediaries for Vietnamese trade with third countries.

THE SOVIET PATTERN OF EXPORTS

Are these trends in the direction of trade bound to last? We can only attempt to answer this question after examining the commodity composition of the trade of the three CMEA developing countries. A

Table 8.3 *The top ten trade partners of Cuba and Vietnam, 1983 (Ranked in order of importance according to the value of trade in millions of US dollars).*

Cuba				Vietnam			
Exports		Imports		Exports		Imports	
USSR	3,628	USSR	4,574	USSR	316	USSR	1,216
GDR	(711)	GDR	(711)	Hong Kong	64	Japan	131
China	202	Canada	324	GDR	(121)	GDR	(121)
Bulgaria	194	Bulgaria	223	Japan	35	India	74
Czechoslovakia	123	Czechoslovakia	195	Czechoslovakia	34	Hong Kong	61
Spain	85	Argentina	141	Singapore	30	Singapore	50
Japan	84	Rumania	140	Poland	19	Czechoslovakia	40
Netherlands	82	Japan	115	Bulgaria	13	France	36
Rumania	80	France	111	Hungary	10	USA	23
Algeria	68	China	107	Malaysia	8	Poland	17

Note: Data for the GDR refer to total trade. They are calculated by converting into US dollars the values in valuta-marks published in *Statistiches Jahrbuch der DDR, 1984.*

Sources: IMF, *Direction of Trade Statistics, Yearbook, 1985;* UN, *Monthly Bulletin of Statistics,* July 1985.

first glance at the trade structure of the Soviet Union with these countries reveals a striking similarity to its commercial relations with Third World countries.[4] The USSR exports mostly machinery and equipment, plus petroleum and petroleum products, in return for mineral raw materials, foodstuffs and agricultural products, handicraft and light consumer goods (see Table 8.4). The second remarkable feature is that the trade structure of the CMEA LDCs is more diversified with the rest of the world than with the USSR. But other interesting trends can be seen in a country by country analysis.

The Soviet export structure shows two relevant contrasting trends over the last fifteen years. The category of machinery and equipment, which was by far the most important item in 1970, lost ground in favor of petroleum products and remains in the lead only with Mongolia, where it still represents 60 per cent of Soviet exports. For Cuba and Vietnam it represents less than one-third of total Soviet exports, 27 per cent and 32 per cent, respectively. It is also interesting to note that, leaving aside military goods, the machinery and equipment imported is meant to expand the production of exports within the CMEA. So, in the case of Mongolia and Cuba one finds mainly mining and drilling equipment, infrastructure and agricultural machinery, while Vietnam also receives a good deal of equipment for its light industrial sector.

Raw materials and intermediate products have become the most dynamic components of Soviet exports, particularly in the 1980s. But this results almost entirely from the export of petroleum and derived products. They alone account today for 15 per cent of Soviet exports to Mongolia (mainly refined products) and have reached the astonishing levels of 36 per cent and 38 per cent respectively in the case of Cuba and Vietnam. Mongolia and Cuba are completely dependent on Soviet oil, while Vietnam receives some supplies from other sources. Not all the petroleum which appears in Soviet statistics for trade with Cuba is really produced in the USSR. The Soviet Union has chosen closer partners for Cuba, in order to reduce its transport costs. Under a swap agreement with Venezuela and Spain, the former supplies oil to Cuba, while the Soviet Union delivers an equal amount to Spain. A similar arrangement is under discussion with Ecuador. Finally, under a triangular agreement with Mexico, the USSR pays for the Mexican oil delivered to Cuba in hard currency. These supplies are inserted into Soviet trade statistics with Cuba, since they originate from a bilateral agreement.

Will the share of oil continue to rise? Cuban domestic production is increasing, but for the moment it provides for only 5 per cent of consumption. Estimates for the near future predict an increase of

Table 8.4 Commodity composition of Soviet trade with Cuba, Mongolia and Vietnam (%)

	Machinery, equipment, means of transport (10–19)		Raw materials intermediate products (2–5)		Of which: petroleum and petroleum products (21+22)		Foodstuffs and agricultural products (6+7+8)		Of which: raw sugar		Consumer goods (9)		Residual	
	X	I	X	I	X	I	X	I	X	I	X	I	X	I
Cuba:														
1970	35.4		34.0	19.4	(11.9)		17.2	80.4		(78.3)	3.6	0.1	9.8	0.1
1975	24.3		40.0	5.2	(21.7)		19.0	94.7		(92.8)	4.5	0.1	12.2	0.1
1980	32.4		40.5	4.1	(26.7)		11.1	95.6		(93.9)	4.3	0.1	11.7	0.2
1984	27.4	negl	49.1	4.8	(35.3)		8.4	94.6		(92.6)	3.8	0.1	11.3	0.5
Mongolia:														
1970	54.9		15.5	58.7	(6.2)		11.4	33.5			14.9	4.8	3.3	3.0
1975	62.4	0.2	8.9	34.2	(3.7)		6.0	56.2			14.9	4.0	7.8	5.4
1980	65.1	0.1	15.8	31.9	(9.8)		4.4	38.3			7.2	5.8	7.5	23.8
1984	60.1	0.2	21.9	60.9	(15.5)		3.6	22.9			8.1	10.6	6.3	5.4
Vietnam:														
1970	42.8		22.3	5.1	(7.4)		22.4	31.4			7.9	59.2	4.6	4.3
1975	42.8		28.9	1.0	(9.0)		11.0	12.7			5.8	82.4	11.5	3.9
1980	47.3		19.6	12.1	(8.4)		16.4	11.8			3.6	57.9	13.1	18.2
1984	32.1		57.0	18.0	(37.9)		1.2	28.4			1.4	39.1	8.3	14.5

Note: X = export. I = import.
Source: Calculated from *Vneshniaia Torgovlia SSSR v . . . g.,* various years.

production to 7–10 per cent of consumption. As for Vietnam, discoveries on the continental shelf in the south have been negligible, although the Soviet Union has committed substantial resources to exploration for petroleum through the jointly established enterprise Vietsovpetro. Finally, Mongolia produces no oil, although intensive exploration is being undertaken. As a consequence, the demand for petroleum by the CMEA LDCs will remain high. But problems will almost certainly occur on the supply side. Because of the well-known difficulties it encounters in oil production, the Soviet Union is tightening up its terms on energy trade with all CMEA members. In 1985 it reduced the quantity sold to them and announced that future supplies would not exceed the 1985 level. Since intra-CMEA prices have begun to incorporate the price cuts experienced on the world market in recent years, we can expect the total value of Soviet oil exports to have reached a ceiling. Thus, petroleum will likely comprise a declining share of the value of total Soviet exports to the CMEA in the near future.

Another trend can be seen in the Soviet export structure: the diminishing importance of foodstuffs and agricultural products (revealing the crisis of Soviet agriculture) and of consumer goods. By comparison, these two categories, as well as machinery and equipment in the case of Cuba, loom much larger in Cuban and Vietnamese imports from the rest of the world.

Finally, we should not forget that roughly 10 per cent of Soviet exports to Cuba and Vietnam, and slightly less in the case of Mongolia, are unidentified by type of commodity and constitute the so-called "residual" in Soviet statistics. The widespread hypothesis that military goods may explain a large portion of them seems plausible, especially for Cuba and Vietnam.

MONGOLIAN RAW MATERIAL EXPORTS

One category stands out in Mongolian exports to the USSR, namely raw materials, which comprised 61 per cent of total exports in 1984 (see Table 8.4). Of these, the largest share is accounted for by metal ores and concentrates (40 per cent as calculated from *Vneshniaia Torgovlia* for 1984), mainly copper and molybdenum. This large yearly flow of resources comes from the Erdenet copper–molybdenum mining and ore dressing complex, founded and run jointly with the USSR. The complex reached full production at the end of 1983. The deposit is estimated to be endowed with half of the total copper reserves in Asia. Another joint enterprise, Mongolsovtsetmet, controls the production of fluorite (particularly important for the steel industry) and gold. The

Soviet Union receives these products in repayment for its credits and investments. The European members of the CMEA show great interest in Mongolian raw materials. With the USSR setting an example, Bulgaria and Czechoslovakia have followed with two other joint enterprises for the extraction of minerals.[5] One striking feature seems to characterize all of these experiences: the mineral concentrates are sold to the European member countries, which process them to obtain the pure metals. Furthermore, Mongolia sells fluorspar and tungsten to the USSR which has become a net importer of both minerals.[6]

Joint action for the exploration and extraction of raw materials in Mongolia has always received much attention from CMEA policy makers. The Agreed Plan for Multilateral Integration Measures for 1976–80 and for 1981–85 have provided for exploration and construction on its soil. The Long Term Specific Programs since 1975 provided for the enlargement and exploitation of the phosphorite deposits. The October 1984 session of CMEA, which approved long-term comprehensive measures in the sphere of raw materials, scheduled the further opening up of nonferrous metal deposits and of phosphorite.[7]

Other primary commodities which rank high in Mongolian exports are wool (9 per cent of Soviet import needs) lumber, hides and skins. Then come foodstuffs and agricultural products (23 per cent), mainly meat, dairy products and livestock for slaughter. And finally there is a growing category of light consumer goods (carpets, leather clothes, knitwear). Here, too, integration into the CMEA meant increased business because the CMEA commission for light industry is promoting the construction of new capacities for the processing of wool and raw materials of animal origin.[8]

CUBA'S SUGAR RELATIONS AND BEYOND

Cuban exports have always been and still are dominated by sugar. With 8 per cent of world production (12 per cent of world cane sugar production) and 24 per cent of world sugar exports, Cuba is among the leading producers and the largest exporter of sugar.[9]

The US embargo of Cuba meant a dramatic reorientation of sugar exports away from the traditional American outlet toward the CMEA market. The latter, which in 1958 accounted for a mere 4 per cent of Cuban exports (calculated on volume), had already reached 59 per cent in 1961, with the USSR taking the lion's share (51 per cent). From 1961 to 1975 the CMEA market never accounted for less than 43 per cent of Cuban exports and since 1975 for never less than 55 per cent (see Table 8.5). The Soviet share has varied considerably over the period. Until

Table 8.5 *Cuban exports of sugar.* (%)

Year	(1) Exports of sugar/ Production of sugar	(2) Exports of sugar/ Total exports	(3) Exports of sugar to the USSR/ Total exports to the USSR	(4) Exports of sugar to the USSR/ Exports of sugar to the world	(5) Exports of sugar to CMEA/ Exports of sugar to the world	(6) Exports of sugar to the free market/ Exports of sugar to the world
1960	96.1	79.1	99.9	28.0	33.2	
1965	87.4	85.5	88.7	46.2	57.0	
1970	91.4	75.1	78.3	45.0	58.7	30.5
1975	89.4	89.0	92.8	55.5	64.3	28.8
1980	91.0	82.7	93.9	44.0	55.9	35.4
1983	91.0	73.7	89.4	48.8	64.3	24.8

Sources: (1) (4) (5) and (6) calculated from data in volume published by the *Sugar Year Book*, various years; (2) calculated from data published by the *Anuario Estadístico de Cuba*, various years; (3) calculated from mirror data published by *Vneshniaia Torgovlia v . . . g.*, various years.

1967 it was always over 40 per cent. Between the end of the 1960s and 1974 this quota fell, while the amount sold on the free market within the framework of the International Sugar Agreement rose. This same contrasting trend seems to have continued over the last ten years, when the Soviet share was higher than 50 per cent for all but three years.

Table 8.5 shows unequivocally that the percentage of Cuban sugar exports to the USSR has always been comparatively greater than the share of sugar exports to the world. This extreme dependency on sugar is very similar to and in some years more pronounced than that experienced previously with the United States as its major client.[10]

Cuba's sugar relations with the European CMEA countries have often been presented as being advantageous only to the exporter which could enjoy a stable outlet and preferential prices well above the world market prices. The most common argument, accepted by many Western and probably Soviet and East European scholars, is the following: the difference between the higher price paid by CMEA members and the lower prices prevailing on the free market multiplied by the quantity sold would give us the amount of subsidy enjoyed by the Cuban economy. In fact, this is integrated into the calculations of Soviet aid to Cuba.[11] However, this procedure raises some questions. How can we compare the reported unit values in a nonconvertible currency to a price in hard currency? Only a negligible share of sugar imports is paid for by the USSR in convertible currencies (not even 1 per cent in 1983). Sugar is then exchanged against a basket of commodities, the price and the quality of which are not easily comparable to world standards (particularly in the case of Soviet equipment). Cuba's past behavior on the international market seems to confirm that these high prices do not matter so much. Whenever possible it has preferred the free market, even in periods of falling prices. It was the Soviet Union that recently stiffened its attitude by requiring that Cuba respect its contractual obligations and even obliging it to buy some sugar on the free market in 1983–84 to fulfill its commitments toward its largest client.

This brings us to the second argument against the "exclusive Cuban advantage" thesis. Cuban sugar is very important to satisfy Soviet as well as Bulgarian, East German and Romanian consumption. All these countries, which produce beet sugar, are no longer self-sufficient in sugar and have had to resort to imports. In fact, Cuban exports cover growing Soviet import needs less and less. Beginning in 1978 the share of sugar imports from Cuba with respect to Soviet global imports of sugar has dropped from a peak of 94 per cent to a low of 55 per cent in 1983.[12]

It should not be forgotten that Cuban sugar is traditionally reexported in various quantities after being refined by the European CMEA

Table 8.6 *Share of CMEA LDCs in Soviet imports of selected commodities,*
1984

Commodity	Country of origin	Share in Soviet imports
Non-metallic minerals, clays and earths	Mongolia	11.7
Natural rubber	Vietnam	8.4
Jute	Vietnam	7.4
Wool	Mongolia	9.3
Raw hides and skins from small cattle	Mongolia	100.0
Coffee	Vietnam	6.7
Tea	Vietnam	4.9
Raw sugar	Cuba	70.6
Fruits (fresh)	Cuba	13.1
	Vietnam	1.3
of which:		
Oranges	Cuba	27.4
Cigarettes	Cuba	0.5
	Vietnam	11.9
Coats (except leather and fur), underwear	Vietnam	2.3

Source: Calculated from *Vneshniaia Torgovlia SSSR v 1984 g.*

countries. This has been the case not only for net exporters like Poland or
Czechoslovakia, but also for net importers, i.e., all the other countries,
except Hungary in the 1980s. Finally, a Soviet journal indicates a further
advantage for the Soviet economy: Cuban deliveries in the first semester
of the year help utilize more fully Soviet sugar factories' productive
capacities in a period when sugar beets are not processed.[13]

The importance of sugar in Cuban exports should not overshadow
two current trends occurring in the Cuban export structure. The first
concerns fresh fruit. Cuba already supplies 13 per cent of Soviet import
needs (27 per cent in the case of oranges, see Table 8.6). Under a general
agreement on citrus fruit signed in 1981, the CMEA countries, with the
exception of Hungary and Romania, set up the largest agro-industrial
program in the region.[14] Cuba was assigned the role of producing and
processing citrus fruit, while most of the equipment and credits came
from the more developed members of the CMEA.

Nickel is the other export item on which Cuba and its CMEA
partners alike are expending increasing efforts. One of the world's
leading nickel producers, Cuba reportedly has reserves totalling 19
million tons of ore. Half of the production is sold to the USSR which is
self-sufficient, but can divert a corresponding amount of its production

to exports. Some other CMEA members, however, meet in this way 85 per cent of their demand.[15] In 1986 a new Soviet assisted nickel-mining facility at Punta Gorda was scheduled to begin producing nickel oxide and cobalt (30,000 tons a year), while a second complex being built at Las Camariocas with the help of all European CMEA members will produce an equal amount of nickel–cobalt concentrate.

Lastly, the Cuban export structure contains an item that Soviet statistics neglect. Since 1978 Cuba reexported some petroleum products for convertible currencies: in 1982, it was the second largest export item after sugar, according to Cuban statistics.

VIETNAMESE EXPORTS: A SEARCH FOR FURTHER DIVERSIFICATION

Of the three Communist LDCs, Vietnam's export structure seems to be the most diversified. Handicrafts, a traditional export item, take the lead: coats, underwear, knitwear, carpets, cane and bamboo articles are the core of this important category, although its share in Soviet imports has dropped in the 1980s. The textile industry, sporting goods and wood-working articles are earmarked for special development by the CMEA light industry commission.

Unlike handicrafts, exports of agricultural products and foodstuffs, a second important category, are increasing rapidly. Tropical fruits and vegetables are at the top of the list of the exports to the USSR. A long-term target program signed in October 1983 forecasts that the amount sold by Vietnam in the period 1981–85 will increase six-fold between 1986–90.[16] The Soviet "Food Program" and the needs of the Soviet Far Eastern regions may be at the root of Soviet interest in this agreement.[17] Coffee, tea, liqueurs and spirits, and fishery commodities complete the list of the major articles exported within this category.

Raw materials and intermediate products are of growing importance in Vietnamese exports: coal (mostly to the West), natural rubber (8 per cent of Soviet import needs), jute (7 per cent), wood flooring, and cotton fabrics. But the time may not be too far off when mineral resources will be exported in greater quantities. Some fifty minerals are said to be present under Vietnamese soil and its continental shelf. Meanwhile, exploration goes on in cooperation with the other CMEA members. The opening up of nonferrous metal deposits and of bauxite ores are scheduled in the near future.

THE CMEA CALL FOR SPECIALIZATION: A NEW
INTERNATIONAL DIVISION OF LABOR?

We cannot calculate the exact degree of Soviet subsidization of the CMEA developing countries. Moreover, the exaggerated emphasis on this aspect may conceal some other relevant issues. It may very well be that the disadvantage for the dominant economy does not result so much from the "opportunity costs" involved in these relations, but rather from the chronic imbalances in foreign trade. Mongolia and Vietnam have always shown a deficit in their balance of trade with the Soviet Union, while Cuba has had a surplus in only seven out of twenty-six years. The cumulative deficits with the USSR are as follows: Mongolia, 1960–84: 6.2 billion foreign-trade rubles (roughly equivalent to $8.2 billion); Cuba, 1959–84: 4.2 billion rubles ($5.6 billion); and Vietnam, 1975–84: 4.0 billion rubles ($5.1 billion).[18] Mongolia and Cuba incurred more than half of their total deficit during the last five years, while three-quarters of Vietnams's deficit was generated during the same period. In 1984 the sum of their deficits with the USSR was 46 per cent of the deficit of CMEA countries and 49 per cent of the deficit of all the developing countries.

As is well known, these deficits involve automatic credits from the surplus country that will eventually be repaid through an adequate amount of goods. To this we should also add the development credits granted by various CMEA countries. When the three CMEA LDCs will be able to repay Soviet and East European credits remains an open question, especially since their debts in convertible currencies towards the West amount to $1.5 billion in the case of Vietnam and $3 billion in the case of Cuba (a situation which has already obliged Vietnam to introduce a recent massive devaluation of the dong).

Although the goods which the Soviet Union receives in exchange from the three LDCs are very limited in quantity, they are nevertheless valuable for its economy. Tropical products and other agricultural products either cannot be grown because of climatic conditions or are not produced in sufficient quantities. Foodstuffs are particularly welcome in the crisis-ridden Soviet agricultural markets.

The other axis on which CMEA integration seems to turn is the development of raw materials for the growing needs of the European members.[19] Moreover, in the socialist international division of labor the LDCs seem to be confined to the first stage of production, leaving the processing and the end products to the more developed countries. Mongolian copper and Cuban nickel are typical example. A third trend which arises from our analysis is the growing Soviet and East European insistence on expanding the production of industrial consumer goods. Their production within the CMEA is seen as a cheaper alternative to buying them on the world market.

In conclusion, we could say that the "CMEA effect," with its cooperative agreements, multilateral schemes, target programs, enforced through the special sections inserted into the national plans, engenders the relative specialization of the different LDCs according to their own resource endowments, whether they are primary commodities or traditional light industrial sectors utilizing local raw materials. These sectors could even show a certain diversification among individual products exported within the same categories.

By comparison, the examples of industrial specialization are too scattered to speak of a trend. However, such examples do exist: Cuban specialization in the manufacturing of microcomputers of the third generation within a multilateral agreement signed in 1980; the Mongolian production of spare parts for Soviet motor vehicles; and the assembly in Vietnam of components for the Czechoslovak electronic industry. All in all, the structure of trade which emerges is essentially one of capital intensive products (Soviet exports), exchanged against relatively high labor-intensive and/or non-energy products (Soviet imports), which is not very different from what we experience in North–South relations.

A final question concerns the degree to which these CMEA LDCs can maintain the current high level of integration within the CMEA. Trade concentration on CMEA partners has probably hit a ceiling, especially in the case of Cuba and Vietnam. Both of these countries are trying to reorient some of their trade toward the West. They feel the need for high technology equipment to run the existing facilities and the pressure to service their debts in convertible currencies. But this by itself may not necessarily mean a change in the overall pattern of trade.

NOTES

1 Peter Wiles, ed., *The New Communist Third World* (London: Croom Helm, 1982).
2 Giovanni Graziani, *Comecon, domination et dépendances* (Paris: Maspero, 1982).
3 Calculated from *Vneshniaia Torgovlia SSSR v 1984 g.*
4 Giovanni Graziani, "Commercial Relations Between Developing Countries and the USSR," paper presented to the first annual scienfic meeting of AISSEC (Associazione Italiana per lo Studio dei Sistemi Economici Comparati), Turin, 25–26 October 1984 (to be published in *Cambridge Journal of Economics*).
5 Giovanni Graziani, "Des multinationales à l'Est?," *Revue d'Economie Industrielle*, no. 28 (1984).

6 *Mining Annual Review*, 1984.

7 *Pravda*, 2 November 1984.

8 Pavel Bagudin, "The CMEA Countries' Coordinated Plan for Multilateral Integration Measures for 1981–1985: Its Implementation and Connection with Mutual Trade," *Foreign Trade*, no. 1 (1983).

9 *Sugar Year Book*, 1983.

10 Carmelo Mesa-Lago, *The Economy of Socialist Cuba: A Two-Decade Appraisal* (Albuquerque: University of New Mexico Press, 1981).

11 Lawrence H. Theriot and JeNelle Matheson, "Soviet Economic Relations with Non-European CMEA: Cuba, Vietnam, and Mongolia," in US Congress, Joint Economic Committee, *Soviet Economy in a Time of Change*, vol. II (Washington, DC: US Government Printing Office, 1979).

12 Calculated from *Sugar Year Book*.

13 *Foreign Trade*, no. 7 (1984).

14 Giovanni Graziani, "Les Mouvements de capital au sein du CMEA," *Economies et Sociétés*, Cahiers de l'ISMEA, series G, no. 40 (1984).

15 TASS, 15 August 1984.

16 *Foreign Trade*, no. 8 (1985).

17 Adam Fforde, *Economic Aspects of the Soviet–Vietnamese Relationship: Their Role and Importance*, Birbeck College Discussion Paper, no. 156 (1984).

18 Calculated from *Vneshniaia Torgovlia v . . . g . . .* various years.

19 Horst Brezinski, "Economic Relations Between European and the Less-Developed CMEA Countries," in US Congress, Joint Economic Committee, *East European Economies: Slow Growth in the 1980s* (Washington: US Government Printing Office, 1986), vol. II.

PART 3

The Soviet Union in the Middle East
and South Asia

9

Soviet policy toward Syria in the Andropov era

ROBERT O. FREEDMAN

The relationship between the Soviet Union and Syria in the Andropov era (November 1982–February 1984) provides a fascinating case study of the limits of a superpower's influence on a client state, particularly when that client becomes the only lever of influence a superpower has in a region deemed of great importance by the superpower's leadership. In order to analyze the Soviet–Syrian relationship, however, it is first necessary to deal with the goals of both the Soviet Union and Syria, and to determine to what degree the assistance each can offer the other is critical to the accomplishment of each country's goals.

As far as the question of Soviet goals in the Middle East is concerned, there are two major schools of thought.[1] While both agree that the Soviet Union wants to be considered as a major factor in Middle Eastern affairs, if only because of the USSR's propinquity to the region, they differ on the ultimate Soviet goal in the Middle East. One school of thought sees Soviet Middle Eastern policy as primarily defensive in nature; that is, directed toward preventing the region from being used as a base for military attack or political subversion against the USSR. The other school of thought sees Soviet policy as primarily offensive in nature, aimed at the limitation and ultimate exclusion of Western influence from the region and its replacement by Soviet influence. It is the opinion of the author that Soviet goals in the Middle East, at least since the mid-1960s, have been primarily offensive in nature; and in the Arab segment of the Middle East, the Soviet Union appears to have been engaged in a zero-sum game competition for influence with the United States.

Moscow, however, has run into serious problems in its quest for influence in the Middle East. The numerous inter-Arab and regional conflicts (Syria–Iraq, North Yemen–South Yemen, Ethiopia–Somalia, Algeria–Morocco, Iran–Iraq, etc.) have usually meant that, when the USSR has favored one party, it has alienated the other, often driving it over to the West. Secondly, the existence of Middle Eastern communist parties has proven to be a handicap for the USSR, as communist activities have, on occasion, caused a sharp deterioration in relations between Moscow and the country in which the communist party has operated. The communist-supported *coup d'état* in Sudan in 1971, communist efforts to organize cells in the Iraqi army in the mid and late 1970s, and the activities of the Tudeh party in Khomeini's Iran are recent examples of this problem. Third, the wealth which flowed to the Arab world (or at least to its major oil producers) since the quadrupling of oil prices in late 1973 enabled the Arabs to buy quality technology from the West and Japan and, thus, helped weaken the economic bond between the USSR and such Arab states as Iraq. Fourth, since 1967 and particularly since the 1973 Arab–Israeli war, Islam has been resurgent throughout the Arab world. The USSR, identified in the Arab world with atheism, has been hampered as a result, particularly since the Soviet invasion of Afghanistan in 1979 where Moscow has been fighting against an essentially Islamic resistance force. Fifth, in the diplomacy surrounding the Arab–Israeli conflict, Moscow is hampered by its lack of diplomatic ties with Israel, a factor which enables the United States alone to talk to both sides of the conflict. Finally, the United States, and to a lesser extent, China and France, have actively opposed Soviet efforts to achieve predominant influence in the region and this has frequently enabled Middle Eastern states to play the extra-regional powers off against each other and thereby prevent any one of them from securing predominant influence.

To overcome these difficulties, Moscow has evolved one overall strategy – the development of an "anti-imperialist" bloc of states in the Arab world. In Moscow's view these states should bury their internecine rivalries, and join together, along with such political organizations as the Arab communist parties and the Palestine Liberation Organization, in a united front against what the USSR has called the "linchpin" of Western imperialism in the Middle East–Israel. Under such circumstances, it is the Soviet hope that the Arab states would then use their collective pressure against Israel's supporters, especially the United States.[2] The ideal scenario for Moscow, and one which Soviet commentators have frequently referred to, was the situation during the 1973 Arab–Israeli war when virtually all the Arab states supported the war effort against Israel, while also imposing an oil embargo against the United States. Not only did the oil embargo create domestic difficulties for the United States, it caused serious problems in the NATO alliance, a development warmly welcomed by Moscow. Unfortunately for the USSR, however, this "anti-imperialist" Arab unit was created not by

Soviet efforts, but by the diplomacy of Egyptian President Anwar Sadat; when Sadat changed his policies and turned toward the United States, the "anti-imperialist" Arab unity sought by the USSR fell apart. Nonetheless, so long as Soviet leaders think in terms of such Leninist categories as "united fronts" ("anti-imperialist" Arab unity, in Soviet parlance, is merely another way of describing a united front of Arab governmental and non-governmental forces) and so long as there is a deep underlying psychological drive for unity in the Arab world, Moscow can be expected to continue to pursue this overall strategy as a long-term goal.

While Moscow has sought to rally the Arab world into an "anti-imperialist" front against the West, Syria's goals are exclusively regional. Syrian objectives since the rise to power of Hafiz Assad in November 1970, seem to be five-fold: (1) the maintenance of the minority Alawite regime in power in the face of domestic and foreign enemies; (2) the acquisition of sufficient military equipment to enable Syria to regain the Golan Heights from Israel militarily or by diplomatic means from "a position of strength"; (3) the acquisition of the position of dominant external force in Lebanon which has very close cultural, political, economic and religious ties to Syria; (4) the establishment of sufficient control over the PLO to prevent it from acting independently in such a way as to jeopardize Syrian interests; and (5) the acquisition of a position of leadership in the Arab world, and in particular in Syria's immediate region (Jordan and Lebanon), in part to reinforce the Assad regime's domestic legitimacy and in part to maintain a credible "eastern front" against Israel, thereby also justifying economic assistance from the oil-rich Arab states.[3]

In order to succeed in these aims Syria needs assistance from the Soviet Union, primarily in the form of military equipment. Moscow could also provide support in the form of political/military action to deter the United States, or a US-backed Israel, from taking actions inimical to Syria, and could provide diplomatic assistance to Syria at the United Nations and, to a lesser extent, in Arab forums. For its part Moscow saw Syria as an ally in its competition for influence with the United States in the Middle East, as a leader of the "anti-imperialist" bloc of Arab states Moscow was hoping to form, and as the source of air and naval bases.[4] Yet, in its deliberations about the degree of aid to give Syria, the Soviet leadership had to be concerned about the risks involved in aiding the regime of Hafiz Assad. In the first place, throughout this period the USSR cultivated its own relationship with both the PLO, which it wanted to form an independent state on the West Bank and Gaza, and with Jordan, which Moscow wished to pull away from the United

States. Syrian efforts at controlling the PLO and Jordan had the potential of working at crosspurposes with Soviet goals in the Middle East. Secondly, Moscow had no desire to become involved in a military conflict with the United States that could escalate into a nuclear confrontation in support of Syria's regional goals. Moscow's concern with the possible dangers of too close an identification with Syria were reflected in the Soviet–Syrian Treaty of Friendship and Cooperation which was signed in October 1980. Thus, the treaty itself was a fairly standard Soviet Friendship and Cooperation treaty, unique only in its denunciation of "Zionism as a form of racism" both in the preamble and in article 3.[5] Moscow, perhaps to maintain Syria's independent image, stated that it would "respect the policy of non-alignment pursued by Syria."[6] As far as military cooperation was concerned, article 10 of the treaty merely stated that, "the parties shall continue to develop cooperation in the military field on the basis of appropriate agreements concluded between them in the interest of strengthening their defense capacity." As in other treaties, both sides promised to consult regularly and to consult immediately in the case of situations jeopardizing the peace and security of one of the parties, although the Soviet–Syrian treaty, perhaps because of Soviet concerns about Assad's tendency to create *faits accomplis*, went a bit farther by adding the phrase "with a view to coordinating their positions and to cooperation in order to remove the threat that had arisen."

Signed in 1980, the treaty had its first major test less than two years later when Israeli forces invaded Lebanon and, in the process, clashed with Syrian troops occupying large sections of the country. Soviet inactivity during the period from the Israeli invasion of Lebanon until the exodus of the PLO from Beirut in August 1982 need only be summarized here.[7] Suffice it to say that, despite the fact that Israel shot down eighty-five Syrian planes and destroyed the Syrian SAM bases established in Lebanon in 1981, contrary to its behavior during the Yom Kippur war of 1973, Moscow provided no military help during the course of the fighting. Its verbal warnings to Israel and to the United States were only of a very general nature – and very ineffectual – until the announcement of the possible deployment of US troops to Beirut. Even then, Brezhnev quickly backed down from his warning after it became clear that the United States was going ahead with the deployment. While Moscow did mount a resupply effort to Syria once the fighting had ended, as soon as it became clear that Israel was not going to invade Syria and was restricting its efforts to destroying the PLO infrastructure in Lebanon (although battering Syrian troops stationed in Lebanon in the process), Moscow took no substantive action, thus demonstrating that the Soviet–Syrian treaty did not cover Syrian activities in Lebanon. To be sure, Moscow did appeal to the Arabs to unite to confront Israel and use their oil weapon against the United States, but the badly divided Arab world, threatened on the East by Iran, was to take neither action. Indeed, the Arab states were unable even to convene a summit conference until after the PLO left Beirut.

Interestingly enough, while there was a spate of Arab criticism of Moscow for its lack of assistance to the PLO and Syria (Libyan leader Muammar Kaddafi went so far as to berate a group of Soviet ambassadors, complaining that Arab friendship with the socialist countries was almost "ready to go up in flames, the way Beirut is going up in flames"),[8] Syria held aloof from the cascade of public criticism against the Soviet Union. Instead, Syrian Information Minister Ahmad Iskander told a press conference in Damascus that the Soviet Union was a "sincere friend" of Syria who had "helped us defend our lands, wives and children," and he called for a strategic alliance with the Soviet Union.[9] While the Syrians appeared to be using their battle losses against Israel and the Iskander press conference as a plot to obtain the weapons and the strategic alliance with the Soviet Union they had long wanted, Moscow utilized the press conference which was given prominent coverage by the Soviet news agency, TASS, to demonstrate its continuing importance in Arab affairs and the major role it had already played in aiding the Arabs.

Nonetheless, it was Washington, not Moscow, which controlled the pace of Middle Eastern events in the period leading up to the PLO exodus from Beirut and the Soviet leadership could do little but sit on the diplomatic sidelines as the American-mediated exodus took place on 20 August. Indeed, to Soviet eyes, the Arab world must have appeared only too susceptible to American diplomacy at this time. Events such as the Camp David agreement between Egypt and Israel, the Soviet invasion of Afghanistan, and the outbreak of the Iran–Iraq war had split the Arab world into three major groupings. On the one hand was the pro-Western grouping led by Egypt and including Sudan, Oman and Somalia. This Arab grouping supported Camp David, opposed the Soviet invasion of Afghanistan, supported Iraq in its war with Iran, and cooperated with the United States in joint military exercises. On the other side of the Arab spectrum was the so-called Front of Steadfastness and Confrontation, led by Syria and including Libya, the Peoples Democratic Republic of Yemen, the PLO and Algeria. This Arab contingent opposed Camp David and, with the exception of Algeria, supported Soviet activity in Afghanistan, and Iran against Iraq. In the center of the Arab spectrum was the group of Arab states composed of

Saudi Arabia, Jordan, Kuwait, the UAE, Morocco, Iraq, North Yemen, Tunisia, Bahrein and Qatar. These "Centrists" opposed Camp David but also opposed the Soviet invasion of Afghanistan and tended to back Iraq in its war with Iran. From the Soviet viewpoint, the diplomatic goal was to move the Centrist Arab grouping as close as possible to the Steadfastness Front so as to isolate Egypt and other members of the pro-Western Arab bloc. Conversely, from the US standpoint, it was important to try to move the Centrist Arabs toward the Egyptian-led Arab states. Reagan exploited the enhanced US diplomatic position in the Middle East following the PLO withdrawal from Beirut for just such an effort. The Reagan plan for a Middle East peace settlement, issued on 1 September, seemed aimed at winning over the Centrist Arabs with its call for no Israeli sovereignty on the West Bank, a stop to the building of Israeli settlements there and a link between a West Bank–Gaza entity and Jordan – something King Hussein had long wanted.[10] The Arab states, finally convening their long-postponed summit in Fez, Morocco, issued their peace plan one week later.[11] With the United States and Arab peace plans now on the table, the USSR hastened to issue its plan in a speech delivered by Brezhnev in mid-September. While a number of its points were repetitions of previous Soviet proposals (a Palestinian state on the West Bank and Gaza; total Israeli withdrawal to the 1967 borders; the right to exist of all states in the region), others seem to have been added to emphasize the similarity between the Fez and Soviet plans.[12] In modeling the Soviet peace plan on Fez, Brezhnev evidently sought to prevent the Arabs from moving to embrace the Reagan plan. Nonetheless, with the United States clearly possessing the diplomatic initiative in the Middle East after the PLO pull-out from Beirut, and Jordan's King Hussein, PLO leader Arafat, and other Arab leaders expressing interest in the Reagan plan, Moscow was on the diplomatic defensive. Given this situation, it is not surprising that Brezhnev seized upon the massacres in the Sabra and Shatilla refugee camps to point to Arafat, "if anyone had any illusions that Washington was going to support the Arabs . . . these illusions have now been drowned in streams of blood in the Palestinian camps . . ."[13]

Nonetheless, despite the massacres, Arafat evidently felt that there was value in pursuing the Reagan plan and he began to meet with his erstwhile enemy, King Hussein of Jordan, to work out a joint approach to the United States. Such maneuvering infuriated Syria, which sought to use pro-Syrian elements within the PLO to pressure Arafat into abandoning his new policy, a development which further exacerbated relations between Assad and Arafat. In addition, evidently fearing the weakening of the Steadfastness Front and the possibility of the PLO (or at least Arafat's followers) defecting from it, Moscow continued to warn the Arabs about what it called US efforts to split the PLO and to draw Jordan and Saudi Arabia into supporting the Reagan plan, which the USSR termed a cover for Camp David.

It was at this point in mid-November that Brezhnev passed from the scene. His successor, Yuri Andropov, had the task of rebuilding the Soviet position in the Middle East which had suffered a major blow during the Israeli invasion of Lebanon.

SOVIET POLICY FROM ANDROPOV'S ACCESSION TO POWER UNTIL THE MAY 1983 WAR SCARE

When Andropov took power in mid-November 1982, he had to face the fact that the Soviet Union's Middle East position had deteriorated in three major areas as a result of the Israeli invasion of Lebanon. In the first place, Soviet credibility had suffered a major blow because its frequent warnings to the United States and Israel during the course of the war had proven to be ineffectual. Second, the quality of Soviet military equipment and, to a lesser degree, the quality of Soviet training had been called into question by the overwhelming victory of US-supplied Israeli weaponry over the military equipment supplied by Moscow to Syria. Finally, Andropov had to deal with a situation where the United States had the diplomatic initiative in the Middle East. Not only was the Reagan plan – and not the Soviet peace plan – the central factor in Middle East diplomatic discussions, but Arafat and King Hussein had begun to meet regularly and the governments of Israel and Lebanon had begun talks on a Lebanese–Israeli peace accord. Under these circumstances the new Soviet leader, although preoccupied with consolidating his power and trying to block the installation of US Pershing II and cruise missiles in Western Europe, evidently felt that Moscow had to move before Soviet influence in the Middle East fell any further.

In an effort to rebuild the Soviet position in the Middle East, Andropov moved both militarily and diplomatically. On the military front in January 1983, he dispatched several batteries of SAM-5 missiles to Syria along with the Soviet soldiers to operate and guard them.[14] This Soviet move went far beyond the resupply efforts of tanks and planes to Syria which had been going on since the end of the Israeli–Syrian fighting in 1982. Indeed, by sending Syria a weapons system that had never been deployed outside the USSR itself, a system that had the capability of engaging Israel's EC-2 aircraft system, which had proven so effective during the Israeli–Syrian air battles in the first week of the Israeli invasion of Lebanon in June, Moscow was demonstrating to the

Arab world – and especially to Syria – that it was willing to stand by its allies.[15] Nonetheless, by manning the SAM-5 missiles with Soviet soldiers, Moscow was also signalling that it, and not Syria, would determine when the missiles would be fired. Given the fact that both in November 1980 and April 1981 Assad had tried to involve the USSR in his military adventures, this was probably a sensible precaution – especially, as will be shown below – when Assad and other Syrian government officials began to issue bellicose statements several months later. Yet another cautionary elements in the dispatch of the missiles was that Moscow never formally announced that its own troops were involved in guarding the missiles, thus enabling the USSR to avoid a direct confrontation with Israel (and possibly the United States) should Israel decide to attack the missile sites.

While Moscow was moving to enhance its political position in the Arab world by sending the SAM-5 missiles to Syria, it was also benefiting from developments in the PLO which challenged Arafat's opening to Washington. Indeed, Moscow's interest in preventing a PLO turn to the United States was shared by both Syria and Libya which actively moved to undermine Arafat's position. The efforts of the anti-Arafat forces were to prove successful as the Palestine National Council which, after a number of postponements, finally convened in mid-February in Algiers, formally stated its refusal to consider the Reagan plan as "a sound basis for a just and lasting solution to the Palestine problem and the Arab–Israeli conflict."[16] Needless to say, Moscow was very pleased with this development with *Pravda* correspondent, Yuri Vladimirov, praising the Council's policy document as a reaffirmation of the organization's determination to continue the struggle against imperialism and Zionism.[17]

Meanwhile, as the Reagan plan was faltering, a development which weakened United States influence in the Middle East, Moscow was seeking to underscore its improved position in the region by issuing a public warning to Israel not to attack Syria. The Soviet warning, issued on 30 March, came after a series of Syrian warnings, yet was limited in nature. Thus, while Moscow warned that Israel was "playing with fire" by preparing to attack Syria, it made no mention of the Soviet–Syrian treaty. Indeed, in listing those on Syria's side in the confrontation with Israel, the Soviet statement merely noted, "on the side of the Syrian people are Arab patriots, the socialist countries, and all who cherish the cause of peace, justice and honor." The statement also emphasized the need to settle the Arab–Israeli conflict politically, not through war.[18]

This rather curious Soviet warning can perhaps be understood if one assumes that Moscow did not seriously expect an Israeli attack on Syria.

With the more cautious Moshe Arens having replaced Ariel Sharon as Israel's Defense Minister, and with rising opposition to Israel's presence in Lebanon being felt in Israel's domestic political scene, it appeared unlikely that Israel would attack Syria, even to take out the newly-installed SAM-5 missiles. Indeed, even the hawkish Israeli Chief of Staff, General Rafael Eitan, in an interview on Israeli armed forces radio, stated that Israel had no intention of starting a war.[19] If Moscow basically assumed that Israel would not go to war, then why the warning? Given the fact that Moscow's credibility in the Arab world had dropped precipitously as a result of the warnings it had issued during the Israeli invasion of Lebanon in the June/July 1982 period – warnings that had been ignored by both Israel and the United States – Moscow possibly saw a chance to increase its credibility in the region. Thus if Moscow, assuming Israel would not attack Syria, issued a warning to Israel not to attack Syria, and Israel then did not attack Syria, Moscow could take credit for the non-attack and could then demonstrate to the Arab world that diplomacy was effective *vis-à-vis* Israel, at least as a deterrent. If this, in fact, was Moscow's thinking, however, not all the Arabs were to be convinced. Indeed, the Saudi paper *Ar-Riyad* expressed a lack of trust in the Soviet warning, noting that the limited value of Soviet statements had been proven during the Israeli invasion of Lebanon, "which dealt a sharp and severe blow to the Kremlin when the Soviet missiles became no more than timber towers in the face of the sophisticated weapons the United States had unconditionally supplied to Israel."[20]

In any case, only three days after the Soviet warning to Israel, Soviet Foreign Minister, Andrei Gromyko, who had recently been promoted to Deputy Prime Minister, held a major press conference in Moscow.[21] While the main emphasis of Gromyko's press conference was on strategic arms issues, he also took the opportunity to make two major points about the Middle East situation. First, in response to a question from a correspondent of the Syrian newspaper *Al-Ba'ath*, Gromyko stated, "the Soviet Union is in favor of the withdrawal of all foreign troops from the territory of Lebanon, all of them. Syria is in favor of this."[22] Secondly, Gromyko noted once again that the USSR supported Israel's existance as a state. "We do not share the point of view of extremist Arab circles that Israel should be eliminated. This is an unrealistic and unjust point of view."[23] The thrust of Gromyko's remarks was clear. By urging the withdrawal of all foreign troops from Lebanon, including Syrian troops, and reemphasizing the Soviet commitment to Israel's existence, the Soviet leader seemed to be telling Syria that, despite the provision of SAM-5 missiles, Moscow did not desire to be dragged into a war in Lebanon on Syria's behalf. If this was indeed the message Gromyko was trying to get across, the rapid pace of Middle Eastern events was soon to pose additional problems for Soviet strategy. Thus, one week later King Hussein announced his refusal to enter into peace negotiations, and then the US embassy in Beirut was blown up by a car bomb with a massive loss of life. Reacting to both events, President Reagan dispatched Secretary of State, George Shultz, to salvage the stalled Israeli–Lebanese talks and regain the momentum for the United States in Middle East diplomacy. As Shultz toured the region and shuttled back and forth between Beirut and Jerusalem, prospects for a Lebanese–Israeli agreement began to improve. For different reasons, both Moscow and Damascus wanted to see the Shultz mission fail. The USSR did not want more Arab states to follow in Egypt's footsteps and agree to a US plan for Middle East peace. Syria, for its part, had long sought the dominant role in Lebanon and feared that any Lebanese–Israeli agreement would strengthen the Israeli position in Lebanon at Syria's expense. In addition, Syria also did not wish any more Arab states to make peace with Israel, since this would leave Syria increasingly isolated among the Arab confrontation states facing Israel. The end result was a rise in tension and yet another war scare in which Moscow was to play a role, albeit perhaps a somewhat unwilling one.

Less than a week after King Hussein refused to enter the peace talks, the Syrian government raised its price for a Lebanese troop withdrawal. While as late as January Syria seemed to have been willing to have a simultaneous withdrawal of Israeli, Syrian and PLO forces, on 16 April the Syrian government, strengthened both by its new Soviet weapons and by the Soviet warning to Israel, stated that Syria would not even discuss the withdrawal of its troops from Lebanon until all Israeli troops had left the country.[24] While the United States sought to assuage Syrian opposition in a letter from Reagan to Assad in which the US President indicated that the United States was still pressing for Israeli withdrawal from the Golan Heights,[25] the US ploy was not successful. Indeed, Syria appeared to step up tension by allowing guerrillas to infiltrate into Israeli lines to attack Israeli troops while simultaneously accusing the Israeli government of reinforcing its troops in Lebanon's Bekaa Valley and of staging "provocative" military exercises on the Golan Heights.[26]

Meanwhile, despite the rise in Syrian–Israeli tension, US Secretary of State, Shultz, continued to work for an Israeli–Lebanese troop withdrawal agreement and on 6 May his efforts were crowned with success as the Israeli government accepted, in principle, a troop withdrawal agreement that had already been agreed to by Lebanon.[27]

(The agreement was formally signed on 17 May). The next US goal was to try to gain Arab support for the agreement so as to pressure Syria also into withdrawing its forces from Lebanon. As might be expected, neither Moscow nor Syria was in favor of a rapid Syrian withdrawal. Although interested in Syria's ultimately withdrawing its troops from Lebanon, Moscow did not want a precipitate withdrawal in the aftermath of the Israeli–Lebanese agreement, lest the United States reap the diplomatic benefit. Syria complained that Israel had obtained too much from the treaty and Damascus Radio asserted that Lebanon had "capitulated to the Israeli aggressor."[28] As the crisis was played out until the end of May, with military maneuvers and threats of war (almost all from the Syrians), it appeared as if Assad was enjoying the opportunity to play a major role once again in Middle East events – and thereby move out of a position of isolation in the Arab world because of his continuing support for Iran in the Iran–Iraq war.

As Syria was exploiting the Lebanese situation for its own ends, Moscow was cautiously supporting its Arab ally. Thus on 9 May, three days after Israel had agreed in principle to the accord, the Soviet Union issued an official statement denouncing the agreement and, in a gesture of support for Syria, demanded that "first and foremost" Israeli troops be withdrawn from Lebanon. The statement added, however, that "American and other foreign troops staying in Lebanon also must be withdrawn from it," an oblique reference to Moscow's continuing desire to see Syrian troops leave the country.[29] At the same time, perhaps to enhance the atmosphere of crisis, Soviet dependents were withdrawn from Beirut, although the Soviet Ambassador to Lebanon stated that the departure of the dependents had occurred because of the beginning of summer camp in the USSR.[30] In helping to enhance the atmosphere of crisis, Moscow may also have seen that the situation could be used as a means of once again playing a role in the Middle East peace process after having been kept on the diplomatic sidelines since Sadat's trip to Jerusalem in 1977. Indeed, on 10 May, Shultz openly urged Moscow to use its influence to get Syria to withdraw its troops and stated that he might meet Soviet Foreign Minister Gromyko to discuss the Middle East along with other international issues.[31] Shultz, however, indicated that the United States was not yet ready for an international conference on the Middle East, still a goal of Soviet diplomacy.[32]

Nonetheless, even in giving Syria a limited degree of support Moscow had to be concerned about the possibility of war erupting, especially as Syria began to issue increasingly bellicose threats which involved Soviet support for Syria in case of war.[33] Thus in an interview on 9 May, Syrian Foreign Minister Khaddam noted that, in case of war between Israel and Syria, "We believe that the USSR will fulfill its commitments in accordance with the [Soviet–Syrian] treaty." The next day Syrian radio warned that any Israeli attack against Syrian forces anywhere, even in Lebanon, would mean an "unlimited war."[34] Syrian bellicosity, however, may have overstepped the bounds of propriety insofar as Moscow was concerned. In a broadcast over Beirut Radio the Soviet Ambassador to Lebanon, Alexander Soldatov, when asked about Khaddam's assertion that Moscow would fully support Syria if war with Israel broke out, replied that "the USSR does not reply to such hypothetical questions."[35] Soldatov added that the USSR continued to support the withdrawal of all foreign forces from Lebanon. These themes of caution were repeated by Soviet officials during the visit of a Soviet delegation to Israel in mid-May to attend ceremonies marking the 38th anniversary of the defeat of Nazi Germany.[36]

Meanwhile, Assad stepped up the political and military pressure in the Bekaa. After refusing to see US envoy Philip Habib, Assad, on 23 May predicted a new war with Israel in which Syria would lose 20,000 men.[37] Two days later Syrian planes fired air-to-air missiles against Israeli jets flying over the Bekaa Valley – the first such encounter since the war in 1982.[38] Assad followed this up by conducting military exercises in the Golan and Bekaa, and the danger of war appeared to heighten.[39] Nonetheless, despite a limited counter-mobilization, Israel responded coolly during the crisis while Moscow kept a very low profile (although it did send a new aircraft carrier into the Mediterranean), supporting Syria politically but issuing no threats against the United States or Israel and again appealing for a full withdrawal of all forces in Lebanon. In any case, by the end of May the crisis had subsided and the dangers of a Syrian–Israeli war in Lebanon had been replaced in the headlines by the growing revolt in the PLO against Arafat's leadership, a development engineered by Assad, as the Syrian leader appeared to want to bring the PLO under Syrian control once and for all.[40]

The revolt against Arafat underlined the PLO leader's weakened position in the aftermath of the Israeli invasion of Lebanon which had eliminated his main base of operations. While he was supported by the bulk of Palestinians living outside Syria and Syrian-controlled regions in Lebanon, and while both Iraq and Algeria gave him support in the Arab world's diplomatic arena, he had no real power to resist Syria's crackdown against him. Thus, as the summer wore on, the positions of Arafat's supporters in the Bekaa Valley were overrun, and Arafat himself was expelled from Syria. In early August the Palestine Central Council, meeting in Tunis, called for an "immediate dialogue" to rebuild relations with Syria[41] but this effort proved to be of no avail. In early September, Arafat, who had once again begun to meet with Jordanian officials, admitted that all attempts at negotiations with Syria had failed.[42]

As the revolt within Fatah developed, Moscow was faced by another of its serious problems of choice. On the one hand, a victory for the Fatah hardliners would make it even more difficult for Moscow to succeed in promoting its Middle East peace plan. In addition, the split within Fatah and the fact that Iraq and Algeria were backing Arafat against the Syrian-supported opposition further underlined the disunity in the Arab world. This was one more obstacle in the way of the "anti-imperialist" Arab unity Moscow had sought for so long. On the other hand, Moscow could not have been too unhappy with the fact that Arafat was being punished for his flirtation with the Reagan plan. In any case, in a showdown between Assad and Arafat, *Realpolitik* impelled Moscow to side with Assad, who, in the aftermath of the Israeli invasion of Lebanon, was the main Arab leader opposing US diplomacy in the Middle East and who had granted to Moscow the use of the Syrian naval and air force facilities as well.[43]

In addition to bringing Arafat's forces in the Bekaa under his control, Assad was profiting from the growing war-weariness of Israel, which was planning a unilateral withdrawal of its forces from the Chouf Mountains, and seemed in no mood to go to war to throw the Syrians out of Lebanon. Indeed, on 1 June Prime Minister Begin had stated that Israel was not preparing to attack Syria.[44] One month later Shultz stated that US Marines would not fill any vacuum created by a unilateral withdrawal by Israel from Lebanon.[45] Under these circumstances Assad was able to fill the vacuum with Syrian-backed forces, in large part because of mistakes by the Lebanese government. By July, the Lebanese government of Amin Gemayel had alienated two of the major forces within Lebanon, the Druze and the Shiites. In part because he did not establish an equitable power sharing system, and in part because Phalangist policies in the Chouf Mountains and in Shiite areas of Beirut angered the Druze and Shiites, they entered into an alignment with Syria. Druze leader Walid Jumblatt did this explicitly by leading a newly proclaimed "National Salvation Front" (which also had as members Rashid Karami, a Sunni Muslim, and Suleiman Franjieh, a Christian opponet of Gemayel), while Shiite leader Nabih Berri gave tacit support to the organization.[46]

The strengthening of the Syrian position in Lebanon was, on balance, a plus for Moscow since by the end of August, American diplomatic efforts to secure a troop withdrawal agreement from Lebanon had all but collapsed and Moscow was again raising the possibility of a joint

US–Soviet effort to bring about a Middle East peace settlement.[47] Yet, the situation also had its dangers for Moscow. As Israel stepped up its planning to withdraw troops from the Chouf Mountains, the possibility that new fighting would erupt became increasingly strong, particularly since no agreement had been reached between the Druze and Gemayel about deploying the Lebanese army in the Chouf to replace the departing Israelis. Exacerbating the situation was the Syrian government statement on 27 August that it would defend its allies against the Lebanese army.[48] The danger for Moscow was that since the United States was backing the Gemayel government, a direct US–Syrian confrontation could occur and then Moscow would again be faced with the problem of how to react to a military conflict in which its principal Arab ally was involved. This time, the opponent would most likely not be Israel backed by the United States, but the United States itself. In short, Moscow faced the prospect of a superpower confrontation over Lebanon. When the crisis did occur, the USSR adopted a very cautious policy so as to avoid any direct involvement.

THE SEPTEMBER 1983 CRISIS

The crisis began at the end of August when warfare broke out between the Lebanese government and the Shiites of Western and Southern Beirut who resisted a Lebanese army push into their neighborhoods on 30 and 31 August. The scale of fighting escalated sharply, however, after the Israeli deployment of 3 September from the Chouf Mountains southward to the Awali River, with Syrian-supported Druze forces clashing both with the Maronite (Phalange) militia and the Lebanese army. While the Phalangist forces were all but driven from the Chouf Mountains, the Lebanese army proved a tougher opponent for the Druze and a major battle was fought for the strategic mountain town of Souk el-Gharb which overlooks Beirut. While Israel refrained from intervening, the United States played an active role in the fighting in support of the Lebanese army which it was training.[49] After holding aloof from the fighting, France also got involved when its forces came under fire. As the fighting escalated, Syria felt constrained to issue threats against the United States, so as to back up its clients in the Chouf Mountains.[50]

As the crisis developed, Moscow reacted very cautiously. A TASS statement published in *Pravda* on 1 September merely noted that the Soviet Union was "deeply concerned" over the US armed intervention in Lebanon. It also called for the end to US intervention, the unconditional withdrawal of Israeli forces from Lebanon, and the withdrawal of US troops and "the foreign troops that arrived with them." Interestingly enough there were no Soviet threats against the US, although Moscow may have balanced its lack of activity with the implicit support of Syria's right to remain in Lebanon, because there was no mention of any Syrian withdrawal in the TASS statement – a clear change from earlier Soviet policy.

The rapid escalation of the crisis, however, posed both problems and opportunities for the USSR. On the one hand, Moscow seized on the US involvement in the fighting to discredit American policy in the Middle East by asserting that the United States was now directly fighting the Arabs. Vladimir Kudriavtsev, one of *Izvestiia's* more colorful commentators, emphasized this Soviet propaganda line with the statement, "By shedding the blood of Arab patriots, the United States has *de facto* declared war on the Arabs." In addition, Soviet commentators also utilized the intervention to discredit the US Rapid Deployment Force whose troops it claimed were fighting in Lebanon.[51] Moscow also sought to exploit the Lebanese fighting to divert attention from its shooting down of a Korean airliner in early September. Nonetheless, as American participation in the fighting grew, Moscow faced the dilemma of whether or not it should get directly involved, particularly as Syrian positions came under American fire. The Soviet press noted the escalation of the fighting and also noted Syria's warning to the United States that it would fire back if fired upon, perhaps to prepare the Soviet public for a heightened crisis. Nonetheless, on 20 September, the day after *Pravda* published the Syrian warning, the same Soviet newspaper published a TASS statement that carefully avoided any hint of Soviet involvement in the fighting. While it accused the United States of trying to intimidate Syria and of seeking to establish its own hegemony in the Middle East, it issued no warning other than to state that Washington would not "evade responsibility" for the consequences of the escalated fighting.[52] To be sure, Moscow did not deny reports in the Kuwaiti press that the USSR had placed its forces in the southern part of the USSR on alert and that a joint Soviet–Syrian operations room was monitoring the situation in Lebanon.[53] In addition, Moscow rejected a US offer to cooperate in limiting Syrian participation in the conflict.[54] Nonetheless, Moscow reportedly refused formally to offer military support to Syria; nor did it react to statements by Syrian officials that Damascus might turn to the USSR for help. It also ignored the leftist Lebanese newspaper *As-Safir's* report that Assad had made a secret trip to Moscow in mid-September.[55] Perhaps most important of all, during the crisis Moscow failed publicly to mention the Soviet–Syrian treaty. In sum, Soviet behavior during the crisis was very cautious, and it is not surprising that Moscow, which feared a superpower confrontation over Lebanon – an area of only tertiary interest to the USSR – warmly welcomed the cease-fire that ended the crisis.[56]

In looking at the September 1983 crisis, it is clear that if differed substantially from the one four months earlier. In May Assad had been basically in control of the situation and maneuvered accordingly. Since that crisis was essentially a political one, over the Israel–Lebanese treaty, Syrian mobilizations and threats of war were essentially political acts, unlikely to get out of control. In September the crisis was essentially a military one that escalated rapidly. Under these circumstances, it is not surprising that the USSR refrained from giving Syria overt support during the crisis; nor did Syria complain publicly about a lack of Soviet aid (thus repeating the strategy it followed during the Israeli invasion of June 1982), although Damascus could not have been happy with the lack of Soviet support. Syria expressed its anger more openly against its fellow Arabs, intimating that whatever the position of the Arab governments, the Arab masses supported Syria.[57] The lack of Soviet and Arab support, coupled with the US Congress's agreement to extend the stay of US Marines in Beirut for an additional eighteen months and the arrival near Beirut of the US battleship, *New Jersey*, seem to have persuaded Assad to agree to a Saudi-mediated cease-fire plan that held out the possibility of a new distribution of power in Lebanon.[58] No sooner had the cease-fire been achieved, however, than Assad moved to strengthen Syria's position in Lebanon further, by expelling the remaining troops loyal to Arafat from the Bekaa Valley and forcing them to go over the mountains to Tripoli where Arafat had suddenly appeared in mid-September.

In the aftermath of the cease-fire the Soviet Union adopted what, on the surface, appeared to be a contradictory policy toward Syria. On the one hand, Moscow dispatched to Syria modern SS-21 ground-to-ground missiles with a range of 70 miles – long enough to strike deep into Israel, and with greater accuracy than the previously supplied SCUD or Frog missiles.[59] On the other hand, Moscow downplayed its military relationship to Syria. With Andropov ill, a major Soviet campaign to prevent the deployment of US Pershing II and cruise missiles underway in Western Europe, and Moscow still trying to overcome the negative effects of the Korean airliner incident, the time was not opportune for the USSR to become involved in a Middle East war. Thus, Soviet treatment of the third anniversary of the Soviet–Syrian treaty was kept in very low key as far as Soviet military aid was concerned. A *New Times* article commemorating the treaty, for example, emphasized that Soviet aid had enabled Syria to enhance its defense potential and that the Syrian leaders had themselves repeatedly stressed that they possessed the means to repulse an aggressor.[60] Similarly, a *Pravda* commentary by Yuri Glukhov on 8 October cited the Syrian Prime Minister's statement that Syria relies on its own efforts first, and only then on the assistance of its friends. Perhaps to reinforce the point that the first friends to whom Syria should look for help were its fellow Arabs, an Arabic-language broadcast commemorating the tenth anniversary of the 1973 Arab–Israeli war asserted that the effectiveness of aid from the socialist countries is increased manyfold if the Arab states themselves unite to fight the aggressor.[61]

THE DECEMBER 1983 CRISIS

Moscow's low-key approach to the simmering Lebanese conflict was jarred by the bombing of the US Marine headquarters in Beirut on 24 October and subsequent American accusations that Syria was at least indirectly responsible.[62] Soviet commentary on US policy in Lebanon became more shrill after the United States invaded Grenada, with the Soviet media warning that such moderate Arab states as Saudi Arabia, Morocco, and even Oman might be next.[63] Meanwhile, as threats of retaliation for the destruction of the Marine headquarters were repeated and the US began flying reconnaissance missions over Syrian lines in Lebanon, the possibility of a Syrian–United States clash grew stronger. At this point, as if to dissociate Moscow from the possibility of intervening, a major Arabic-language broadcast minimized the Soviet military presence in Syria, repeating the now-familiar Soviet practice of citing Syrian statements that, "Syria has enough means at its disposal to defend itself." In addition, the broadcast asserted that, "there is no Soviet military presence in Syria at all, only experts helping Syria bolster its defense capability," and that Syria has "repeatedly replied vehemently to the lie of the alleged Soviet military presence on its soil."[64]

Nonetheless, as tension rose in Lebanon, Moscow evidently felt constrained to issue another warning to the United States, if only to show its support of the "progressive" Lebanese forces which were backed by Syria. Thus, on 4 November a Soviet government TASS statement, citing remarks by Reagan, Weinberger and Shultz that the United States was planning a "massive strike against Lebanese national patriotic forces," warned the United States "with all seriousness" about taking such action.[65] As in the case of the 30 March warning to Israel, the Soviet warning of 4 November was very limited. Not only was there no mention of Syria, let alone the Soviet–Syrian treaty, but there was not even the usual Soviet statement that the Middle East lay close to the southern borders of the USSR. While *Pravda* commentator Pavel Demchenko two days later mentioned specifically that the United States was preparing "an act of retribution against Syria," he omitted any Soviet warning to the United States and also failed to mention the Soviet–Syrian treaty.[66]

While Moscow was seeking to limit its involvement in the period of rising tensions, Assad was exploiting the possibility of an escalated Syrian–United States confrontation to crack down on the last redoubt of Arafat's supporters, the refugee camps north of Tripoli. At the same time it was announced that Syrian Foreign Minister Khaddam would shortly visit the Soviet Union.[67] Whoever initiated it, it was clearly Damascus which was to exploit the atmosphere surrounding the visit. Thus, despite American and Israeli statements that they were not going to attack Syria, Assad mobilized his army on 8 November. While Moscow noted the Syrian mobilization in an Arabic-language broadcast on 9 November, and stated that Syria was exerting its additional defense efforts with the help of the USSR on the basis of their bilateral treaty, the broadcast also stated that "the substance of this treaty is very well known."[68] The purpose of this qualification to the treaty may well have been to remind the Arabs that the treaty did not cover Syrian activities in Lebanon.

While Moscow was urging the Arabs to unite on an "anti-imperialist" basis, Assad appeared to be painting his Soviet allies into a corner in which they had no choice but to support him, regardless of what he did to Arafat's forces. On the eve of Khaddam's visit to the USSR, Syrian forces opened fire on four American reconnaissance planes.[69] Thus, the Syrian Foreign Minister flew to Moscow in the midst of a crisis which, like the one in May, seemed to have been orchestrated by Assad who at this critical moment, however, suddenly become seriously ill. For its part Moscow could not have been too pleased either with Syrian claims to Soviet aid in a widened conflict or to Syria's crackdown on Arafat's forces in the Tripoli area since Moscow still appeared to wish to see Arafat, and the PLO, as independent actors in the Middle East who would need Soviet support, rather than as a dependent element of the Syrian army. Gromyko's luncheon speech to Khaddam made this point very clear: "We regard as highly important and urgent the need for overcoming strife and restoring unity within the ranks of the liberation movement of the Arab people of Palestine which must remain an active and effective factor of the anti-imperialist struggle in the Middle East."[70]

Gromyko also pointedly called for increased Arab unity, stating "the fact is that the enemies of the Arabs seek, in no small measure, to rely in their aggressive policy precisely on their disunity." While Gromyko also condemned US and Israeli threats against the Lebanese National Patriotic Forces and Syria, he pointedly refrained from mentioning the Soviet–Syrian treaty. In his speech, Khaddam totally ignored the Palestinian issue, while pointedly mentioning, in a segment of his speech ignored by *Pravda* but reported by Damascus Radio, that Soviet support "helped Syria in its steadfastness" and "enabled it to confront aggression."[71] Khaddam did, however, state Syrian aims in Lebanon that seemed to coincide with those of the Soviet Union: the renunciation of the 17 May agreement; the full withdrawal of Israeli and multi-national forces; and the achievement of national unity and the restoration of security in Lebanon. The joint communiqué issued at the conclusion of the talks reflected the differing viewpoints of the two sides as it reported an exchange of opinions – the usual Soviet code words for disagreement – "regarding the US and Israeli threats against Syria and the danger of aggression against Syria in this connection."[72] Moscow did, however, give a general statement of support for Syria against "the intrigues of imperialism and Zionism," and "confirmed its adherence" to its commitments under the Soviet–Syrian treaty.

If Moscow felt that it had succeeded in getting Syria to moderate its pressure on Arafat as a result of the Khaddam visit to Moscow, this proved not to be the case. Indeed, soon after Khaddam's return to Damascus, Syrian-backed troops stepped up their attacks on Arafat's forces and drove them out of the two Palestinian refugee camps north of Tripoli into the city itself.

As the Tripoli fighting escalated despite the Soviet pleas to end it, Moscow stepped up the level of its public complaints with an appeal from the Soviet Afro-Asian Peoples Solidarity Organization. Reminiscent of similar pleas at the time of Syrian–PLO fighting during the Syrian intervention in Lebanon in 1976, the AAPSO called for an end to the "senseless bloodshed" and the restoration of unity in the ranks of the Palestinians, and the consolidation of all Arab anti-imperialist forces "in the face of the mounting military and political pressure on the part of the USA, Israel and their allies."[73]

Fortunately for Moscow an uneasy ceasefire was achieved in Tripoli, although to what degree Assad's agreement to halt the fighting was due to Saudi inducement, Soviet pressure, or the realization that Arafat continued to have widespread support in the Arab world and among Palestinians, is not yet clear. In any case, Moscow warmly praised the cease-fire[74] and three days later, a joint Soviet party–government statement on the "international day of solidarity with the Palestinian people" saluted Arafat as the Chairman of the PLO executive committee.[75] At the same time it called for unity within the organization and its "close collaboration" with "those countries that are in the forefront of resistance to the US and Israel" (i.e., Syria), as Moscow continued to try to maintain good relations with both Arafat and Assad.

While Moscow was relieved by the Tripoli ceasefire, however tentative it may have been, it had to be concerned with the rise in Syrian–United States tensions. US Defense Secretary Weinberger had asserted on 11 November that the attack on the Marine headquarters had been undertaken by Iranians with the "sponsorship and knowledge and authority of the Syrian government."[76] While Syria rejected the charge, it also again asserted that its planes had driven off US jets flying over Syrian-controlled areas.[77] At this point, with the ceasefire holding in Tripoli, Moscow moved again to champion Syria, as a Novosti article by Demchenko that was distributed to Western correspondents, warned that Syria was an ally of Moscow with which it had a Treaty of Friendship and Cooperation, and that aggression against Syria was an "extremely dangerous venture." He had noted that the potential of forces opposing US and Israeli policy in Syria and Lebanon did not compare "in any way with what the Pentagon faced on Grenada."[78] This was the strongest warning given by Moscow to the United States thus far in the Lebanese crisis and was perhaps aimed at deterring the United States from any strike against Syria, although the fact that it took the form of a Novosti article, and not a TASS statement, indicated it was still low level. Nonetheless, such a warning again raised questions of Soviet credibility should a Syrian–American confrontation take place, either in the form of an American retaliation for the Marine headquarters explosion or an attack on Syrian positions in Lebanon in retaliation for the firing on US reconnaissance planes. Syrian government statements, such as the one broadcast on Syrian radio on 29 November that "Syria expresses its pride – before the Arab nation and the world – at the fact that it agitates a superpower," appeared to make some form of confrontation even more likely.[79]

The US attack came on 4 December, following Syrian anti-aircraft fire on US reconnaissance planes the previous day. Under these circumstances Moscow was again faced with the dilemma of either supporting its clients policies in Lebanon – policies with which the USSR did not thoroughly agree – or once again losing some of its diplomatic credibility, particularly since Reagan was threatening to strike Syrian positions again if US forces continued to come under attack.[80] Once again Moscow was to take a cautious stand, although its diplomatic credibility was to suffer. Thus, a TASS statement merely noted that the Soviet Union "declared its solidarity with the peoples of Lebanon, Syria, and other Arab countries in defending their independence" and that "the aggressive actions of the United States against Syria constitute a serious threat to peace not only in the Middle East region."[81] While the TASS statement also sought propaganda advantage by tying the US attack to the strategic cooperation agreement concluded between President Reagan and the new Israeli Prime Minister, the failure of the TASS statement to mention the Soviet–Syrian treaty indicated that Syria could not expect more than Soviet moral support against the United States so long as the confrontation was limited to Lebanon.

While Moscow was not willing to aid Syria militarily to confront the United States, it did seek to utilize the American attack against Syria to undermine the US position in the Middle East. Thus a *Pravda* editorial on 10 December repeated the TASS statement themes that the United States no longer qualified as a mediator in the Arab–Israeli conflict and that the United States attack was the outgrowth of United States–Israeli strategic cooperation. The editorial went on to assert that the United States was now being opposed even in conservative Arab countries, and Moscow once again appealed for Arab unity on an "anti-imperialist" basis. It seems clear that Moscow, unwilling to use force to aid Syria, had gone back to the course of action it had pursued since the September crisis – an appeal to the Arabs to help Syria themselves. Unfortunately for the USSR, which hoped that the US attack would force the Centrist Arabs to rally again around Syria and what was left of the Steadfastness Front, this was not to happen. With Syria's ally Iran again threatening to close the Straits of Hormuz, the Centrist Arabs, and particularly the members of the Gulf Cooperation Council, had no choice but to rely on the United States for help. Syria also realized this soon after the US attack, as the Syrian media bewailed the lack of Arab support.[82] The end result was that Syria, without Soviet or Arab support against the United States and with its efforts to topple Arafat as leader of the PLO unsuccessful (the PLO leader, who continued to command widespread Palestinian support, left Tripoli under the UN flag), moved to de-escalate the tension. Thus it returned the body of the dead US airman, agreed to talk to US mediator Donald Rumsfeld, and finally, in a gesture which it said was aimed at "creating a circumstance conducive to the withdrawal of US forces from Lebanon," released the captured US airman, Lt. Goodman.[83] This was a major Syrian concession, given the fact that Syrian leaders had earlier said that he would not be released until after the "war" was over and US forces had withdrawn from Lebanon.[84]

It is possible that Assad was trying to exploit the rising tide of opposition in the United States to the Marine presence in Lebanon; nonetheless, to release Lt. Goodman at a time when US naval guns were still pounding positions held by Syria and its Lebanese allies indicated that the Syrian leader realized that his confrontation with the United States held the danger of getting out of control at a time when he could not count on either Soviet or Arab support. Fortunately for Assad, however, the ineptitude of the Gemayel government and war weariness in both the United States and Israel were soon to enable the Syrian leader to regain predominant influence in Lebanon, a development from which Moscow sought to profit.

The release of Lt. Goodman, coupled with the publication a few days earlier of the Long Commission report which analyzed the US political/military mistakes in Lebanon in the period leading up to the destruction of the Marine headquarters, increased the clamor in the United States for a pullout of the Marines. At the same time the position of Amin Gemayel weakened considerably as negotiations for a disengagement plan among the various warring Lebanese factions broke down at the end of January. The diplomatic impasse was followed by heavy fighting in the Beirut area between the Lebanese army and Druze and Shiite forces – a development which led to the virtual collapse of the Lebanese army, the resignation of Prime Minister Wazzan and the seizure of West Beirut by Moslem militias. As chaos appeared to reign in Beirut, President Reagan suddenly announced the "redeployment" of US Marines to Navy ships off the coast of Lebanon. The US redeployment, which was soon to be followed by that of the other members of the multinational force, was accompanied by American naval shelling of anti-government positions in the vicinity of Beirut. Indeed, the general course of US policy during this period seemed confused at best, and whatever the mistakes the United States had made in backing the Gemayel government up until this point, the hurried exodus of the Marines from Beirut, coupled with what appeared to be indiscriminate artillery fire into the Lebanese mountains, could only hurt the US image, not only in Lebanon, but in the Middle East as a whole. Naturally, such a weakening of the US position was welcomed by Moscow, which moved to coordinate policy directly with Syria following the Moslem takeover of West Beirut. On 8 February *Pravda* announced that Geydar Aliyev, the only Politburo member of Shiite Moslem extraction, would go to Syria for a "working visit." Just before Aliyev was to depart, however, Andropov died, prior to a major accomplishment for Syrian – and Soviet – policy, the abrogation in March of the US-mediated treaty between Lebanon and Israel.

CONCLUSIONS

In examining Soviet–Syrian relations under Andropov two central conclusions can be drawn. In the first place, Syria proved to be Moscow's primary ally in opposing American policy in the Middle East, particularly in Lebanon. As a result Syria's success in thwarting US policy initiatives in Lebanon could also be considered, to a limited extent, a victory for the Soviet Union, given Moscow's zero-sum game view of the Soviet–American influence competition in the Middle East. A second major conclusion that can be drawn from this study, however, is that Moscow paid a stiff price for its support of Syria, both in terms of the risk of a confrontation with the United States and in terms of its larger policy aims in the Middle East.

Moscow's problem in the aftermath of Brezhnev's death was that while it was reinforcing Syria's ability to thwart US diplomacy, if faced the dilemma that Damascus was exploiting Soviet support to achieve its own goals, both in Lebanon and in the Arab world as a whole (goals that were not always compatible with those of the Soviet Union). Thus, Syria sought predominant, if not exclusive, influence in Lebanon, control over the PLO, and a leading role in the Arab world during this period. To be sure, Moscow was not averse to Syria's obtaining a position of Arab leadership. This would mean that Syria would move out of the position of isolation in the Arab world caused by its support for Iran in the Iran–Iraq war, and Moscow may have hoped that Syria would thereby win over some of the more important Centrist Arab states or at least keep them from a reconciliation with Egypt. Nonetheless, Syrian attempts to confront first Israel in May 1983 and then the United States in the September–December 1983 period – confrontations which the Syrian leadership attempted to portray as Syria's "defense of the Arab nation against Zionism and imperialism" – did not appear to meet with full Soviet approval. This was the case not only because most Arab states continued to remain cool to Syria, but also because Syrian leaders threatened to drag in the Soviet Union to help Syria fight its Lebanese battles, especially by claiming that the Soviet–Syrian treaty covered Syrian actions in Lebanon. Similarly, Assad's efforts to split Fatah and his subsequent crackdown on Arafat's supporters in Lebanon appeared to be unpopular in Moscow. In the first place, it further splintered the already badly divided Arab world, with not only Iraq but also Steadfastness Front member Algeria supporting Arafat, thus making Moscow's long-sought "anti-imperialist" Arab unity even more difficult to achieve. Secondly, despite its unhappiness with Arafat's flirtation with the Reagan plan, Moscow gave every appearance of wanting to keep the PLO as an independent actor in Arab politics – one open to Soviet influence – rather than having it become a mere appendage of Syrian policy. Finally, should the hard-liners in the Syrian-backed anti-Arafat movement in Fatah win out, it would be far more difficult for Moscow to gain acceptance for its Middle East peace plan which called for the existence of a Palestinian state alongside, not in place of, Israel.

Thus, the Soviet–Syrian relationship in the Andropov period was an uneasy one, as each country sought to use the other to help further its goals. Nonetheless, if one asks which country profited more from the relationship, the answer would appear to be Syria. While Moscow benefited from Syrian opposition to US diplomatic initiatives, the USSR also had to make important concessions to Damascus during this period. First, after initially demanding that all foreign forces, including Syrian, leave Lebanon by September 1983 the USSR, although realizing that the continued presence of Syrian troops in Lebanon carried with it the danger of a confrontation with the United States, no longer publicly called for a Syrian troop withdrawal. Secondly, after resisting a number of Syrian demands for more advanced weaponry so that it could have a degree of military power equivalent to that of Israel, Moscow agreed to send to Damascus two major weapons systems, the SAM-5 anti-aircraft system and the SS-21 surface-to-surface missile. Both systems had never before been deployed outside the Warsaw Pact area. Interestingly enough, both weapons systems were sent after Moscow failed to give Syria support in a major military confrontation – the SAM-5 after Syria had been defeated by Israel during the Israeli invasion of Lebanon and the SS-21 after the September 1983 Syrian–American confrontation. By sending the two sophisticated weapons systems Moscow may have tried to assuage Syrian unhappiness at the lack of Soviet support. It is, of course, quite possible that the weapons systems were sent to Syria with the primary purpose of aiding it in deterring an attack, thus making Soviet support in a crisis situation unnecessary. In addition, Moscow emphasized during the Syrian military buildup and the subsequent crises that Syrian goals were defensive, another ploy aimed at averting the outbreak of war. Nonetheless, the reason that Soviet troops manned the SAM-5s, and appeared to control the SS-21s as well, may have been that Moscow was concerned that otherwise Syria would exploit the new weaponry to go to war in pursuit of its Lebanese or Middle Eastern goals. Indeed, by sending Assad such weapons, as well as by replenishing his 1982 losses to Israel, the USSR not only enhanced the Syrian leader's bargaining position *vis-à-vis* Israel, the United States and the other Arab states, but also gave him the means to wage war more successfully, should he so choose, as Syria approached its long-sought strategic equivalence with Israel.

In taking such action, Moscow clearly ran a risk. On the one hand, its own credibility and that of its weaponry had come under strong attack by the Arabs during the Israeli invasion of Lebanon in 1982; by providing such advanced weaponry to Syria and by issuing warnings to both Israel and the United States, Moscow evidently hoped to regain some of its lost credibility. The dilemma for the Soviet leadership was that Assad tended to exploit both the new weaponry and the Soviet warnings – limited as they may have been – to further his ambitions in Lebanon and elsewhere in the Arab world. What made matters so dangerous for the Kremlin, particularly at a time when Andropov was ill, was that both in September 1983 and in December 1983, Assad provoked the United States into a military confrontation, thus putting Moscow in the unenviable position of either backing its most important Arab ally, thereby risking a confrontation with the United States, or remaining silent and losing credibility as it had in 1982. Moscow was to choose the latter course, although it may have hoped that the United States–Syrian confrontation would so undermine the American position in the Arab world that the lack of direct Soviet support to Syria would be overlooked. Fortunately for Moscow, the growing war weariness in the United States which led Reagan to withdraw US troops in February 1984, together with an increasingly large consensus in Israel calling for another troop withdrawal, left Syria in the dominant position in Lebanon without the need of direct Soviet support. Nonetheless, the successive crises in Lebanon in the 1982–84 period underlined not only Syria's independence of action *vis-à-vis* the USSR, but also the dangers Moscow faced by being closely tied to the Assad regime.

NOTES

1 For studies of Soviet policy in the Middle East, see Robert O. Freedman, *Soviet Policy Toward the Middle East Since 1970*, 3rd edn (New York: Praeger, 1982); Jon D. Glassman, *Arms for the Arabs: The Soviet Union and War in the Middle East* (Baltimore: Johns Hopkins, 1975); Galia Golan, *Yom Kippur and After: The Soviet Union and the Middle East Crisis* (Cambridge: Cambridge University Press, 1977); Yaacov Ro'i, *From Encroachment to Involvement: A Documentary Study of Soviet Policy in the Middle East* (Jerusalem: Israel Universities Press, 1974); and Adeed Dawisha and Karen Dawisha, eds., *The Soviet Union in the Middle East: Policies and Perspectives* (New York: Holmes and Meier, 1982). See also Yaacov Ro'i, ed., *The Limits to Power* (London: Croom Helm, 1979). For an Arab viewpoint, see Mohamed Heikal, *The Sphinx and the Commissar* (New York: Harper and Row, 1978). For a Soviet view, see E. M. Primakov, *Anatomiia blizhnevostochnogo konflikta* (Moscow: Mysl', 1978).

2 For a Soviet view of the importance of "anti-imperialist" Arab unity, see the comments by Soviet Foreign Minister Andrei Gromyko to PLO chairman Yasser Arafat, during Arafat's visit to the Kremlin in 1979. The minutes of the conversation were captured during the Israeli invasion of Lebanon in 1982. See *PLO in Lebanon: Selected Documents*, Raphael Israeli, ed. (New York: St Martin's Press, 1983), p. 47.

3 For analyses of the domestic situation in Syria, see Nikolas van Dam, *The Struggle for Power in Syria* (New York: St Martin's Press, 1979); Stanley Reed, III, "Dateline Syria: Fin De Régime?," *Foreign Policy*, no. 39 (Summer 1980), pp. 176–90; and Chris Kutscheria, "Sticks and Carrots, " *The Middle East*, no. 80 (June 1981), pp. 8–9.

4 For background analyses of Soviet–Syrian relations, see Freedman, *Soviet Policy Toward the Middle East Since 1970*; Galia Golan, "Syria and the Soviet Union Since the Yom Kippur War," *Orbis*, vol. XXI, no. 4 (Winter 1978), pp. 77–801; and Galia Golan and Itamar Rabinovich, "The Soviet Union and Syria: The Limits of Cooperation," in *The Limits to Power*, Ro'i, ed., pp. 213–31.

5 *Pravda*, 9 October 1980. For a detailed analysis of the treaty, see Amiram Nir, *The Soviet–Syrian Friendship and Cooperation Treaty: Unfulfilled Expectations* (Tel Aviv: Jaffa Center for Strategic Studies, 1983).

6 *Pravda*, 6 December 1978.

7 The central reasons for Soviet inactivity during the Israeli invasion would appear to be (1) the failure of the other Arab states to aid Syria and the PLO; (2) Israeli air supremacy in the region; and (3) uncertainty over the possible US reaction to a Soviet intervention. The reasons for Soviet inactivity are discussed in Robert O. Freedman, "The Soviet Union and the Middle East: Failure to Match the United States as a Regional Power," *Middle East Contemporary Survey*, vol. VI, *1981–82*, Colin Legum, Haim Shaked, and Daniel Dishon, eds. (New York: Holmes and Meier, 1984), pp. 40–48, and Karen Dawisha, "The USSR in the Middle East: Super Power in Eclipse," *Foreign Affairs* (Winter 1982–83), pp. 438–52.

8 Tripoli, *Jana*, 26 June 1982 (*Foreign Broadcast Information Service Daily Report: The Middle East* (hereafter *FBIS: ME*), 26 June 1982, pp. Q-2, Q-3.

9 TASS, 22 June 1982 (*FBIS: USSR*, 22 June 1982, p. H-3).

10 For a description of the Reagan plan, see Barry Rubin, "The United States and the Middle East from Camp David to the Reagan Plan," *Middle East Contemporary Survey*, *1981–82*, pp. 30–31.

11 For a description of the Fez Plan, see *The Middle East Journal*, vol. XXXVII, no. 1 (Winter 1983), p. 71.

12 *Pravda*, 16 September 1982. For an analysis of the status of the Soviet Middle East peace plan on the eve of the Israeli invasion of Lebanon, see Robert O. Freedman, "Moscow, Washington and the Gulf," *American–Arab Affairs*, no. 1 (Summer 1982), pp. 132–34.

13 *Pravda*, 21 September 1982.

14 See report by Edward Walsh, *Washington Post*, 5 January 1983 and Thomas L. Friedman, *New York Times*, 21 March 1983.

15 It is also possible that the Soviet move, in part, was a response to the emplacement of the US troops in Beirut, as well as a means of hampering US air operations in the Eastern Mediterranean near Lebanon.

16 Cited in a report by Thomas L. Friedman, *New York Times*, 23 February 1983.

17 *Pravda*, 25 February 1983.

18 *Pravda*, 31 March 1983.

19 Cited in *Christian Science Monitor*, 30 March 1983.

20 Riyadh *SPA*, 2 April 1983 (*FBIS:ME*, 4 April 1983, p. C-6).

21 The text of Gromyko's press conference may be found in *FBIS: USSR*, 4 April 1983, pp. AA-1 - AA-17.

22 *Ibid.*, p. AA-15.

23 *Ibid.*, p. AA-16.

24 Cited in Reuters report, *New York Times*, April 17 1983.

25 See report by David Landau, *Jerusalem Post*, 20 April 1983.

26 See report by Herbert Denton, *Washington Post*, 22 April 1983.

27 For an analysis of the dynamics of the process leading to the Israeli–Lebanon agreement, see the report by Bernard Gwertzman, *New York Times*, 10 May 1983.

28 See report by Herbert Denton, *Washington Post*, 7 May 1983.

29 TASS report, 9 May 1983 (*FBIS: USSR*, 10 May 1983, p. H-1.)

30 See reports by Thomas Friedman, *New York Times*, 10 May 1983, and Nora Bustany, *Washington Post*, 10 May 1983.

31 See report by Bernard Gwertzman, *New York Times*, 11 May 1983.

32 See report by John Goshko, *Washington Post*, 11 May 1983.

33 Damascus, *Sana*, 9 May 1983 (*FBIS: ME*, May 9, 1983, p. H-2).

34 Reuters report, *New York Times*, 11 May 1983.

35 Beirut Domestic Service in Arabic, 10 May 1983 (*FBIS: ME*, 16 May 1983, p. H-8). This has become the standard Soviet response when Soviet officials are asked about Soviet intervention in Middle East crises.

36 See *Jerusalem Post*, 15 May 1983, for statements by Igor Belaev and Karen Khachaturev.

37 See report in *Jerusalem Post*, 24 May 1983.

38 See report by William E. Farrell, *New York Times*, 26 May 1983.

39 See report by Hirsh Goodman, *Jerusalem Post*, 27 May 1983.

40 For an analysis of Syrian–PLO relations at this time, see the article by Eric Rouleau, *Manchester Guardian Weekly*, 15 May 1983.

41 See *FBIS:Me*, 5 August 1983, p. A-1.

42 See *Al-Watan Al-Arabi*, cited by INA (*FBIS: ME*, 2 September 1983, p. A-1).

43 For a description of Soviet military facilities in Syria, see *Near East Report*, vol. xxvii, no. 23 (10 June 1983), p. 2.

44 Cited in report by David Shipler, *New York Times*, 2 June 1983.

45 Cited in report by Don Oberdorfer, *Washington Post*, 8 July 1983.

46 See report by Nora Bustany, *Washington Post*, 24 July 1983.

47 Novosti article by Pavel Demchenko, cited in AP report in the *Jerusalem Post*, 3 August 1983. Novosti reports are often used as a direct means of trying to influence Western nations.

48 *Tishrin* editorial, cited in Reuters report, *Washington Post*, 28 August 1983.

49 See reports by E. J. Donne, Jr, *New York Times*, 20 September 1983; and by David Ottaway, *Washington Post*, 29 September 1983.

50 See reports by Thomas L. Friedman, *New York Times*, 23 September 1983; and by Trudy Rubin, *Christian Science Monitor*, 19 September 1983.

51 *Izvestiia*, 4 September 1983 (*FBIS: USSR*, 7 September 1983, p. H-4); Editorial, *New Times*, no. 38 (1983), p. 1.

52 *Pravda*, 19 September 1983 and 20 September 1983.

53 See *Al-Qabas* (Kuwait), 20 September 1983 (*FBIS: USSR*, 22 September 1983, p. H-1).

54 Cited in report by Bernard Gwertzman, *New York Times*, 23 September 1983.

55 See *Tishrin*, 12 September 1983, cited on Radio Monte Carlo (*FBIS:ME*, 13 September 1983, p. H-1); Radio Monte Carlo, 23 September 1983 (*FBIS: ME*, 23 September 1983, p. H-1).

56 Andropov himself praised the ceasefire (*Pravda*, 30 September 1983) in a page one report of his meeting with PDRY leader Ali Nasser Mohammed.

57 See Damascus Domestic Service, 15 September 1983 (*FBIS: ME*, 15 September 1983, p. H-1), 18 September 1983 (*FBIS: ME*, 19 September 1983, p. H-3), and 14 September 1983 (*FBIS: ME*, 20 September 1983, pp. H-1, H-2).

58 For the text of the ceasefire agreement, see the AP report, *New York Times*, 27 September 1983.

59 See report by Michael Getler, *Washington Post*, 7 October 1983. A report in the Arabic-language *Al-Majallah* asserted that Moscow had told Damascus that the missiles could only be used in self-defense (*FBIS: ME*, 31 October 1983, p. ii).

60 A. Stepanov, "Consistent Support," *New Times*, no. 42 (1983), p. 13.

61 Moscow Radio in Arabic, commentary by Alexander Timoshkin, 6 October 1983, (*FBIS: USSR*, 7 October 1983, pp. H-2, H-3).

62 See Pavel Demchenko's comments in *Pravda*, 25 October 1983.

63 See Moscow Radio in Arabic, commentary by Aleksei Zlatorunskii, 2 November 1983 (*FBIS: USSR*, 3 November 1983, pp. H-1, H-2).

64 Moscow Radio in Arabic, Rafael Artonov commentary, 3 November 1983 (*FBIS: USSR*, 4 November 1983, p. H-3).

65 *Pravda*, 5 November 1983.

66 *Pravda*, 6 November 1983.

67 TASS, 4 November 1983 (*FBIS: USSR*, 8 November 1983, p. H-2).

68 See report by Bernard Gwertzman, *New York Times*, 8 November 1983; see *FBIS: USSR*, 10 November 1983, p. H-2.

69 See report by Thomas Friedman, *New York Times*, 11 November 1983.

70 FBIS: USSR, 15 November 1983, p. H-2.

71 *FBIS: ME*, 14 November 1983, p. H-2.

72 *Pravda*, 13 November 1983.

73 See *Pravda*, 19 November 1983; Freedman, *Soviet Policy Toward the Middle East Since 1970*, p. 255; TASS, 20 November 1983 (*FBIS: USSR*, 21 November 1983, p. H-2).

74 *FBIS: USSR*, 29 November 1983, p. H-8. There was some indication that Arafat was publicly angry with the lack of Soviet aid, but he moved quickly to deny the report published to that effect in the Egyptian newspaper *Al-Akhbar* (see Kuwait *KUNA*, 29 November 1983; *FBIS: USSR*, 29 November 1983, p. H-I).

75 *Pravda*, 29 November 1983.

76 Cited in report by Richard Halloran, *New York Times*, 23 November 1983.

77 UPI report, *Washington Post*, 24 November 1983; cited in report by David Ottaway, *Washington Post*, 27 November 1983.

78 Cited in AP report, *New York Times*, 27 November 1983.

79 Damascus Domestic Service, 29 November 1983 (*FBIS: ME*, 30 November 1983, p. H-2).

80 Cited in *New York Times*, 5 December 1983.

81 *FBIS: USSR*, 6 December 1983, p. H-1; see, also, *FBIS: USSR*, 14 December 1983, p. H-1.

82 See Damascus Radio, 8 December 1983 (*FBIS: ME*, 8 December 1983, p. H-4).

83 Damascus Domestic Service, 3 January 1984 (*FBIS: ME*, 3 January 1984, p. H-2).

84 This point had been repeatedly emphasized by Defense Minister Mustapha Tlas, while Syrian Foreign Minister Khaddam only a few days earlier had linked the airman's release to the suspension of US reconnaissance flights over Syrian positions (Radio Monte Carlo, 1 January 1984; *FBIS: ME*, 3 January 1984, pp. H-1, H-2).

IO

Indo-Soviet security relations

JYOTIRMOY BANERJEE

Indo-Soviet relations in the politico-security realm have flourished in part because of a lack of American willingness to help India. Significantly, the Nehru government had approached the United States in the 1950s and the 1960s to help build India's major steel projects in Bhilai and Bokaro. But Washington turned down India's requests because the projects were to be in the state sector of the economy. Again in late 1962, during India's *débâcle* in its border war with China, the Nehru government turned to the Kennedy Administration for assistance. While the latter responded promptly with small arms supply, Washington hesitated to comply with a subsequent Indian request for a long-term modernization of India's armed forces.[1] The Pentagon feared that such US cooperation with the Indian armed forces would result in Pakistani retaliation in terms of closure of the US intelligence base in Peshawar targeted at the USSR. Paradoxically, Pakistan closed it down anyway a few years later. In all three cases (Bhilai, Bokaro and the Indian armed forces) Moscow was only too happy to fill the vacuum. All three today are, therefore, symbols of Indo-Soviet, rather than Indo-American friendship.

While Stalinist Russia looked upon newly independent India's non-alignment with as much suspicion as did US Secretary of State Dulles, following Stalin's demise in 1953 the Soviets were quicker to appreciate Third World nationalism and changed their Cold War perceptions and policy accordingly. The widely divergent geopolitical perceptions of the superpowers relating to South Asia resulted in closer identification of views on a number of political issues between Moscow and New Delhi than between the latter and Washington. Since Washington militarily backed India's rival, Pakistan, in South Asia in the 1950s, early 1960s and again in 1971 during the Bangladesh crisis, the largest nation in the area was antagonized and looked to Moscow for economic, political and military support. And such support was, and continues to be, forthcoming. Even though the United States provided a significant measure of bilateral economic aid to India (around $10 billion until 1980),[2] the Pentagon seems to have been the most significant obstacle to an improvement of Indo-American political relations. Though both India and the United States pride themselves on being democracies, they apparently find it easier to deal with non-democratic regimes than with each other.

After these preliminary observations, we turn to an analysis of Indo-Soviet relations. These relations have blossomed over the past three decades. This chapter cannot and need not take the entire gamut of those relations into account; it will, instead, concentrate on the key elements – namely, the politico-security ties. An assessment of those ties will be attempted within the framework of the following questions: (1) How have Indo-Soviet political relations fared over the past three decades; i.e., in the post-Stalin era? (2) How does Moscow perceive these relations and how do they serve Soviet interests? (3) Have these ties helped or hindered India's national interest? (4) Has India grown over-dependent on Moscow and, if so, what could be done to create a more genuine non-alignment that does not remain tilted towards Moscow?

While the February 1955 agreement on the Bhilai steel project marked an early turning point in post-independence India's relations with the USSR, the beginning of military cooperation coincided with the Soviet decision to cut off aid to China in 1960. In August 1962, at a time when China's relations with both India and the USSR had reached a low point, Moscow granted New Delhi a license to produce the MiG-21 jet fighter, which became the backbone of the Indian Air Force. Significantly, India was the first non-communist country to receive such a "favor." As already noted, Washington declined India's request for long-term military aid in the 1960s for fear of upsetting its own security collaboration with Pakistan. Moscow then stepped in to fill India's defense needs. The death of India's first Premier, Jawaharlal Nehru, and the ouster of Nikita Khrushchev from power in 1964 marked the end of the euphoric days of Indo-Soviet friendship. For about half a decade following the Indo-Pakistani war of 1965, the post-Khrushchev triumvirate – Brezhnev, Kosygin and Podgorny – tried a more balanced approach towards the subcontinent. This was partly with a view to offset growing Chinese influence in Pakistan (especially in the sphere of security cooperation), which was replacing US influence; Washington was becoming increasingly involved further east, in Vietnam. However, the 1971 Bangladesh crisis against the background of heightened Sino-Soviet tension since 1969 and the opening of China to the United States decisively reestablished Moscow's Indian orientation. The Indo-Soviet

Friendship Treaty signed that year provided the strategic cover under which Indira Gandhi's India assisted in the dismemberment of Pakistan.[3] New Delhi's Moscow connection had paid off, as the Soviets unfailingly point out today.[4]

While Brezhnev visited New Delhi in December 1973, the then Defense Minister Grechko led a high-level military team there fourteen months later amidst reports that two Pakistani divisions were being equipped by China and that the United States might resume arms aid to Islamabad. Grechko's talks in India culminated in an agreement to expand defense production in the host country, including production of an improved version of the MiG-21. While other high-level political visits were exchanged between Moscow and New Delhi over the next few years, in October 1979 K. Subrahmanyam, India's ranking defense expert, led a delegation to the USSR to discuss ongoing programs and ways to increase the rate of indigenization of the Soviet-supplied equipment.[5]

Meanwhile, the evolution of the strategic environment around India seemed to call for closer security cooperation with Moscow. In the second half of the 1970s, with a post-Vietnam United States in an introspective and uncertain mood, Soviet power appeared to be rising dramatically. Along the volatile "arc of instability" stretching eastward from the African Horn, Soviet and allied involvement in regional conflicts became increasingly noticeable. Moscow's ability to project force overseas by air or sea was no longer in doubt. In May 1978, NATO adopted a long-term modernization plan, while President Carter's security adviser Zbigniew Brzezinski reached an understanding of sorts during his visit to Beijing. In August, the Sino-Japanese Friendship Treaty was signed, the text containing a reference to "hegemonism" which irked Moscow. In November and December, the latter signed its own Friendship Treaties with Hanoi and Kabul, respectively. With the next few months, as Iran shook from an elemental upheaval, there occurred the Hanoi-backed overthrow of the Pol Pot regime in Kampuchea, Deng Xiaoping's hurried visit to the United States, the establishment of Sino-American diplomatic ties, and the outbreak of the Sino-Vietnamese border war. By the end of 1979 the Soviet military intervention in Afghanistan introduced yet another element of tension, since it brought the oil-rich Persian Gulf, seen as the jugular of the West, well within the strike range of Soviet tactical aircraft. The Carter Doctrine followed in January 1980, which declared the Gulf to be within the West's vital sphere of interest, and the accelerated program of putting together a Rapid Deployment Joint Task Force, elevated to an independent Central Command by President Reagan for the defense of the West's sea lines of communication with the Gulf. Moscow's rivalry with the United States and China brought Pakistan into the picture because of its geographic proximity to the Gulf and a Soviet-dominated Afghanistan and because of its close politico-military ties with the United States and China.[6] Little wonder that India's strategic value for Moscow as a counterweight to China and Pakistan rose further in recent years. To be sure, the Janata interregnum in India of 1977–79 had made Moscow nervous, since the Janata leaders had started diversifying the source of India's arms procurements so as to lessen dependence on Moscow, and had even discouraged the Maldives from granting a naval facility to the USSR.

With the collapse of the Janata government and Mrs Gandhi's return to power, Soviet anxieties were laid to rest. Mrs Gandhi's government reversed Janata policy and quickly recognized the Vietnamese-backed Heng Samrin government in Phnom Penh. In June 1980, New Delhi signed a $1.63 billion arms deal with Moscow.[7] In December of that year, shortly after Brezhnev's second visit to India in the course of which the Soviet leader announced an abortive peace plan on the Persian Gulf, it was announced that the Indian Air Force would buy the high-flying MiG-25 Foxbat in its trainer and reconnaissance versions.[8] In November 1981, Indo-Soviet security ties were symbolized by the establishment of an all-weather, multi-channel troposcatter communication link between the two capitals. In March 1982, an unusually high-powered Soviet military delegation headed by then Defense Minister and Politburo member Dmitri Ustinov arrived in New Delhi on a five-day visit.[9] The delegation included the Soviet air and navy chiefs, Kutakhov and Gorshkov, respectively, army deputy chief Vitali Shabanov, thirty majors and lieutenant generals and at least ten other senior officials. This was the most powerful military team ever sent by the Kremlin to a non-communist country. Its members inspected the naval base and other military installations in Bombay, aeronautical plants run by Hindusthan Aeronautics in Bangalore, and other defense establishments in Agra, Jodhpur (MiG base) and Babina (armored corps base). On the day of his arrival Ustinov conferred with Mrs Gandhi for ninety minutes and for forty-five minutes with then newly-appointed Indian Defense Minister, R. Venkataraman. The absence of aides in the Ustinov–Gandhi talks pointed to the probability that broad security perceptions were exchanged and compared. Ustinov that evening revealed the kind of talks he had had with the Indian Premier and Defense Minister during the day. He observed that the two sides had found "a common language" on the questions concerning the security of Asia and the world, that the Indo-Soviet Friendship Treaty of 1971 "plays a particularly great role in present-day conditions when the international situation has sharply deteriorated," and that the "aggressive imperialist circles" were to be blamed for this.[10] He then transparently referred to Pakistan's security cooperation with the United States: "Imperialist reaction is also striving to spread the sphere of its so-called 'vital interests' to South Asia, pinning special hopes on the stockpiling of armaments by some countries of the region. And we are well aware that this cannot but cause concern in India."[11]

He also quoted Brezhnev to underline Moscow's desire to see India as "a strong country capable of protecting successfully its independence [and] consolidating the cause of peace in Asia." He went on to add that "the Soviet Union regards its assistance to the strengthening of India's defense potential precisely within this context."[12] This was nothing short of publicizing the view that India neatly fitted into the Soviet scheme of things in Asia, notwithstanding New Delhi's endeavors to normalize relations with both Islamabad and Beijing. The Indian side reportedly urged the Soviets to provide the latest MiGs and to speed up the delivery of spare parts, to all of which the latter agreed. Ustinov, who had an impressive background in defense production, agreed to help further expand the already noticeable defense production base in India.

Shortly before his death Ustinov paid another visit to India in March 1984. This time Gorshkov and Vitali Shabanov accompanied him along with the First Deputy Chief of the General Staff, Marshal Sergei Akhromeyev, and other officials. On the day of his arrival, 5 March, Ustinov held talks with Indira Gandhi and R. Venkataraman, and later with President Zail Singh and Foreign Minister Rao. The team visited the Nasik factory of the Hindusthan Aeronautics, the naval base at Visakhapatnam, probably the tank factory at Avadi and a military unit at Dehradun.[13]

The questions which arise in this connection are: What was the meaning of all these high-level military visits and how do the Soviets perceive security ties with India? The Ustinov visits reflected Moscow's anxiety to help India in the military realm to balance the growing American–Pakistani security link and to demonstrate to Islamabad and its allies that Pakistan continued to remain precariously sandwiched between a Soviet-dominated Afghanistan and a "pro-Soviet" India. Hard-headed business considerations must also have played a part, a possibility reinforced by the disclosures following the massive spy scandal in New Delhi in early 1985, in which the USSR, Poland and GDR from the Soviet bloc and France from the West were found to be in cahoots with business firms and government officials for the purpose of conducting *inter alia*, industrial espionage.[14] After all, New Delhi has been diversifying the sources on its arms procurement since the Janata days. France, England and West Germany are among the countries supplying India with modern arms; there has been periodic press speculation both in the United States and in India in the 1980s that $1 billion arms deal might come off between Washington and New Delhi. There was talk of India possibly buying US F-5G Tigershark jet fighters, when Mrs Gandhi visited Washington in mid-1982.[15] All this must have alarmed the Soviets somewhat. The visits by the Soviet elite were at least partly meant to ensure the Soviet arms market in India. They also served to reinforce Western suspicion that India was really not so non-aligned – an impression which Moscow takes pains to keep alive.

This brings us to the question of the Soviet perception of security ties with New Delhi and the latter's relations with neighboring Pakistan and China. Ever since the Afghan crisis Soviet publications have increasingly focused on Pakistan's security links with China and the United States and the allegedly negative impact of these links on India's security.[16] Soviet commentators have consistently seized upon doubts or disapprovals which New Delhi or the Indian media might have expressed regarding US, Pakistani or Chinese policies and then expanded on them. Soviet scholars have delved into the recent past to discover that the Sino-Indian border conflicts of 1959 and 1962 had been initiated by Beijing with the objective of complicating Moscow's relations with New Delhi. Though Beijing had failed in this, its South Asian policy "regrettably" remained unchanged.[17] The Soviets amplify India's reservations about the package proposal that the Chinese have advanced in recent years to settle the border problem on the ground that India would be the net loser in the territorial transactions involved. Soviet commentators express skepticism about the recent moves towards Sino-Indian normalization, since in their view India and the states of Indochina constitute roadblocks to China's drive to gain access to the Indian Ocean and domination over South and Southeast Asia. To undermine the Indian obstacle, China is allegedly engaged in training and arming separatists from India, partly in centers located in Pakistan. The aim of such Sino-Pakistani collusion is the destabilization of the northeast and northwest regions of the "Hindustan subcontinent."[18] The US secret service also plays a role in China's game since, as one Soviet observer noted, "The Chinese–American alliance has acquired a global strategic character . . ."[19] At a seminar on Indo-Soviet relations held in Tbilisi on the eve of Brezhnev's visit to India in December 1980, a Soviet scholar even called for a kind of collective security against the onslaught of the Sinocentric view of history propounded by Chinese historians.[20]

Turning to the specifics of Sino-American military cooperation with Islamabad, Soviet commentaries allege that such cooperation stretched from waging an "undeclared war" against the Karmal government in Kabul to the Karakoram-80 project involving mountain-based electronic surveillance of India, Afghanistan and the Soviet south. The Chinese-built all-weather, 535-mile Karakoram Highway connecting China's Xinjiang province with Pakistan, it is maintained, had evil implications for India's security. Pakistan has been allegedly conducting more conventional types of espionage against India and has concentrated the bulk of its army on India's border.[21] To top it all, Islamabad's nuclear activities were geared to harm India since past experience showed that whenever the United States gave arms to Pakistan, the latter chose to attack India. Current Pakistani acquisition of US arms exceeded that country's legitimate defense needs and boded ill for its eastern neighbor. The transparent implication of these Soviet discussions is that, since both Moscow and New Delhi faced threats from common adversaries, they should not only never part company but come ever closer together.

Soviet observers carefully note the exchange of political and military visits between Pakistan, the United States and China, and maintain that the latter two countries are secretly acquiring base facilities on Pakistan's Baluch coast on the Arabian Sea. Pakistan has a key role to play in the US Central Command's strategy for the Persian Gulf, while China seeks access to the Indian Ocean via the Karakoram Highway connected with Pakistan's forward positions along the line of actual control in Kashmir. In such an environment, it is concluded with smug satisfaction, Moscow remains the only reliable friend of India. Indeed, top Soviet leaders have loudly reiterated Moscow's eagerness to see India's defense capabilities further improved. Brezhnev said so in December 1980, Gromyko repeated it the next August and, as already seen, Ustinov took it up again subsequently. Further, in August 1981, when Soviet Deputy Foreign Minister N. Firyubin failed in his mission in Islamabad to make the Pakistanis talk with Kabul, he made an unscheduled detour to New Delhi to confer with Indian officials. Such Soviet moves are hardly calculated to stimulate friendship between India and Pakistan. The late Soviet Premier Kosygin had pulled the issue of Kashmir off the backburner during his hurried India visit in March 1979 against the tense background of the Vietnamese–Kampuchean and Sino-Vietnamese hostilities. What is remarkable about all these Soviet pronouncements and discussions about India's relations with Pakistan, China or the United States, is not that they are not based on facts but rather the one-sided selection of the negative aspects of those relations. The more positive aspects – like India's normalization talks with Pakistan and China, its attempt at cooperation with the former in the form of South Asian Regional Cooperation and such other cooperative moves – are either ignored or treated with underlying cynicism. New Delhi does not necessarily feel cheerful about unsolicited Soviet proclamations on its relations with third countries, even if those proclamations might run close to Indian views.

Other issues of concern to India are also cleverly manipulated by the Soviets. New Delhi's long-standing call for making the Indian Ocean a peace zone has been verbally backed by Moscow. The peace zone concept primarily implies that the United States should wind down its military presence in the region, especially on the Diego Garcia atoll, although the Indian call has been formally addressed to both super-powers. Moscow cheerfully maintains that it is ready to withdraw militarily provided the United States does the same and blames the latter for the failure of talks on the demilitarization of the Indian Ocean in 1978. Its apparent willingness to withdraw seems cynical in light of the fact that the USSR and its allies have been actively supporting various revolutionary forces and dictatorships in Africa, including the Horn. The cynicism appears all the more blatant, since Moscow makes its withdrawal conditional on US withdrawal; the upgrading of Carter's Rapid Deployment Joint Task Force to the Central Command under Reagan, as noted earlier, is hardly a signal of the US willingness to withdraw from the Indian Ocean. Moscow, therefore, is in the happy position of squarely blaming the United States for the ongoing rivalry in the region. Also, because of their military presence in Afghanistan, the Soviets will still be in the proximity of the Persian Gulf even if their naval forces withdrew from South Yemen. The West, on the other hand, has to project force from overseas; their naval withdrawal would mean the end of their military presence in the area, which the West can ill afford, given the importance of the Gulf oil. All Moscow has to do is to encourage more non-alignment in the region, as reflected in Brezhnev's proposal for the Gulf made on 10 December 1980, in New Delhi. The West, on the other hand, has to find local partners willing to cooperate and run the risk of being identified as pro-West.

An important reason behind Moscow's cultivation of strategic relations with India is the historic fear of being encircled, coupled with its drive to expand southwards, and its long-term strategy to block China's southward advance. Hence it opposes any attempt at a Sino-Indian understanding on improving bilateral relations and will do the same if Hanoi were to reach an understanding on outstanding issues with Beijing. It is also interesting to note that, while Moscow blames the United States for creating tension whenever the latter supplies arms anywhere – be it the Pershing II or cruise missiles for West Europe or F-16s for Pakistan – it explains away its own arms-peddling or that of its allies Cuba, the GDR or Czechoslovakia as peaceful cooperation.

MOSCOW AND MRS GANDHI

Significantly, Moscow consistently chose to ignore the differences which persisted between its views and those of Mrs Gandhi's government on Afghanistan and other issues.[22] Although Mrs Gandhi refused to join the US-orchestrated "hue and cry" over the Soviet military intervention in Afghanistan, her government conveyed to the Soviets in private India's concern at the continued Soviet military presence in that country. The Indo-Soviet communiqués following Brezhnev's summit in New Delhi in December 1980 and Mrs Gandhi's summit in Moscow in the fall of 1982 were silent on the Afghan question. But Soviet pronouncements and scholarly analyses simply sidetracked the stumbling block when discussing India's attitude towards the Afghan problem in the context of Indo-Soviet relations. Mrs Gandhi's attitude towards Karmal in Kabul and Samrin in Phnom Penh stemmed from her *Weltanschauung* of opposing the United States, Pakistan and China on the international political plane rather than from an automatic pro-Soviet orientation. But the result was the same, and Moscow played it up. Over the past one and a half decades the Kremlin has considered Indira Gandhi as the best available alternative in terms of India's foreign policy orientation, a consideration which also resulted in a split in the Communist Party of India. Soviet media carefully noted each minor attempt on or alleged plots of assassination of Mrs Gandhi and immediately blamed the CIA for them.[23] Soviet allegations of the CIA's hand in Mrs Gandhi's actual assassination made George Shultz, the US Secretary of State, display open anger in the presence of Soviet Premier Tikhonov during the funeral in early November 1984 in New Delhi. Mrs Gandhi's importance to Moscow was reflected, *inter alia*, in the fact that only an alternate member of the Party Politburo attended the Congress of the Communist Party of India (CPI) at the end of March 1982, which disappointed the latter party. Even that Soviet Party representative, Eduard Shevardnadze, who would rise to the position of a full Politburo member and Foreign Minister under Gorbachev, was required to convey to Mrs Gandhi "warm greetings" from Brezhnev so as to mollify her. *New Times* quoted only that part of a message from the Soviet Party's Central Committee to the CPI Congress which strongly suggested that the CPI ought to throw in its lot once again with Mrs Gandhi's government.[24] Brezhnev had earlier underlined Mrs Gandhi's political importance for the USSR in his key report to the 26th Congress of his Party in early 1981.[25] At both his summits with her in 1980 and 1982 he called her an "outstanding" stateswoman. The recipient of these eulogies was, however, less lavish in reciprocation.[26] If Subramaniam Swamy is correct, Mrs Gandhi had even maneuvered a demonstration organized by him against the Soviet leader on the Afghan issue during Brezhnev's New Delhi visit in 1980, because the latter had allegedly avoided meeting her when she visited Moscow while being out of office.[27] With Mrs Gandhi's removal from the Indian political scene and India's transition to the Rajiv Gandhi era, the Soviets, as the Americans, are carefully monitoring their relations with India.

THE POST-INDIRA ERA

Rajiv Gandhi, who succeeded his mother as Prime Minister and obtained an unprecedented electoral victory in December 1984, has been widely billed as a young man of forty with a modern and technical outlook and without ideological hangups characteristic of the older generation of politicians who resisted British imperialism. Characteristically, upon his rather reluctant entry into politics in the early 1980s, he introduced business management techniques and the use of computers into the ruling Congress (I.) Party. On being elected Prime Minister he coopted former pilot and business executive friends into important positions in the party and government and launched an unprecedented Reagan-type budget that promised to unleash the private sector, while making India's stodgy state sector more accountable. His maiden speeches as the elected Prime Minister were remarkably free of rhetoric about "socialism."

All this made the powerful pro-Soviet lobby in India nervous about the future orientation of that country's domestic and foreign policies. The Soviets had seen Mrs Gandhi as a politically reliable partner, even though the economic liberalization process had started following her comeback to power in 1980. Her assassination in October 1984 introduced new uncertainties in the Kremlin. Because of the pressure from the pro-Soviet lobby, partly embedded within the Congress (I.), Rajiv Gandhi and other prominent party members belatedly made public pronouncements with the reassurance that their policies were in full consonance with "socialism" and that they had no intention of deviating from the "socialist path." From the Kremlin's point of view the stakes are high, i.e., a thirty-year economic partnership, a twenty-five-year military relationship and a fourteen-year Friendship Treaty with India. As noted earlier, the Afghan crisis and the consequent renewal of US security ties with Pakistan have increased India's importance to the Kremlin, quite apart from India's role in Soviet eyes as a counterweight to China. India's recent chairmanship of the non-aligned movement has added to that importance. Moscow's rupee-trade with India, which grew from a meager $1.3 million (Rs 1.3 crores) in 1953–54 to $4.6 billion (Rs 4,620 crores) in 1985,[28] enables the Soviets to divert part of their massive rupee holdings to political purposes. The espionage scandal in New Delhi already mentioned revealed illegal Soviet access to the Indian government's secrets, paradoxically through private firms enjoying big export orders from the USSR. It is revealing that the Indian private sector accounts for 90 per cent of all India's exports to the USSR, but only 10 per cent of India's imports from that country.[29]

While the Soviets may have drawn satisfaction from the Bhopal carnage caused by a poison gas leak from a pesticide plant of a US multinational at a politically sensitive time in India, Rajiv's retention of the External Affairs and Science and Technology portfolios following his election as Prime Minister may have seemed like indicators of future change in these areas under his guidance, the overall results of which would be better ties with the West. Some of the Soviet trepidations following Mrs Gandhi's unexpected death came through in a number of early statements. A message to Rajiv from the Soviet Council of Ministers following his landslide electoral victory and released on 2 January 1985, sounded as if the Kremlin was seeking reassurance: "In the Soviet Union you are known as a firm adherent of the course of Jawaharlal Nehru-Indira Gandhi . . . Following this course, India has scored impressive successes in solving socio-economic problems, in developing science, technology and culture and in strengthening its international positions . . ."[30] The "course" is clear. The Soviets understand thereby India's non-alignment which is tilted towards Moscow, especially in the politico-security realm. Remarkable was the Soviet attempt in this message to pre-commit Rajiv. If up to the point of his election he was "known" at all, it was for his perceived pro-technology – and, therefore, image-wise at least – pro-Western leanings. Three weeks later another Soviet message reminded the young Indian leader of "the time-tested Soviet–Indian friendly relations based on the solid foundation" of the Friendship Treaty. It further noted that bilateral relations were marked by "the ties of close friendship" and were "an increasingly tangible factor of peace and stability in Asia and in the world as a whole."[31]

To be sure, in his foreign policy statements Rajiv has stressed continuity rather than change, especially in the context of relations with

Washington and Moscow. Even at his mother's funeral he reportedly expressed concern to Secretary of State George Shultz over US arms supply to Pakistan. In his first radio broadcast to the nation on 12 November 1984, Rajiv appeared even-handed in stressing the import- ance of relations with the two superpowers and emphasized economic and technological, as distinct from political, ties with the United States. In his next broadcast on 5 January 1985, which followed his electoral triumph, he said nothing specific on Moscow or Washington. While reiterating adherence to the "basic approach" of his illustrious pre- decessors, he revealed what was suggestive of flexibility to say that "like them we shall be dynamic in our responses to the changing context . . ."[32]

As his official foreign tours loomed large on the horizon in mid-1985, Rajiv began raising issues of international relations which revealed that his party was not about to dispense with past rhetoric on East–West issues, even though young technocrats had filled its many key positions. On 4 May 1985, in his first address as the President of All-India Congress Committee (I.), the Prime Minister raised the issues of Pakistan's suspected nuclear activity and acquisition of arms, both of which pointed to US responsibility.[33] Interestingly enough, the following day the party congress unanimously adopted the economic resolution reiterating commitment to "socialism" and, in the same breath, endorsed the new government's economic liberalization drive. While top Pentagon official Fred C. Ikle was conferring at this time in New Delhi,[34] and President Reagan praised Rajiv's economic liberalization as a "revolution" in an address in Madrid on 7 May,[35] India's foreign policy posture after Mrs Gandhi seemed to continue in the familiar anti- US slant. On 10 May, India's envoy to the United Nations regretted "new forms of pressure and coercion" in connection with a Nicaraguan proposal directed against US economic sanctions.[36]

On the eve of Rajiv's arrival in Moscow on 21 May, the new Soviet leader, Mikhail Gorbachev, who had met his Indian counterpart briefly at Chernenko's funeral in March, granted his first interview since he took over in the Kremlin to a foreign journalist, an Indian, to say that Rajiv Gandhi was greatly respected in the USSR.[37] Rajiv's Moscow talks went off well. In keeping with past usage established by his mother, during his six-day visit to the USSR he was critical of the United States for arming Pakistan, militarizing the Indian Ocean and for its policy towards Latin America, even though his official US visit was scheduled for the following month. If there was a partial US satisfaction, it lay in the Prime Minister's remark that India was opposed to outside interference anywhere, which would apply not only to Nicaragua but also to Afghanistan. Gorbachev broke protocol to arrive at Rajiv's apartment in Moscow ten minutes earlier than scheduled on 22 May, invited the latter to walk together to their meeting place, and with apparent spontaneity picked up flowers from the Kremlin compound to offer to his guest. Their talks without aides lasted three and a-half hours, a half-hour more than scheduled.[38]

The Soviets signed two economic agreements with India on 22 May, one of which would provide one billion rubles of credit to finance the purchase of Soviet goods and services for joint projects in oil, power coal, machine-building, etc.[39] The second one set out guidelines for economic trade, scientific and technical joint ventures in third countries. The subsequent toasting with soft-drinks (as an indication of his campaign against alcohol abuse) symbolized Gorbachev's determination to reorient his country towards greater efficiency, a point he had in common with his Indian guest. The Soviets gave Rajiv the Lenin Peace Prize to honor his departed mother and named a square in Moscow after her, just as they had named another square after his grandfather, Nehru, during Indira Gandhi's Moscow visit in the fall of 1982. They also indicated a desire to hold a Festival of India like the ones which would open shortly in France and the United States. Rajiv kept up the anti-United States rhetoric. At a press conference in Moscow he accused the United States of turning a "blind eye" to Pakistan's suspect nuclear activity. He also contrasted Soviet and US attitudes towards the six-nation Delhi Declaration on nuclear disarmament; while Moscow had supported it, the United States "did not even bother to pick up the declaration," he said. He added that he would raise the question of US support for the Punjab terrorists when he visited Washington and voiced suspicion that the FBI disclosure of 13 May on the unearthing of a Sikh terrorist plot to assassinate him during his forthcoming US visit was not exhaustive.[40] Such critical remarks on the United States, which were made in the USSR, must have been pure music to Soviet ears. At the same time his visit to the USSR did not immediately spawn an agreement on the transfer of the MiG-29 to India, presumed to be a counter to the US-supplied Pakistani F-16. Rajiv also revealed that the Soviet offer to help build a nuclear power station had safeguard implications and that India was, therefore, in no hurry to grab for it.

Rajiv continued with his anti-United States rhetoric following the conclusion of his USSR visit. The Indo-Soviet Joint Statement sounded like other such statements from Indira Gandhi's days, with the list of demands including the closing of all foreign bases in the Indian Ocean, recognition of Mauritius' claim to Diego Garcia (a major US base), strict respect for Nicaragua's rights, and cessation of the militarization of outer space, etc. As in the past, Afghanistan was not mentioned, revealing the continued residue of Indo-Soviet differences.[41] It was somewhat startling that the Indian Premier made an issue out of his disapproval of Reagan's space defense initiative or "star wars" program. While visiting UNESCO in Paris on 7 June, Rajiv called for international support to that organization and its like, which "strong nations," meaning primarily the United States were "bending."[42] The Premier continued with his US critique in Algiers and Washington itself during his subsequent visit to these capitals.[43] If he, nevertheless, made a favorable impression on the whole in the United States, it was not the result of the contents of his speeches and remarks but rather of his youth, warmth and sincerity. Contrary to expectations, his visit to the United States did not lead to a military deal, even though top US Defense Department officials had visited New Delhi in May, as already noted, and a memorandum of understanding had been signed there with Commerce Secretary Malcolm Baldrige on hi-tech transfer on 17 May.

Rajiv's rhetoric seemed to have been partly designed to reassure the Soviets, who after all have stood by India in critical times in the past. It was also probably tailored to the perceived need to balance his pro-West image and that of his government – an image which had been reinforced by his Reagan-style budget. The rhetoric also responded to the pressure of the pro-Soviet lobby, both inside and outside the ruling party. It was a further reassurance that the great tradition of Nehru and Mrs Gandhi would continue, if only in words. Finally, Rajiv and his advisors had to be mindful of not only domestic votes, but also of the international constituency of the non-aligned club. Rajiv's rhetoric, if nothing else, must have pleased the Soviets for its propaganda value. His concern for remote issues like Nicaragua and space defense instead of the more immediate issue of neighboring Afghanistan could not but have pleased the Kremlin.

India remains the only country in South Asia with an overwhelming identity of views in international issues with Moscow. Mrs Gandhi had deftly put the Soviet connection into domestic–political use, i.e., affecting a pseudo-leftist posture so as to capture votes and take the wind out of the sail of the pro-Soviet Communist Party of India. Indo-Soviet politico-security relations at this time of writing seem slated to continue as in the past. This is especially so, as the prospects for a change in the different political and geopolitical perceptions of Washington and New Delhi seem as remote as ever, despite the Rajiv–Reagan summit in June 1985. Rajiv's critique of US foreign policy, it must be noted, was not merely rhetoric. It reflected India's substantial national consensus which the ultra-right in the United States did little to modify. Also, the impression that Sikh terrorists are apparently flourishing in the United

States and that certain sections of influential Americans continue to sympathize actively with them has not helped mitigate the suspicion of even the apolitical Indian that the United States does not really like Third World nations to show their independence. This impression is reinforced by Soviet propaganda.[44] The Soviets attach special importance to cultivating India, not only as a counter to Pakistan and China, but also as a leading actor in the non-aligned movement. There is not-too-subtle patronizing tone in Soviet commentaries regarding India's prestige in the Third World and the non-aligned movement, for which they credit the USSR.[45]

Both Washington and New Delhi could still help each other to build better political relations by mutual give and take. India could afford to tone down anti-US rhetoric on issues that are of little direct concern to it. The United States, in turn, could mollify India's public opinion by supplying weapons that would match its F-16s and Harpoon missiles given to Pakistan. If these hi-tech weapons can be entrusted to the latter, there is no reason why similar weapons cannot be entrusted to India. The Pentagon's fear of hi-tech leakage from India to the Soviets seems justified in the light of the spy scandal mentioned earlier, but such leaks may also take place from Pakistan. Indeed, the United States itself is hardly immune from the KGB's espionage. And in any case, the Soviets are going to get US technology from West Europe. A Pentagon official denied that stringent leak-proof measures had been demanded of India,[46] in case the Pentagon decided to supply hi-tech arms to the latter. Rajiv went on record saying that the hitch in an Indo-American arms deal lay in a clause that would enable the US Congress to legislate on the deal retroactively.[47] Whatever the real reasons, periodic press speculation in both the United States and India since 1980 that an arms deal might be in the offing have so far proven false. The political will to achieve this seems to be lacking. US intransigence, however, will only push India further towards eager Soviet arms as in the past.

Moscow is surely worried about the international implications of India's economic liberalization drive because this opens a hitherto closed window for Western private capital and, perhaps, influence. At this time of writing the situation is still in both Moscow and New Delhi. The successive leadership changes in the Kremlin and the replacement of the veteran Foreign Minister Andrei Gromyko by Eduard Shevardnadze, who has little experience in foreign affairs, show that the Kremlin itself is in a flux. Rajiv Gandhi also introduced many changes in his government following his election. Both leaderships, hence, are involved in a process of finding their bearings. It will be worthwhile to monitor the evolution of Indo-Soviet relations in the politico-security realm in the Rajiv–Gorbachev era.

NOTES

1 Details in John Kenneth Galbraith, *Ambassador's Journal* (New York: Signet, 1969), pp. 376–422; and Chester Bowles, *Promises to Keep* (New York: Harper and Row, 1971), pp. 472–84.

2 The National Advisory Council on International Monetary and Financial Policies, *International Finance, Annual Report*, FY 1981 (Washington: US Government Printing Office, no date), Statistical Appendix, Section B, Table B-1, p. 234. Total US net aid to India during 1 July 1945 to 31 December 1980 was $9,608 million.

3 Details in Robert Jackson, *South Asian Crisis: India, Pakistan and Bangla Desh* (New York: Praeger, 1975).

4 For instance, G. G. Kotovsky, "Soviet–Indian Cooperation: Factor of Stability in Asia," *Soviet Review*, USSR Embassy, New Delhi, vol. XVII, no. 57 (8 December 1980), pp. 10–11; B. Levchenko, "A Major Factor of Peace in Asia," *International Affairs*, Moscow, no. 9 (1981), 19. Soviet military aid to India until 1971 probably exceeded $1 billion in value, and from 1 November of that year, on the eve of the Indo-Pakistani war over Bangladesh, Moscow started airlifting additional military equipment to India. *World Military Expenditures and Arms Transfers, 1965–1974* (Washington: US Arms Control and Disarmament Agency, 1976), Table 5, pp. 73–76.

5 *Indian & Foreign Review*, New Delhi, vol. XVII, no. 2 (1–15 November 1979), p. 29.

6 On Pakistan's importance for the US Central Command, see *US Security Interests and Policies in Southwest Asia*, Senate Foreign Relations Committee hearings, 96th Congress, 2nd session, February–March 1980 (Washington: US Government Printing Office, 1980).

7 The deal involved 17-year credit at 2.5 per cent interest. Drew Middleton, "Pakistan Aid: Frail Shield?" *New York Times*, 12 July 1981.

8 *The Statesman*, Calcutta, 14 December 1980.

9 *Soviet Review*, vol. XIX, no. 14 (25 March 1982), pp. 17–24; *The Statesman*, 14–21 March 1982; Diip Bobb, "The Soviet Tour de Force," and Bhabani Sen Gupta, "From Russia with Verve," *India Today*, New Delhi, vol. VIII, no. 7 (15 April 1982), pp. 32–34 and 120–23, respectively.

10 *Ibid.*, p. 19.

11 *Ibid.*, p. 20.

12 *Ibid.*

13 *Soviet Review*, vol. XXII, no. 4 (28 January 1985), pp. 24–26.

14 "Bureaucrat, Diplomat, Industrialist, Spy," *Sunday*, Calcutta, vol. XXII, no. 13 (3–9 February 1985), pp. 14–31; "Red Spies in India," *The Week*, Cochin, vol. III, no. 11 (3–9 March 1985), pp. 18–27; *India Today*, 28 February 1985, pp. 31–32.

15 *Newsweek*, 9 August 1982, p. 30; *India Today*, 31 August 1982, pp. 66–72 and 73–78.

16 Boris Chekhonin, "India: Looking Into the Future," *New Times*, Moscow, no. 4 (January 1980), pp. 10–11; Sergei Irodox, "India and the Indian Ocean Problem," *New Times*, no. 26 (June 1981), pp. 12–13; Andrei Leonid Zhegalov, "Why the Dialogue Has Not Continued," *New Times*, no. 13 (March 1982), pp. 10–11; D. Borisov, "Who Is Behind the Afghan Counter-Revolution," *International Affairs*, no. 1 (1982), pp. 36–43; and editorial, *Far Eastern Affairs*, Moscow, no. 1 (1982), pp. 3–16.

17 Kotovsky, "Soviet–Indian Cooperation," p. 11.

18 G. Astafyev, "Great Power Hegemonistic Policy of Present Chinese Leadership in Asia," *Soviet Review*, vol. XVII, no. 57 (8 December 1980), pp. 37–44.

19 *Ibid.*, p. 39.

20 *Ibid.*, p. 42.
21 *The Statesman*, 22 October 1982, p. 5.
22 *The Statesman*, 9, 12 December 1980; *Soviet Review*, vol. XIX, no. 43 (30 September 1982), pp. 26–32.
23 *New Times*, no. 16 (April 1980), p. 4; no. 40 (October 1981), p. 4; Richard Owen, "Russia Points the Finger at CIA," *The Times*, London, 1 November 1984, p. 5.
24 *New Times*, no. 13 (March 1982), p. 3.
25 Text in *Europa Archiv*, Bonn, no. 8 (25 April 1981), p. 212.
26 Leonid I. Brezhnev, *Socialism, Peace, the Freedom and Independence of the Peoples* (New Delhi: Allied Publishers, 1982), p. 119; *Soviet Review*, vol. XIX, no. 43 (30 September 1982), pp. 19, 23.
27 Subramaniam Swamy, "Mrs Gandhi Has All the Aces, Brezhnev None," *The Telegraph*, Calcutta, 17 September 1982.
28 I. Semyonov, "Bright Prospects of Soviet–Indian Trade," *Soviet Review*, vol. XXII, no. 27 (15 July 1985), p. 18. Figures in US dollars are approximate only.
29 *Ibid.*, p. 29.
30 *Soviet Review*, vol. XXII, no. 2 (10 January 1985), p. 4.
31 *Soviet Review*, vol. XXII, no. 6 (7 February 1985), p. 2.
32 "Rajiv's Foreign Policy Projections," *Mainstream*, New Delhi, vol. XXIII, no. 20 (12 January 1985), pp. 3–4.
33 *The Statesman*, 5 May 1985, p. 1.
34 *Ibid.*, 6 May 1985, p. 5.
35 *Ibid.*, 11 May 1985, p. 5.
36 *Ibid.*
37 *The Telegraph*, 19 May 1985, p. 3.
38 *The Statesman*, 22, 23, 25, 26 May 1985, p. 1. *The Telegraph*, 22, 23, 25, 26 May 1985, p. 1.
39 *The Telegraph*, 23 May 1985, p. 1.
40 Rajiv's Press Conference in Moscow on 22 May 1985, *The Statesman*, 23 May 1985, p. 1, and *The Telegraph*, 23 May 1985, p. 1. His remarks to *Newsweek* on the FBI probably holding back information on Sikh terrorists are quoted in *The Statesman*, 26 May 1985, p. 1.
41 *The Telegraph*, 27 May 1985, p. 1.
42 *Ibid.*, 8 June 1985, p. 4.
43 *The Telegraph*, 11 June 1985, p. 1; *The Statesman*, 13, 14 and 15 June 1985, p. 1. (Rajiv–Reagan talks without aides on 12 June, Rajiv's address to the joint Congress session on 13 June, his address to the National Press Club on 14 June 1985).
44 V. Georgiev, "South Asia: Strategic Goals of US Imperialism," *International Affairs*, no. 2 (February 1985), pp. 105–13; M. Kapustin, "The CIA Against India," *International Affairs*, no. 5 (1985), pp. 138–41; a *Pravda* editorial of 2 August 1985 pointed at a link between terrorism in India and Frank Camper's commando training school in Alabama, quoted in *The Telegraph*, 3 August 1985, p. 3.
45 V. Georgiev, "India: A Milestone on the Path of Independence," *International Affairs*, no. 4 (1985), p. 47. The Soviet conviction that Moscow is a natural ally of New Delhi and that the latter's non-alignment has flourished thanks to the Soviet security umbrella has reached emotional proportions. At a seminar on "India's Foreign Policy: Post-Nehru Years," held at Jadavpur University, Calcutta, on 20 March 1985 the present author was taken aback when a Soviet diplomat present in the audience reacted very emotionally to his thesis that Moscow heeded New Delhi more than vice-versa.
46 *The Telegraph*, 19 June 1985, p. 1.
47 Rajiv's 16 June 1985 Meet the Press TV interview, *The Telegraph*, 17 June 1985, p. 1.

Index

Academic analysts, Soviet, 24–38
"Active measures", 86
Afghanistan
  civil war in, 15, 25, 42, 51–2
  Soviet invasion of, 13, 51, 77
  Soviet policy in, 14, 16, 17–8, 42, 56–7, 59
  Soviet views of, 56–7, 105–6
  US support to resistance, 52
Africa
  and USSR, 11, 13
  Soviet propaganda about, 106–7
Albania
  and USSR, 7
Algeria
  and USSR, 25
Alizov, Iu., 35
Allende, Salvador, 9
America, Latin
  Soviet propaganda about, 107–8
  US policy in, 107
  and USSR, 13
Amin, Hafizullah, 18, 51
Amin, Samir, 29
Andropov, Iurii, 15, 189
Angola
  civil war in, 15, 28, 44–6
  Cuban role in, 10, 12, 42, 45
  and South Africa, 45
  US policy toward, 45
  and USSR, 4, 10, 14, 16
"Anti-Soviet" Insurgencies, 42–65
  Soviet policy toward, 54–60
  US aid to, 61–3
  US policy toward, 60–5
Arab–Israeli Conflict
  1956 Suez War, 6
  1973 October War, 8
Arafat, Yasir, 188, 194–5, 200

Arens, Moshe, 191
Argentina
  and USSR, 11, 17
Arms races, Third World, 103–4
ASEAN (Association of Southeast Asian
  Nations)
  and Kampuchea, 50
Asia
  and USSR, 13
Asia, South
  Soviet propaganda about, 105–6
Asia, Southeast
  and USSR, 4, 10
Assad, Hafiz, 185, 190, 194, 196, 198, 204

Baldridge, Malcolm, 224
Barghoorn, Frederick C., 84
"Basket 3", 77, 81
"Bay of Pigs", 43
Begin, Menahem, 195
Beglov, S., 73
Boshevik Revolution
  and world revolutionary process, 92–3
Bovin, Aleksandr, 13
Brezhnev, Leonid I., 7, 13, 14, 215, 217
  in India, 213
  on propaganda, 76
Brutents, Karen, 24, 36, 91
Brzezinski, Zbigniew, 213

Cambodia (see Kampuchea)
Carr, E.H., 84
Central Intelligence Agency (CIA), 10
Chandra, Ramesh, 96
Chernenko, Konstantin, 71
Chile, 9
China, Peoples Republic of
  hegemonism of, 98

and USSR, 7, 9, 18
and Vietnam, 49–50
Clark Amendment, 45
"Clearing Agreements"
  in East European trade, 154–5
  in Soviet trade, 122–3
Clients, Third world
  of USSR, 14
Colonialism
  collapse of, 7, 12
Communist Party of the Soviet Union
  International Department, 86
  Internatinal Information Department, 86
  26th Congress of, 71
  27th Congress of, 13
Conference on Security and Cooperation in
    Europe (CSCE, Helsinki Conference),
    75, 76
  Belgrade Follow-up Meeting, 77
  Madrid Follow-up Meeting, 81–2
Conflicts in third World, 12
Congo Crisis, 1960, 6
Congo, republic of, 25
Containment, US policy of, 3
Contras, 53–4
  US support for, 53
"Correlation of Forces", 95
Council for Mutual Economic Assistance,
    (CMEA)
  non-European membes of, 163–78
  International Investment Bank, 127
  specialization in, 177–8
Cuba, 43
  Bay of Pigs, 43
  foreign economic relations of, 163–78
  and Nicaragua, 52, 57
  and USSR, 7
    trade, 164–6, 172–6
  role in Angola, 45
  Soviet aid to, 15
  trade of
    with developing countries, 167
    with OECD countries, 167
Cuban Missile Crisis, 6

Debts, Third World, 102
Detente
  and Soviet foreign policy, 9
Development
  capitalist model of, 33
Developing countries (*see* Third World)
Development policy of Third World
  Soviet views of, 28–32

Dhlakama, Alfonso, 46
Disinformation, 77, 85

East–West economic relations, 19
  embargo on USSR, 123
Economic assistance
  Soviet, 11, 12, 124–8
    amount of, 125
    bilateral nature of, 127
    changes in, 135–6
    grants in, 128–9
    objectives of 136–7
    as percentage of GNP, 125–6
    recipients of, 127–8
    terms of, 128–30
  Western as exploitation, 102
Economic relations, foreign
  of USSR and Third World, 117–38
  of Eastern Europe and Third World,
    141–58
Egypt
  and USSR, 5, 12, 17
Eitan, Rafael, 191
Elianov, A. Ia., 33
Eritrea, 48
  Cuban aid to rebels in, 48
  Soviet aid to rebels in, 48
Ethiopia
  civil war in, 48–9
  Cuban role in, 10, 59
  and Ogaden War, 48
  and Somalia, 48
  and USSR, 4, 10, 14
Europe, Eastern
  Soviet aid to, 15
  and Third World, 141–58
Exports, Soviet
  to developing countries, 120–3

Firyubin, N., 217
FNLA (National front for the Liberation of
    Angola), 44, 59
FRELIMO (Front for the Liberation of
    Mozambique), 46
  Soviet aid to, 46–7
Friedgut, Theodore H., 95

Gandhi, Indira, 213, 214
  alleged CIA plot against, 219
Gandhi, Rajiv, 220–2
Genscher, Hans-Dietrich, 76
Glukhov, Yuri, 199

Gorbachev, Mikhail, 14, 60, 222
    foreign policy of, 37
Gorshkov, S.G., 215
Grechko, A.A., 9, 95
Grenada
    US invasion of, 199
Gromyko, Anatolii, 24, 94
Gromyko, Andrei, 95, 191, 193, 200

Hazan, Baruch, 85, 88
Helsinki Conference (see Conference on
        Security and Cooperation in Europe)
Heng Samrin, 51, 58
Hizb-i-Islami, 52
Hussein, King, 188, 192

Imperialism, Western, 93–4, 97–8
India
    importance of to USSR, 221
    and Pakistan, 8, 216–17
    Soviet economic aid to, 223
    Soviet military aid to, 212–13, 214, 223
    Soviet propaganda about, 106, 219, 224
    and US, 211, 235
    and USSR, 5, 11, 12, 16, 17, 211–25
    security relations, 216–19
Indian Ocean Peace Zone, 218
Indo-Pakistani War, 1973, 8
Information
    free flow of, 73, 75, 78, 101
        Soviet opposition to, 79
    Soviet policy on 71–2, 79, 82
Insurgencies (see "Anti-Soviet" Insurgencies)
International Fronts
    and propaganda, 89, 90
    and United Nations, 96
International Program for the Development
        of Communication 80
Intervention, military
    of USSR, 59
Iran
    Tudeh Party in 184
    and USSR, 11
Iran-Iraq War, 18
Iraq
    and USSR, 11
Iskander, Ahmad, 187
Islam
    Soviet views of, 33–4
Israel
    invasion of Lebanon, 186
    and Lebanon, 189
    and Syria, 186, 189ff.

Kaddafi, Muammar, 187
Kampuchea
    and ASEAN, 50
    civil war in, 42, 49–51
    Soviet policy toward, 58
    Vietnamese control of, 16, 42, 49–51
Karmal, Babrak, 51
Kashlev, Iu., 76, 79, 81, 82, 100
KGB, Service "A", 86–7
Khadaam, Abdel Halim, 201
Khmer Rouge, 49–50
Khomeini, Ayatollah Ruhollah, 184
Khoros, V., 34
Khrushchev, Nikita S.
    and national liberation movement, 91
    foreign economic policy of, 117
    foreign policy of, 5
Kim, G., 33–4, 94
Korean airliner
    Soviet shooting down of, 197
Kudriavtsev, Vladimir, 197

Lavigne, Marie, 141
Lawson, C.W., 135
Lebanon
    civil war in, 18
    and Israel, 189
    Israeli invasion of, 186
    US marines in 199
Lenin, Vladimir I., 71
Li, vladimir, 27
Losev, S., 78

MacBride Report, 77–9
    Soviet influence on, 78
MacFarlane, S. Neil, 91
Machel, Samora, 17
Mandzhulo, A., 30
Marxist Regimes in Third World, 42
Mass Media
    Soviet policy on, 70–1
Mengistu, Haile Mariam, 102
Middle East
    Soviet peace plan for, 188
    Soviet propaganda about, 106
    US policy in, 185
    USSR policy in, 6, 95, 183
Military assistance
    of USSR, 11, 12
        and National Liberation Movements,
MNR (Mozambican National Resistance),
    46–8

Mongolia, People's Republic of
  foreign economic relations of, 163–78
  trade
    with developing countries, 167
    with OECD countries, 167
    with USSR, 164, 171–2
Mozambique, 37
  civil war in, 46–8
  and South Africa, 47
  Soviet aid to, 16
  and Zimbabwe, 46–7
MPLA (Movement for the Popular
    Liberation of Angola), 17, 44, 59
Mugabe, Robert, 46

Namibia, 45
  Soviet propaganda about, 107
National Liberation Movements
  and imperialism, 93–4
  Soviet military and, 95
  Soviet support of, 13, 93–4
  Soviet views of, 91–2
Nehru, Jawaharlal, 211
Neto, Agostinho, 44
New International Ecomomic Order (NIEO),
    131–2
  Soviet policy toward, 101–3, 133–5
  Soviet views on, 29, 30
New World Information Order (NWIO), 70
  and Third World, 72–3
  Soviet policy on, 70–82, 100–1
Nicaragua
  civil war in, 15, 28, 52–4
  and the Contras, 53–4
  Cuban aid to, 52, 57
  Soviet aid to, 57
  US policy toward, 52–3
  and USSR, 37
Nkomati Accord, 47
"Non-aligned movement" 35
  New Delhi Conference of, 35–6
"Non-capitalist" path of development, 24, 94
  obstacles to, 15, 25
  and Soviet model, 94
North Atlantic Treaty Organization
    (NATO)
  and USSR, 9, 19
Novosti, 72

OAU (Organization of African Unity), 35
  Soviet views of, 106–7
OPEC (Organization of Petroleum
    Exporting Countries), 35

Pakistan
  and China, 217
  and US, 217
  and USSR, 60, 217
Paktiawal, Akhtar Mohammed, 79
Palestine Liberation Organization (PLO),
    185–6, 194–5, 200, 202
  Exodus from Beirut, 187
  and USSR, 202
Pol Pot, 50
Ponomarev, Boris, 24, 26
Primakov, Evgenii, 24, 33
Propaganda
  definition of, 85
  impregnational, 88
  and international fronts, 89, 90
  operational, 88
  of USSR, 71, 84–108

"Radio war", 80
Reagan, Ronald
  foreign policy of, 13, 19, 43
Regional power
  USSR as, 3
Reisner, L.I., 33, 34
Rejectionist Front (*see* Steadfastness Front)
Roberto, Holden, 44
Romania
  and USSR, 7
Rumsfeld, Donald, 203
Rybkin, E., 54–5

Sanakoev, Sh. P., 71
Sandinistas, 52–4
  Cuban aid to, 52, 57
Savimbi, Jonas, 44
Shabanov, Vitali, 215
Sheinis, V.L., 33, 24
Shulz, George, 193, 196
Simoniia, N.A., 33, 34, 35
Slavnyi, B., 29
Somalia
  and Ethiopia, 48
  and USSR, 17
Stalin, I.V., 72
"State of Socialist Orientation"
  Soviet views of, 24, 30, 31, 99–100
Steadfastness Front, 187
  and USSR, 18, 184–5
Stukalin, V., 80
Sudan
  and USSR, 184
Suez War, 1956, 6

SWAPO (South West African People's
    Organization), 45
Syria
    and Israel, 186, 189ff.
    Soviet military aid to, 189–90, 193, 198
    and US, 199–200
    and USSR, 11, 16, 183–207
Taraki, Noor Mohammad, 18, 51
TASS, 72
Television, satellite, 81
Third World
    arms races in, 103–4
    clients of USSR, 14
    conflicts in, 12
        US as source of, 98
    debts of, 102
    definition of, 5
    and Eastern Europe, 141–58
        economic relations with, 142–3
            clearing agreements in, 154–5
            commodity composition of, 148–51
            surpluses in, 143
            trade settlements in, 151–5
            foreign economic relations with
                USSR, 117–38
        foreign policies of, 35
    and New World Information Policy, 72ff.
    reduced Soviet support for, 14, 15
    Soviet objectives in, 10, 11
    Soviet perceptions of, 23–8
    Soviet political support for, 11
    and the United States, 10, 98
    and the West, 7, 10
Tiagunenko, V., 92
Toynbee, Arnold J., 32
Trade
    East European with Third World, 142–3
        clearing agreements in, 154–5
        commodity composition of, 148–51
        surpluses in, 143
        settlements in, 151
    Soviet with Third World, 11, 118–24
    Soviet with non-European CMEA
        members, 164–7
Turkey
    and USSR, 11

UNESCO
    MacBride Report, 77–9
    19th Conference of, 74–5
        USSR and, 75–6
    21st Conference of, 79–80
    Soviet policy in, 72ff.

Union of Soviet Socialist Republics
    academic analysts of, 24–38
    and Angola, 4, 10, 14, 16
    "Anti-Soviet" Insurgencies, 42–65
    and Arab–Israeli Conflict, 18, 184
    and Argentina, 11, 17
    armed forces, role of, 9
    development policy for Third World,
        28–32
    economy of, 19
    economic assistance of, 124–8
        amount of, 125
        bilateral nature of, 127
        changes in, 135–6
        to CMEA developing countries, 125
        grants in, 128–9
        objectives of, 136–7
        as percentage of GNP, 125–7
        recipients of, 127–8
        terms of, 128–9
    expansionism of, 4
    foreign economic relations of, 117–38
        changes in, 135–6
        nature of, 118
        with non-European CMEA members,
            164–7
        objectives of, 118
    foreign policy of
        limitations on, 17
        objectives of, 6, 10, 11, 183
        under Stalin, 4
    as global power, 4–5, 7, 11, 95
    "globalism of", 7, 9
    and India, 5, 11, 12, 16, 17, 211–25
        importance of to USSR, 221
        Soviet economic aid to, 223
        Soviet military aid to, 212–3, 214, 223
        Soviet propaganda about, 106, 219, 224
        security relations, 216–9
    influence of, 3
    information policy of, 71–2, 82
    isolation of, 4
    mass media policy of, 70–1
    and Middle East, 6, 95, 183
        Soviet peace plan for, 188
        Soviet propaganda about, 106
    military of
        and national liberation movements, 95
    military assistance of, 11, 12
    military capabilities of, 5, 7, 8, 19
        air transport, 7
    military facilities, overseas, 11
        navy, 7, 12

nuclear capabilities, 8
power projection, 7, 8
and National Liberation Movements
Soviet support of, 13, 93–4
Soviet views of, 91–2
and New International Economic Order
Soviet support of, 13, 93–4
Soviet views of, 91–2
and New World Information Order
Soviet policy on, 70–82, 100–1
and Nicaragua, 37
Soviet aid to, 57
and Organization for African Unity,
106–7
and Pakistan, 60, 217
propaganda of, 71, 84–108
channels of, 86–8
dissemination of, 84–5
nature of, 88–91
themes (general) of, 92–98
themes (regional) of, 104–108
themes (specific) of, 99–108
as regional power, 3
and Somalia, 17
and Steadfastness Front, 18, 184–5
and Sudan 184
as superpower, 12
support of for Third World, 14, 15
costs of 15, 16, 19, 37
and Syria, 11, 16, 183–207
military aid to, 189–90, 193, 198
trade of, 11, 12, 124–8
export structure of, 167–71
with Cuba, 164–6, 172–6
with Mongolia, 164, 171–2
with Third World, 11, 118–24
exports in, 120–2
export surplus, 122
growth of, 118–20
with Vietnam, 164, 171–2
and vanguard parties, 99–100
and USA
competition with, 5, 7–8
and Vietnam, 13, 166, 176
and Yemen, South, 11, 18
UNITA (Union for the Total Independence
of Angola), 43, 44, 59
US aid to, 45
United Nations, Conference on Trade and
Development (UNCTAD)
UNCTAD V, 29

United States
and Afghanistan 58
and Cuban Missile Crisis, 6
economic embargo of on USSR, 123
foreign policy of, 43
invasion of Grenada, 199
and Latin America
marines in Lebanon, 199
military aid of, 43, 103–4
Rapid Deployment Force, 187, 213
strategic superiority of, 6
and the Third World, 10, 11, 98
and Vietnam, 10
Ustinov, Dmitri, 214–5

Vanguard Parties
leadership of, 27
problems of, 16, 26
Soviet views of, 99–100
Venkataraman, R., 214, 215
Vietnam
foreign economic relations of, 163–78
trade of
with developing countries, 167
with OECD countries, 167
with USSR, 166, 176
and the United States, 10
and USSR, 13
Vietnam War
Soviet views of, 55
Vladimirov, Yuri, 190
Volsky, Dmitry, 97

Watergate, 10
War, local
Soviet views of, 55
World Peace Council, 96
World revolutionary process, 92–3

Xiaoping, Deng, 213

Yemen, South, 43,
and USSR, 11, 18
Yugoslavia
and USSR, 5

Zia al-Haq, 60
Zimbabwe
aid of to Mozambique, 46–7
Zubkov, Ivan, 71

Publications of the Third World Congress for Soviet and East European Studies

I   *Social Sciences:* Published by Cambridge University Press

Planned Economies: Confronting the challenges of the 1980s, edited by John P. Hardt (Library of Congress) and Carl H. McMillan (Carleton University)

The Soviet Union, Eastern Europe and the Third World, edited by Roger E. Kanet (University of Illinois at Urbana-Champaign)

The Soviet Union: Party and society, edited by Peter J. Potichnyj (McMaster University)

II *Social Sciences:* Published by Lynne Rienner Publishers, 948 North Street, No. 8, Boulder, Colorado, 80302

Environmental Problems in the USSR and Eastern Europe: Do the Greens threaten the Reds?, edited by Fred Singleton (University of Bradford).

Religion and Nationalism in Eastern Europe and the Soviet Union, edited by Dennis J. Dunn (Southwest Texas State University)

III *Literature and History:* Published by Slavica Publishers, P.O. Box 14388, Columbus, Ohio, 43214

Issues in Russian Literature before 1917: Selected Papers from the III World Congress for Soviet and East European Studies, edited by J. Douglas Clayton (University of Ottawa)

Aspects of Modern Russian and Czech Literature, edited by Arnold McMillan (University of London)

Imperial Power and Development: Papers on Pre-Revolutionary Russian History, edited by Don Karl Rowney (Bowling Green State University)

East European History, edited by Stanislav J. Kirschbaum (York University)

Essays on Revolutionary Culture and Stalinism, edited by John W. Strong (Carleton University)

IV *Special Volumes*

Books, Libraries and Information in Slavic and East European Studies: Proceedings of the Second International Conference of Slavic Librarians and Information Specialists, edited by Marianna Tax Choldin (University of Illinois at Urbana-Champaign). Available from Russica Publishers, 799 Broadway, New York, NY 10003

Soviet Education under Scrutiny, edited by N. J. Dunstan (University of Birmingham). Available from Jordanhill College Publications, Southbrae Drive, Glasgow, Scotland, G13 1PP

The Distinctiveness of Socialist Law, vol. 34 in the series *Law in Eastern Europe*, edited by F. J. M. Feldbrugge (Rijksuniversiteit te Leiden). Available from Martinus Nijhoff Publishers, P.O. Box 163, 3300 Dordrecht, The Netherlands

Problems of European Minorities: The Slovene Case, special issue of *Slovene Studies*, vol. VIII, no. 1 (1986), edited by Tom M. S. Priestly (University of Alberta). Available from W. W. Derbyshire, Slavic Department, 324 Scott Hall, Rutgers University, New Brunswick, New Jersey, 08903

Special issue on Linguistics in *Folia Slavica*, vol. VIII, edited by Benjamin A. Stolz (University of Michigan). Available from Slavica Publishers, P.O. Box 14388, Columbus, Ohio, 43214